One

Dr John Viney is Chairman of Heidrick & Struggles International, one of the leading executive search firms worldwide, and has been a headhunter for over 12 years.

Dr Stephanie Jones is a professional author, with eight books published since 1986. She runs her own freelance writing company, International Business Writing Limited, based in London.

Together, they have written *Career Turnaround*, also published by Thorsons.

One Man Band

How to Set Up Your Own Service Business

John Viney

and

Stephanie Jones

Thorsons

An Imprint of HarperCollins*Publishers*

Thorsons
An Imprint of HarperCollins*Publishers*
77–85 Fulham Palace Road,
Hammersmith, London W6 8JB

Published by Thorsons 1992
1   3   5   7   9   10   8   6   4   2

Dr John Viney and Dr Stephanie Jones assert
the moral right to be identified as the
authors of this work

A catalogue record for this book
is available from the British Library

ISBN 0 7225 2646 6

Typeset by Harper Phototypesetters Limited,
Northampton, England
Printed in Great Britain by
Mackays of Chatham, Kent

To our mothers, Alice Viney and Decima Jones –
early examples of "One Man Bands"

Contents

Acknowledgements

The authors would like to thank all the case study contributors (including those not selected in the end!), the valuable input of Olya Khaleelee of Pintab Associates and Lynne Smitham of Teamwork (on the *One Man Band* tests), Roger O'Brart of ManuLife Financial (on money management), and Ljilijana Bogdanovic for accurate typing and useful editorial comment.

Preface

I've never been really convinced about career planning. All you can really do is give yourself options, to create more choice for yourself. This book is about exploring one option, that of setting up on your own, as a One Man Band.

Dr John Viney

This book has been written in the belief that being a one man band is a viable and potentially very profitable alternative to working in a large company; an alternative that can be more challenging, creative, flexible and fun. The one man band route can be especially appropriate following redundancy from big companies, or for women returning to work after having children who want to build their own ventures rather than losing their independence by working for someone else. It is also a logical follow-on for those contemplating a radical career change, and was a popular decision of the people chosen as case studies for our previous Thorsons book, *Career Turnaround*.

One man bands are now emerging in numbers larger than ever before, especially in the service sector. The majority of businesses starting up in Britain today are small consultancy-type service businesses, operating from people's homes or in temporary office space. Most are begun with little capital, and many by choice continue to be low-cost operations, in which quality is tightly controlled by the founder. Others grow into larger, even international organizations, becoming leaders in their chosen fields.

This book aims to help anyone who wants to set up his or her own one man band business – and also offers pointers and advice to those already tackling this challenge – who need help or want to know how others are dealing with the problems encountered. Every one man band is of course unique in some aspects, but all have certain challenges in common.

We have called this book *One Man Band*, but of course no sexism is intended here, and indeed the majority of our case studies are 'one woman bands'.

The Demand for Service-orientated One Man Bands

More and more large companies are now using services outside their own organization: in recruitment, training, management consultancy, marketing, Public Relations, advertising, Desk Top Publishing, speech-writing, travel, import/export and many other types of consultancy and service work.

Companies are also using outside suppliers for in-house catering, for supplies of pure drinking water, and for interior decorating; i.e. for services that are not necessarily needed full-time, that are expensive to maintain in-house, and that are often handled more effectively by outside professionals.

Such large companies are making greater use of small specialist service operations in particular, operations which are in many cases one man band businesses, or which may have been one man band businesses at one time. Often a great deal better in quality and performance than specialist groups within companies, these business-to-business one man bands can offer highly creative, quality service at minimal cost.

Other one man bands are geared more towards offering a personal service to individual consumers. They relate and respond to changes in our working habits: many of us have less time to go shopping, so products and services must come to us. Obvious examples include personal catering services, car valeting, party and entertainment organizing, individually-tailored gift items, and hairdressing and health and beauty services. With the increasing sophistication of merchandising, these products and services must be different and exotic, distinct from chain-store and mass-produced wares. In this context one man bands can offer the stylish and unusual as well as the convenient and accessible.

Which, How and Why?

One Man Band is targeted towards anyone who is thinking about breaking away and setting up on his or her own. What are your motives in taking this decision? Could they be sustained over a period of time? Which particular one man band service or services could you offer? This book suggests a wide range of options, looking at the skills and qualities needed for each. How can your one man band be special? You should aim to be different, in at least some respects, otherwise it may be difficult to establish yourself.

As a one man band, you will want to know how to establish your business from day one, and how then to keep it quality-conscious. You will want to know how to operate from a small capital-base, with minimal resources, and how to maximize profits while minimizing costs. If your business then needs to grow, you will want to know how to handle this growth in the most appropriate way.

Be Prepared!

One Man Band is also intended, albeit to a lesser degree, for those who have already taken the plunge. Up-and-running one man bands have already learned many of the necessary lessons, probably the hard way. They will have also found that operating a one man band leaves practically no time for reading books such as this one! This is one reason why it is vital to prepare as much as possible in advance, because trying to go back over ground that should have been covered straight away, but that was neglected while you were in the midst of developing your business and serving your customers, is practically impossible. Most of the one man bands that fail do so because of a lack of knowledge about oneself and the marketplace. This analysis must come long before the ink is dry on the new stationery and the bright new sign is nailed on the wall.

Our object is to introduce the potential one man band-er to the main issues, to suggest other sources of information and to offer inspiration and encouraging advice (coupled with hints of caution). Not everyone can be a one man band, so first of all you have to know if you have what it takes to do it successfully.

Can You Pass the One Man Band Test?

For example, can you cope with working on your own? Feelings of loneliness and isolation have led to the abandonment of many potentially effective one man bands. It is easy to underestimate the difference between the companionship offered by employment in a large corporate and the solitude of being entirely on your own. *One Man Band* offers two test-yourself exercises to see how you score and to help you identify your strengths and weaknesses.

These exercises include a detailed questionnaire designed specially for this book by Olya Khaleelee of Pintab Associates. These are the sort of questions asked by those consultants who's job it is to advise people following redundancy (outplacement consultants) and by those who find people to fit certain jobs (headhunters). Successful one man bands have specific qualities, and a preponderance of independent and self-motivating traits. They can often be quite eccentric – an eccentricity born of long hours of lone endeavour – but they are nearly always very determined and single-minded. Fear of failure can be a very important attribute. You must be self-reliant, self-motivating, and must actually enjoy working partly on your own and doing your own thing. You must also be prepared, in true one man band style, to do *everything* yourself. It can be a great shock to someone who has been employed in a large organization to have to stick stamps on letters, order new stationery, and clean the equipment regularly. If you think any task is beneath you, then being a one man band is not for you.

Taking the Plunge

The structure of *One Man Band* will let you decide whether you are the right type of person to set up on your own, and what sort of business will appeal to you. It takes you through each new problem, with inspiring case studies/success stories, showing in detail how people from a variety of backgrounds have used the one man band route to find an independent, fulfilling and creative career. They are all true stories, addressing and solving very real challenges. At the end of each business-to-business case study there is an approximate summary of the start-up costs involved and the potential profitability. These tend towards the successful side, and should be seen as targets rather than the norm. They are pitched at the costs of starting up such a one man band business in 1992, and are intended as a guide to the sort of costs involved and potential profits which can be made.

Not an Easy Option

Inevitably, the difficulties are such that many small service businesses do not succeed, and *One Man Band* examines the many pitfalls and problems that cause a large number of one man bands to fade away. Why do some one man bands fail? Did they target the wrong specialization? Were they unable to get enough work to make the business viable, maybe because of setting up at a bad time? Was the individual behind the enterprise not cut out to do it in the first place? Was he or she always hankering for a more conventional, corporate role? Was it the lack of an inner will to overcome setbacks? In a one man band situation, you have to know and judge yourself well, because your weaknesses will stare at you daily. Many people cannot really face themselves, but hide behind masks, and when things go wrong look elsewhere, not at themselves. However, there are cases of one man bands 'failing' for more positive reasons, such as the transformation of a consultant-to-client relationship into an employee-to-employer relationship, i.e. when your best client offers you a full-time job.

One Man Band Prospects and Exit Routes

One man bands do not, of course, always remain as they began. They grow, change, become something different. It is very important from the outset to consider how you see your one man band in the future. A one man band business can tick over or not, depending on your talents. It's personal quality that counts: did you set up in business just as a vehicle for your own personal skills and talents? To promote your own personal money-making activities? To achieve fame and glory by being the best in your chosen field?

Or do you see your business as an embryonic corporate entity, to nurture and build up so that you can then sell it? Yet a one man band business in the service sector is difficult to sell. A value can only be calculated if a buyer believes that future profits will be there. Many investors might shy away from doing a deal with a one man band, when the sole proprietor could fall sick or suffer injury – although you can, of course, insure against this.

Growing a One Man Band

For many one man bands, once the business is established it may be necessary to broaden the initial concept to include one or more partners. This can help spread the risk, but you will want to minimize loss of control. Partners can be great assets or great liabilities. They should complement your skills and talents, so that you can work together as a team.

Developing a one man band business into something larger, or leaving it as it is, are options to choose from according to your particular strategy. Some one man band businesses maintain their status quo due to the nature of the market they serve and the product they offer. If one man band businesses are really successful there will be a lot of pressure on them to grow larger, but there will always be those that remain static (whether their proprietors want it that way or not!).

The constraints to growing a one man band business are not just the amount of business that can be obtained. Expanding means hiring people, finding larger premises, and operating with a higher cost-base, which some one man bands are not able to do, or do not want to do. There are great advantages in growing the business, not turning work away, expanding the client base, feeling a stronger sense of security, fulfilling ambitions and watching your small empire grow. But there are also disadvantages: feeling less in control, spending all your time managing rather than doing, worrying about mounting overheads and the need to maintain business volumes, and concerning yourself with ensuring continued high-quality work while much of it is being handled by someone else who may not be as motivated and dedicated as you are. How do you check product and service quality when it is no longer you doing the work? How do you select and train your assistants, and keep them? How do you convince your valued customers that your partner and/or assistant can serve them as well as you can? What if they only want you? In growing a one man band, you need to leverage the skills of others as you have leveraged yourself in the past, and this is not always easy. Ability to bring on others and develop their skills is not always part of the one man band skill-set, but it is essential if the one man band is to grow.

One Man Band argues that you can stay a one man band and be highly successful in a niche market. Some entrepreneurs who started one man bands have gone on to build something quite large, but here we are concentrating especially on those who have mostly chosen to keep their businesses small, to minimize the management problems and to keep their businesses highly personal.

Dr John Viney
Dr Stephanie Jones
London, March 1992

Contemplating a One Man Band

Why are you leaving your current position? Why are you convinced that you want to set up your own business? What do you hope to achieve in the end? Are you motivated by the desire for wealth, recognition, independence, self-expression – or perhaps a mixture of these?

Your skills and qualities will be important in making your one man band a success, but in the first instance you must analyse your motives for going it alone.

Reasons for Considering Setting Up a One Man Band

The most common scenarios for setting up a one man band are:

- losing your job (either through redundancy or some other change of circumstance)
- ill health/the need to change your lifestyle
- not being able to return to the corporate world
- not wanting to return to the corporate world
- a change of personal circumstances, such as a broken marriage.

Many things can cause change and discontentment. Often the need to earn more money and/or to be independent can lead to the start-up of a one man band. One man bands are born out of circumstances where you feel you want to break out and do better.

You may be motivated to start a one man band to raise your self-esteem, to prove to yourself that you can do it. You may feel an urge to gain recognition for your work, after feeling swallowed up in a big organization. One man bands are sometimes the result of a powerful ego finding his or her self-expression thwarted in a company. One man bands are created by people with drive who are impatient to achieve goals, who find that their drive is being restrained. This drive will later be invaluable in sustaining you through the bad times.

The need for independence is a big motivator for many people in corporations, who develop a desire not to be restricted by other people. You may be attracted to a one man band business because you won't have to take orders and will gain respect from others for what you have done. Those who don't fit comfortably within corporations often end up as one man bands. There can be a paradox here, if that person later sub-contracts his or her services back to this company. This is perfectly understandable and common: you might achieve part of your one man band goals serving your former company while at the same remaining unwavering in your decision not to work full-time within the company.

You may feel that you have always wanted to do something more but that for one reason or another circumstances have kept you from achieving it. In such a case it is likely that you want to prove yourself. You may feel under-confident, but with a burning need to improve, and therefore proving yourself through setting up a one man business and making a success of it is one way of trying to establish that you *can* do it for yourself.

Mentors

The role of mentors is very important. You have to be good yourself, but if you work with very good people then you will be even better. If you admire an outstanding one man band, and to a certain extent model yourself on him or her, this can help enormously not only in terms of motivating yourself but in making your venture a success. Mentors, who should embody strong leadership qualities, can be very powerful motivators.

If you meet a particularly successful one man band when you're young, for example, this can have a considerable influence on you. You may look on him or her not only as a mentor but as a hero. A hero is somebody you aspire to be like, but mentors can be heroes too.

Mentors are usually people you know personally, who have or who you think can help you. They can be excellent in helping you set up your one man band; if you have a good and enthusiastic mentor you are extremely fortunate and you should count yourself lucky – you are also fairly unusual.

Mentors are rare in the case of one man bands, because as a species mentors are more often found within organizations. But it could be that while you were receiving training, or while you were an apprentice – before you decided to go freelance and do your own thing – there was a mentor who was very helpful to you. Mentors give us standards to aspire to, and they shape the style and approach of our work, whether it be in high-level consulting in a business-to-business one man band, or a practical business-to-consumer one man band such as hairdressing or car-cleaning. It may be even worth reading biographies of famous and successful businesspeople for inspiration.

Moving from a Corporate to a One Man Band

If you're in a company and you are thinking of starting a one man band, you must try and work in an area where you can accumulate more confidence. Try to get experience in a more focused sector, even if this means giving up the possibility of going up the organization. Stay in an area where you're gaining confidence, so that you really know your business to the extent that your first point of reference is your particular business specialism rather than the company itself.

From a company's point of view, they want to broaden you so you'll be of most use to them, but if you're planning to leave the company and set up on your own, the option which is best for you as an individual is reinforcing particular, focused skills, which you can later offer as your personal service to selected clients.

So if you are in a corporate and you are thinking of setting up a one man band, you should start preparing for it as soon as possible, improving your competence in the specific areas that will be necessary to you, and not trying to be a jack of all trades. There are many paths to take, but remember always that the company will try to use you for their own purposes. You can command good fees only if you've got a very good singular skill; it is this skill that will be your *differentiator*.

Obviously, don't let the company know what you're doing. But you're not necessarily doing them a disservice: by staying in one area the company will get the benefit of the enhancement of your skills, although they probably won't see you as such a good bet long term, because you won't have the breadth of skills they require.

Leaving a Corporate to Become a One Man Band

Many people in organizations become clones, heavily influenced by the corporate culture, and get to the stage where they lack creativity and imagination. Arguably, some of the best people leave companies and set themselves up on their own. People pursuing one man bands become much more effective than do those people who stay in companies. One man band-ers are more energetic, try harder and out-perform those who have stayed in a corporate environment. They are more motivated, and know they must do equal quality work in less time to cope with the spasmodic commissioning of pieces of work. Out-workers can offer a better service at less cost for the company, often because they are more able and competent than those within the company.

The tendency for big corporates to use one man bands means that their departments are smaller. They need fewer people because of the quality of the one man bands advising them. Arguably, the best people in any sector are often in private practice. Second- or third-level people will remain in the companies, while the first-level people are more likely to operate independently. Top professional people are able to attract the best clients in any line of work, and are sustained in business because they provide the best service. They have more security, as the demand for their work will be continual, whereas they could face redundancy from a legal department precisely because of its preference for using an outside service.

The best people, individually and collectively, can generate big rewards because of the efficiency of a group of able people, who can gain a reputation for being the best. If you look, for example, at in-house lawyers, accountants and public relations people, the second division become in-house in companies, while the first division offer external services. The logic behind this is that if you are really good you won't want just one client. But, to achieve this you will have to be better, offering different features and more benefits, than the in-house people. You will wish to stretch yourself to be measured against your peers, to be the best in your industry.

Many people who work in companies argue an anti-sales thesis, suggesting that hustling is like prostitution, that selling yourself is somehow disreputable, and certainly unattractive. If you feel this way, that's OK: one man banding is not for everyone, and under no circumstances should you let others tell you to strike out on your own if you don't want to.

A New Way of Working for Your Existing Company

There is a way in which you can become a one man band and still stay in your company, if you don't feel justified in leaving it. As we have pointed out there is an increasing incidence of large companies going to one man bands for need-based out-housed services, and in many cases they would prefer to hire someone who has worked for them before on a full-time basis. Large companies often prefer to hire people on a consultancy basis, to get them off the payroll.

In the first instance, the company knows you and you know them. You know the people and the products, and have some idea of the balance of work through the year and how seasonal it is. It should be easy to keep close contact with the company, to be able to sit down with them and know how much work there is and which projects should be undertaken in which year. But, when leaving a company to become self-employed, it is important to have more than one client. Having the company you worked for in the past behind you means that you have some security, but you should use this as a stepping-stone to gain more business. It's a good motivator, but it shouldn't be your only resource.

People in one man bands need to be self-motivated and constantly on the look-out for new opportunities, and always hungry for new business. If they are provided with long-term security, and are just working for their old company in a different way, the chances are that they won't work as well, and may not be able to develop other clients successfully. This is risky, and negates the whole point of a successful one man band.

One Man Bands Born Out of Redundancy

Some people who have been made redundant end up running a one man band because they feel they can't do anything else, and because they can't easily get another job. If this is their only motivation, then it is probably not enough. In this case, running a one man band is second or third best choice, and for this reason these people should perhaps be advised not to undertake it. Perhaps in such an instance they should find a partner, or it may be even better to get re-trained in something else, in another skill. Just doing it because there's nothing else to do is not a valid enough reason.

If you have been made redundant and think that now is the time to make a break and do something you have always wanted to do but have never had the nerve or opportunity to do before, then that is a very positive move. But if you decide to try the one man band option only after looking around for nine months at different jobs within organizations but not finding one which will employ you, this is not positive thinking, and you may be fooling yourself.

Out of the Rat Race

In many remote country villages, far from the stresses and strains of city life, there are often people who originally came from London and other big cities. They live in these villages because they found that they couldn't take the rat race any longer; they are running guest-houses, or making local crafts. Because of the freedom and lack of a boss telling you what to do, running a low-key one man band can be quite restful and relaxing. However, if this is what you're looking for, it's important to have a degree of financial independence, otherwise running the business will be too stressful.

One Woman Bands

The need to achieve recognition can apply to women more than to men. Often women don't have much confidence in setting up their own businesses at a younger age, such as when they are in their teens or early twenties. There are some women of that age who have done it, but they are often exceptional, and they have had important mentors, or have a particularly entrepreneurial outlook.

There are definitely cases where women have set up one man band businesses to overcome obstacles in life, as a way in which they can prove themselves. They can be women who've got married, perhaps have a couple of kids, and who basically want to do that little bit more with their lives. Some of them may have reached a stage in their lives when they want to have a go.

In some cases an idea which started off as a hobby becomes

almost the main source of income. But the motivation, the push factors, come from the inner psyche of the women who go ahead and do it. There is something which is part of their personality. They may have been restricted from doing it before because of lack of money. It hadn't been a time to take risk. If they've got husbands with some income, then the risk is covered a little.

Setting up a one man band is one of the best ways for women with the right temperament and skills to get started in business. There is actually less sexism to be faced as their career progresses. If they go into a corporation they are then layered and looked at in terms of their grade and what they do. By contrast, if they're on their own, then they're outside all that. In Britain there seems to be a great need to pin people down, in terms of where they come from and who they are. This is less easy to do when confronted with a one man band business, because it exists outside the structure, and its owner won't be evaluated in the same way. This can suit women particularly well.

One Man Bands

Men as one man bands fall into two main groups. The 18- to 24-year-olds have nothing to lose; they have not acquired substantial property or commitments, and are able to take a risk. The 50+ age group has experienced heavy financial commitments, but has paid most of them off, and their children are probably grown up, so they've got the freedom to set up a risky business. However, in between these ages it is often quite difficult for men to feel they can do this. It doesn't stop everybody, but it stops some people. By contrast, women can go ahead, if they have the support of their husbands. Thus, the majority of the case studies in this book have women as their subject.

Time of Your Life

There are a number of successful one man bands who have always been one man bands, who started off in their 20s. These people often have never had a corporate background, nor have they wished to. They have never worked for anyone else. Frequently they come from a background of one man bands, and have inherited an entrepreneurial and independent streak. These people have nothing to compare the one man band to; for them, it's a natural way of life.

There can be signs of a tendency towards being a one man band in a very entrepreneurial childhood: for example, Richard Branson ran a magazine while at school, and always had a very enterprising outlook. Many schoolchildren may be very adept at raising money for something they want by doing odd jobs, and even early on may demonstrate a flair for moving beyond more established, traditional ways of raising money. Many successful one man bands have this almost in-born entrepreneurial streak. In the One Man Band Test Part I, several questions centre around this point, as it can be very significant in assessing how entrepreneurial you are by nature.

Older One Man Bands

Many one man bands are begun much later in life, but if a person is 40 and has not done it yet, he or she may well never do so. In some cases these people may be better off finding a partner, or joining a group of one man bands who share office facilities and marketing ideas.

For people in their early 40s, who may well have had quite a lot of experience in other types of organizations, the experience of setting up a one man band is going to be quite different from that of a younger person. They are going to find it very hard, as they are probably at a point where they have their greatest need for money – contemplating what it is they may have to give up is even harder. The older people get the more difficult it is, of course, to learn new tricks. But if they really want to do it, they will find a way. The fact that they are chained in by financial burdens such as a mortgage, school fees, etc. may slow them down at first, but should not daunt them if their commitment to their business is strong.

Starting up a one man band when you are older can be particularly difficult if you are set in your ways, even if you have financial independence and the freedom to make a career change that may be risky. Some people have a very narrow view of life, and cannot imagine working outside the security of a big corporate. It all depends on the perception of risk. Many one man bands are influenced by the activities of one's parents or other relatives, who may have a tradition of being entrepreneurial. One of the qualities most crucial is a sense of independence, and some of the most successful one man bands were the eldest child in their families, or even the only child. They tend to be more rebellious and less compliant. Good one man bands are often takers rather than givers, and lack the streak of fatalism sometimes found in givers.

Not Everyone Can Be a One Man Band

Being a one man band is challenging, it's not for everybody, and it takes a lot of nerve, courage and daring. It's difficult – and doubly so if you don't really want to do it. Many failed one man bands are people who didn't really want to do it in the first place. People who really believe they'll succeed will take a lot of knocks, they'll have the attitude that says 'I'm still building up the business, even if I've still got a lot of problems', and they will keep with it, believing that it will work in the end.

Our first case study concerns Julia, who moved from a large corporate to becoming a one man band. She was able to leverage the skills she learned in her corporate career.

CASE STUDY 1: OCCUPATIONAL PSYCHOLOGY AND ORGANIZATIONAL DEVELOPMENT

Julia, with a BSc in Psychology from Birmingham, gained an MSc in Occupational Psychology at Birkbeck College, London. She'd always thought that she would be an independent management consultant in organization and management development, but she realized that she needed experience in industry first. From about the age of 14 she first discovered an interest in psychology, and this has continued unabated.

After getting her MSc she worked for three different major blue-chip companies. She found them comfortable places to be, and found pleasure in being an employee, even to the point of nearly becoming derailed from her original ambitions; yet she always remembered her reason for being in those companies: she was just passing through until she had enough experience to set up on her own.

Now aged 37, Julia has run her own business for six years – and she is about to form a network of like-minded colleagues working as a group to serve clients even more effectively, while still retaining her own one man band style.

Corporate Background

Julia learned a lot about management while working within the blue-chip firms; she received particularly good training as an organizational development consultant, which she believes would have been harder to do by herself: it would have been expensive to fund such training from her own resources. Julia always wanted to be self-employed, finding while in the corporate sector that she always had job responsibilities other than the tasks she really wanted to do. Also, she was attracted to being self-employed so that she could have a range of clients, and continue to grow and gain broader expertise.

Making the Decision

Julia was aware of the risks involved in leaving the comfortable confines of a big company and setting up on her own. She hesitated, despite her long-held ambitions, and really took the plunge when a particular friend pushed her into actually going it on her own, reminding her of her old goals. When she left her last company, she had only 20 to 30 days' work in hand with a new client. However, Julia resisted the idea of undertaking consultancy work for them: she thought this would be like 'taking your huggy blanket with you'. Her husband was a senior manager there, so she felt there was an ethics issue and that it would not be appropriate to expect work from them, and in any case wanted to be independent.

Of push and pull factors, most of the impetus for Julia to set up her own business came from the latter, although had she been offered a plum organizational development job she might have stayed on. The fact that her further career development was blocked was significant in persuading her to take the plunge. She also felt she was never a good corporate person, as she doesn't like authority or being an employee. Nor had she ever wanted to be entirely full time, as she'd decided she wanted to be able to see her children more than just at weekends.

Start-up Costs

Julia needed little initial investment in setting up her own business, initially just £100 for an answering machine and a further investment in a personal computer, but less than a £2,500 in total. In organizational and management development you and your expertise are the products. Julia did not spend any money on brochures or specific marketing exercises, but news of her work spread by word of mouth, and from referrals from existing clients, contacts through her jobs, and through friends from university.

Early Marketing

Julia's first client led to more business. She feels she's been lucky in always having had enough work, without low points. The nature of her work has meant that she has always had many contacts, so she simply rang up people she knew and the work came. She told people she had set up on her own, with a simple USP (unique selling point): that she could be the right person for their organization, and that if her qualifications suited them she could work at a senior level in a very cost-effective way. Big consultancy companies cost much more, and the client may not always be sure precisely whom they are getting.

Limitations

Julia has since found herself limited in the size and scope of her assignments by the fact that she is a one man band, without resources and without a large team behind her. One solution which she is currently engaged in is setting up a consultancy of four people who have worked together for a long time. For the first time Julia is aiming specifically to market this network, and is creating a brochure and other marketing tools, to sell the consultancy as a service which can pitch for the larger jobs. This has emerged from her discovery that many clients need more people to help in the task once she has started work. She often has to bring in others to help her in any case.

She is no longer sure if she will continue to have her own business separately, as increasingly she is working with colleagues within this network. A second person helping in an assignment is especially useful in ensuring quality of service in such tasks as running strategic workshops and organizational studies. Workshops represent a significant investment by the client, and are more effective if run by two people. It is hard to be a one man band permanently, Julia feels, but nevertheless she wants to stick to having a small business, as she doesn't want to be a manager. She feels this isn't what she's good at. Similarly, her colleagues in her consultancy see the value of working together but want to continue to keep their overheads low so that they can concentrate on delivering quality consultancy work.

Julia can identify three significant mentors in her work, who were all organizational development consultants. They were important role models for her and kept her on course for her aim of setting up her own business. They showed her how running this sort of business was possible. Her husband was a support rather than a mentor, with his line manager role under-pinning Julia's consultancy work. Despite their different approaches to work, they both share the same values.

The challenge of Julia's work is that she is only as good as her last assignment, and she gains satisfaction from gaining repeat business. All her business comes from referrals, and although some are inevitably less successful than others, she maintains a steady flow of work. She feels privileged in this, and feels as if she is almost indulging in a favourite hobby. She admits that this sounds frivolous, but in fact she takes her work very seriously indeed and believes that what she is doing is very important. She also likes the income and the independence it gives her. When she had time off to have her children, she missed this income considerably. She also gains considerable self-worth from carrying on her own business, gaining clients, making a difference to people's lives, working professionally and getting paid for it! She likes all her clients and would not work for ones she did not like. She has established good relationships with individuals within organizations, and continues to work with them even if they move.

The Value of this One Man Band

Julia's work involves, for instance, working with clients who have already been analysed by major consultancy firms and have had new policy initiatives and mission statements, but need to implement these policies. Julia carries out implementation of these new policies, working with the Board. Another example would be working with a policy group that may be experiencing difficulties among themselves, helping to sort out the roles of different members of the team. Often a department will need to sort out its own mission and implement the necessary developmental activities. Julia also carries out some management development with individuals, in the form of career counselling, but feels she is not an expert in this field.

How the One Man Band Operates

Julia works from home, but sub-contracts typing and administrative support. In her work she is not influenced by different economic trends, and finds a consistent demand for her services. She feels that her work is quite innovative, that she is breaking new ground. She faces competition, and while there are many people in the same field she believes there are few who do it well. Increasingly she is working with her consulting partners to offer a fresh perspective, challenge assumptions and ask difficult questions. Nevertheless, much of her work is still on a one man band basis, as she has considerable experience through working in a variety of different industries.

Advantages and Disadvantages

Julia feels that the main disadvantage of being a one man band is the financial and emotional risk. You may find occasionally that you feel lonely, or concerned that work isn't forthcoming, but you need to be able to ride through these times. The main advantage is the opportunity for enhanced professional development through working for different clients and companies. Julia enjoys the freedom of managing her clients and indulging her passion for her work.

Start-up Costs
- Telephone installation – £100
- Answering machine – £100
- Fax machine – £300
- Stationery – £500
- Computer equipment – £1,000
- **Total start-up costs – £2,000**

Running Costs
These include telephone, travel, use of secretary (only £4–£4.50/hour where Julia lives, in the north of England). Most of these costs can be offset to clients. Her office is in her house.

Typical Length of Time to Become Established
Immediately, from first client.

Typical Rate of Growth
30 to 50 per cent at first, now 20 to 30 per cent after a few years, for a business similar to this.

Typical Personal Income
£40,000–£75,000, according to amount of time available.

Typical Turnover
£50,000–£100,000, according to time spent on marketing and developing new business. The potential is great but is limited by the amount of time Julia has available.

As in the other case studies, the information contained in the boxes does not directly relate to the particular case, but relates typically to businesses of this nature generally.

Analysing Your Skills and Qualities

Your Background

Your background is very important in deciding whether or not you can make it as a one man band. You can break away from your background entirely – and many people have done this – but it can be a great asset if you have been brought up to be entrepreneurial and a self-starter. What did your parents do? What was their attitude to being adventurous and risk-taking? Perhaps there is no evidence of their having been entrepreneurial, but perhaps other members of your family were. Perhaps a generation was skipped, and your grandparents were really the entrepreneurial ones among your relatives?

Nationality

Being entrepreneurial can often depend on your nationality. Being a one man band is a more compelling option in the USA than it is in the UK, and a number of one man bands set up in Britain are run by people who were not born there, particularly because elsewhere the business culture can favour one man bands more. Also, immigrants may find it difficult to fit into an established business, or may spot a niche serving other members of the immigrant community to which they belong.

Religion

Religion also plays a role in determining whether you are interested in setting up a one man band. Some religions, such as Catholicism and Anglicanism, are very conformist and do not necessarily encourage risk and entrepreneurship, but rather try to foster loyalty and tolerance, and even a certain discomfort about money. This is very different from Judaism, which as a faith is more likely to encourage people to improve themselves while on Earth, and to live for today, and is a religion which is extremely pragmatic about business, and very supportive. Hinduism also encourages self-improvement, so that in the next incarnation you will come back a better person, in a higher caste. Part of this self-improvement means being generous to needy relatives and to the poor generally, which you can only do if you are successful in business.

Attitude towards Money

People from different backgrounds have differing views about money. Some people have been brought up to have scruples about collecting money from others, and making money. Money is a slightly distasteful subject, and some will never borrow any. These people will have difficulty agreeing on a budget for costing a piece of work, and may not even like having to talk about money at all. If you are from such a background and are thinking about setting up a one man band, then you may be doomed to failure, or may have a very uncomfortable time. You can't run a business if you don't have any cultural affinity with business and making money and profits.

One Woman Bands

Women can be more successful at running one man bands than men. They can avoid established networks, being judged and compared with men, and they often have a greater need for the flexibility of working hours which come with a one man band business. It is not unusual for women one man bands to have husbands who are much less entrepreneurial and less able to run a business. A number of them employ their husbands in their one man bands, in roles such as that of accountant. Often less financial-orientated men have highly successful, go-getting wives. At the same time women running one man bands can find it all quite stressful; they 'live off their nerves' and, in a rapidly changing world, their husbands provide them with some constancy.

Personal Networks

Through background, education and good connections socially, good personal networks can be developed for business use. When someone has got good school and family connections, he or she would obviously have a network that might yield business, whereas someone who hasn't had these advantages will have to develop a network, later and in a more deliberate way. There are some people who have got a good network already in place even if they don't use it for business purposes at all, while others have very few contacts.

Coming Out of Big Companies

For those who have come out of big businesses into a one man band, there will be particular problems, even if they think they have a very enterprising streak. It is psychologically very different working by yourself after working for a large company. You have to worry about things you never had to worry about before. You have to worry about cash, and if there is any money in the bank. You have to worry about your clients paying you. You have to deal with both creditors and debtors. You can't pass the whole problem onto accountants or a finance department: you have to deal with it yourself. There are many aspects to running a one man band that those from a big business environment just don't think about. For example, if you run out of coffee, then you have to go and get it. You can find that communications are more difficult, because you have to do everything yourself. There are no more secretaries or telephone operators. Suddenly all the support you have been used to is taken away.

Your Track Record

You must examine yourself honestly to see if you have the necessary qualities to be a one man band, and this involves looking back on your life so far. Don't just think about your skills related to business, but consider times in your life when you have been in some crisis – moving school or home, losing a best friend, a change in job, a change in personal relationships – and look at how you reacted to these moments of change. For instance, did you console yourself with a lot of other people around you, did you turn to alcohol or drugs? Did your behaviour change, or were you relatively unaffected? Did you truly overcome the obstacles, i.e. did you move from one job to a better one, did things work out well, or were you filled with regret and remorse? From this kind of self-assessment you will be able to build up a picture of your qualities and judgement generally.

Why did you do certain things? And why do certain things happen to you? Does the occurrence of these events show generally good or poor judgement? Or do you just react to things which happen? Do you find things come up because you are challenging and forcing a change to take place, for yourself or other people? Or do these things happen to you almost as a matter of course? Is there any plan going on in your life, an overall ambition which you are determined to achieve, or are you just waiting for things to happen?

Key One Man Band Qualities

Independence

Do you have the feeling that you would like to do something for yourself rather than other people? If you are team person who really gets your kicks, success and identity from a group, you will find it much harder to start out on your own and leave all of that behind. It will be easier if you are someone who has an independent streak, who can be comfortable with your own company. That's not to say that you are anti-social in any sense, but you must have an ability to stand alone. If you are dependent on people, is this an emotional dependence, or are you an autonomous person able to ride the ups and downs? Do you find that you cross swords with people in authority frequently, and like best being able to work on your own? A feeling of and a need for independence is a good quality for a one man band, but you are still dependent on your clients or customers, so this quality must not be exaggerated unduly.

Problem-solving Ability

Starting off and growing a business requires dedication, effort, will-power and energy, but you also need to be able to problem-solve. One man bands are an attractive option for good problem-solvers, because they like finding a way of overcoming obstacles, and tend to rise to challenges. Even if you can't solve the problem yourself, you need to know whom you can get in to solve it for you: good problem-solvers are also good at taking advice from others. Successful one man bands are autonomous, with values based around not wanting to fail; they are people who will go a long way to overcome obstacles and solve problems. One man bands are tenacious, practical, down-to-earth, and are usually action-orientated. They do not put the problem aside, but they try and solve it before going on to anything else.

Optimism

If you are naturally someone who thinks that tomorrow is going to be better than today, and can pick yourself up after something goes wrong, you are much more likely to be successful in a one man band situation. If you are someone who goes into a fit of despondency, however, you are unlikely to be temperamentally or emotionally fit for a one man band way of life. You must have tremendous resilience and optimism. Arguably there is something genetic about this. Certain families are known for nurturing a certain breed of optimism, which may well come out in family values and experience. These attitudes can be quite deep-seated, in so far that they do not suddenly appear in someone at the age of 35, but have always been there.

The question of whether you worry or not is important. If you are a natural worrier, who always has anxieties about this or that, one man band businesses are not for you, as the possibilities of ill-health or mental anguish are quite high. This relates back to problem-solving ability and tenacity. If you have these qualities, then they will effectively banish the worries. You've got to be able to do the job, you've got to be able to come back from the knocks and falls, and you've got to be resilient. You've also got to be quite self-contained and resourceful, to have the ability to come back, to do what you do well. When you make a marketing call which goes really badly, when someone is quite rude to you, you must be able to pick up the telephone again and talk immediately to someone else; keep going, and put the bad experience behind you, rather than sit there worrying about it and feeling depressed for the rest of the day.

Being Risk-orientated

Being able to take risks is a vital part of a one man band make-up. How risk-orientated are you? Have you taken any big risks in your life before? When you got married, did you marry the guy or girl down the street, or did you marry someone from an entirely different culture and background? As a young school-leaver, did you go off to New Guinea or other places off the beaten track? Have you ever done anything that is completely different?

In setting up a one man band, are you ready to take the plunge and give up everything to do it? There are some people with the wit, the will and the drive to carry on with their own jobs and pursue their one man band activities in the evenings or at weekends. This

does therefore make the jump – when you finally decide to make it –
much easier, but the most successful in many cases will be those
who truly want to make the jump, and go the whole way, from the
beginning. Many people would love to set up one man bands, but
perhaps the majority who want to haven't got the courage to actually
go ahead and take the risk.

Need to Prove Yourself

Many one man bands are regarded as odd or not truly normal, in
so far that they do not fit in with conventional employment
situations, and feel a need to express themselves beyond the normal
channels. They may have a need to do this for seemingly 'odd'
reasons which others do not recognize in themselves. Those
establishing one man bands have a need to prove themselves. It is
not that they are quirky or strange necessarily, but they have a make-
up that provides the dynamo which makes them want to prove
themselves, and running a one man band is one way of doing this.

The most essential quality needed in a one man band operation
is determination – an essential part of wanting to prove yourself.
There is no point in doing anything in which you are going to be
unhappy. You should never put yourself into a situation where you
will be unfulfilled. You have to know what you want to do, and you
have to really want to do it.

Need for Control

Whether or not you have it in you to set up a one man band business
successfully depends upon how much personal control you want.
What is your personal need for control, and how does this emerge
in your everyday life? Do you have a strong need to control what
is happening to you? In a one man band business you are going to
be in control of yourself as far as possible, answerable only to your
clients, and you should aim to be in a position to work only for those
for whom you want to work.

Disinterest in Power or Position

Of power, position, influence, and money, which one really interests
you? In a one man band you are not going to have the power that
comes from controlling the destinies of many other people in a
workplace situation. You are providing services, so the best you can
do is have influence, rather than power. If you want power, then go
into politics or a big corporation.

Open-mindedness

In running a one man band business, you must keep an open and flexible mind. You can't be too puritanical about things, or you may miss important opportunities. If you want to get ahead as a one man band business, you have to take what's on offer, you have to be pragmatic, yet you must still not lose sight of your goals for the business.

Prepared to Make Sacrifices

Being able to spare time is another important factor among one man band qualities. If your life is busy with lots of different things, whether they be spare-time hobbies or just spending time with your family, do you really have the time to set up a one man band? This is an important consideration, because most one man bands will admit that they have very little time for leisure pursuits or family once the business has been started and is being built up.

You have to live with a one man band 24 hours a day, and if you are not prepared to give up your hobbies and at least some of the time with your family, then it will not work. There can be no compromise, as most things in your life will become subservient to your business. Does your partner accept this? If not this will inevitably cause tension in the relationship, which will subsequently cause you problems in your one man band business. Make it clear to those around you that this is what will happen. Enlist their support as much as possible.

You may also have to make financial sacrifices. In the short term it may well be that the business won't be viable, so little money will be coming out of it, and you may be heavily in debt. That which is coming through you will want to keep in the business to buy equipment and to get things on a proper footing. In a one man band you have to accept deferred gratification – giving up the short term for the longer-term benefits – and most of the population are not prepared to do this. No one really wants to make financial sacrifices, but to be a successful one man band you must think towards the future. If you are only living for today, then you are not the ideal candidate for a one man band, because you must accept that you might be comparatively poor for a while.

Prepared to Work Hard

Most people who establish one man bands and other small businesses are shocked at how hard they have to work, and many may think 'If I am working this hard, then I should pay myself more,' but this is not necessarily rational. You have to equate work with revenues coming in. Many people who make such statements have come from large corporates or places where they worked for a set salary, which was not performance-related. The real truth in many cases is that in a corporation they were not doing very much, and not adding much value to the business. They fail to understand the relationship between individual work and the bottom-line profit. In your one man band you also have to undergo an overall positioning and planning process so that you say to yourself, 'If I do this now, it will position me to do such-and-such a task well in the future.' So you must work hard, and to a purpose, for future benefits. Too many people in one man bands work extremely hard but only see the short term, and as a result never seem to make much money.

Ability to Project Manage

Good project management skills and being able to manage yourself are crucial to the success of a one man band. If your past experience is in large companies you would never have had to do much of this, especially in terms of handling all aspects of a project. This is a tough problem for many ex-big company people who want to strike out on their own. Within a large company you are not managing a project, but instead you are managing a process which is a part of something else. You are in a team, and work is processed by a number of people. This is quite different from project work. You have to be able to work out how you will manage the project effectively, in terms of your time and expenses. This is often one of the most difficult aspects of running a one man band.

Often in a service company there are a number of projects being managed at the same time. So you have to be able to manage yourself, and this only comes from training and discipline. You need these skills to progress successfully from an idea to a one man band.

Business Experience

If you are setting up a business-to-business one man band, practical business experience can be very important. A business background inherited from your family can also be relevant. Do you have anything in your background connected with business? Did you have an entrepreneurial streak as a youngster, selling sweets or running the school tuck shop? Real business experience counts in running a one man band: it's no good working for Big Petrol Co Ltd or Wessex Borough Council and thinking that you know how to run a business, these do not count, they are not the same thing. Instead, have you been involved in running something smaller and more precarious, where your individual decisions count for something and are immediately related to the bottom line? Small businesses with tight cash flow are very different from big businesses or institutions. Generally, it is also very useful to have studied for a business qualification, such as an MBA or a marketing diploma. It can certainly enhance your image when you first set up your business.

Good Mental and Physical Health

Your medical make-up, and how you withstand pressure and stress, are further important factors in being a successful one man band. There is a history of mental disorders and problems caused through being a one man band business, and if there is any possibility that this might happen to you, then it isn't necessarily the thing for you. You have to be emotionally stable and confident of your ability and reliability. You have to have the physical stamina to cope with an increased work load and increased emotional stress and anxiety.

You Don't Have to be Clever

In theory, if you're offering a service which is within your capabilities – even if these are limited – and you have a pleasant personality and get on with people, there is no reason why you should not succeed. If yours is a consumer-orientated one man band, targeting people who want to buy what you have to offer even if it's not particularly sophisticated, then the chances are you will be successful. You can offer home-minding or cat-sitting services, requiring few skills or qualifications, if you're reliable, cost-effective, and personable. If you can do this type of service well, there is always a need for it, and it does not require advanced qualifications at all.

Have You Got What it Takes?

The two one man band tests that follow in the next two chapters will help you to decide if you could actually make it as a one man band, in terms of qualities. But there are skills which can be learned and skills which are innate to your personal character and make-up. You should then consider which particular technical skills and qualities are required for what you would like to do: sales skills, interpersonal skills, financial skills? Have you got what it takes to break out and run your own business?

The One Man Band Test, Part I

This is an informal, not-overly-serious test of your entrepreneurial qualities; it is not intended to be definitive. It is not widely validated, but has been tested against a number of the case studies in this book, together with a control sample of entrepreneurial and non-entrepreneurial people. This test has been specially commissioned for this book, tailored for start-up one man bands in the service sector, working both business-to-business and business-to-consumer.

Go through the test by deciding your option in each case. It is important to answer all the questions, or your score will not be valid.

1) Have you ever had the idea of running your
   own business?   Yes   No

2) Have you ever had a desire to:

   a) Join one of the Armed Forces?   Yes   No
   b) Join the Civil Service?   Yes   No
   c) Teach?   Yes   No
   d) Join the caring professions?   Yes   No
   e) Be a member of a political party?   Yes   No

3) Tick the four people you most admire:

   Margaret Thatcher   Jimmy Savile
   Richard Branson   Glenda Jackson
   Anita Roddick   Jeffrey Archer
   Robin Day   Harriet Harman
   Steffi Graf   Lord Hanson

Clive Sinclair   Your father
Mother Teresa   William Waldegrave
Nigel Mansell   Madonna
Teresa Gorman   Bishop of Durham
Andrew Lloyd Webber   Paul Gascoigne (Gazza)
Your mother   Yourself
Stephen Hawking   Princess of Wales

4) a) Do you enjoy working on your own? Yes No
   b) Do you enjoy being a member of a work
      group? Yes No
   c) If you answered yes to 4b, do you find you
      are usually a leader or a follower? L F
   d) Do you enjoy a challenge? Yes No
   e) Do you enjoy routine work? Yes No

5) a) Do you ever speculate on stocks and shares,
      property or other commodities? Yes No
   b) Do you enjoy bucking the odds? Yes No

6) Do you bet on:
   a) The dogs? Yes No
   b) The horses? Yes No
   c) Football pools? Yes No

7) Do you play any of the following for financial
   gain?
   a) Backgammon Yes No
   b) Poker Yes No
   c) Bridge Yes No
   d) Blackjack Yes No
   e) Dice Yes No

8) Where you bet or play cards, do you:
   a) Calculate the odds? Yes No
   b) Vary your bets? Yes No
   c) Believe you can win? Yes No
   d) Devise a system to enable you to win? Yes No
   e) Double your bet until you win? Yes No

9) a) Do you have 'gut' feelings about things? Yes No
   b) Do you ignore these feelings and rely on
      thinking things through? Yes No
   c) Do you take note of these feelings and base
      your decisions on them? Yes No

10) Do you enjoy making ideas a reality?   Yes   No

11) Would you say you are:
    a) Optimistic?   Yes   No
    b) Pessimistic?   Yes   No
    c) Extroverted?   Yes   No
    d) Introverted?   Yes   No
    e) Very self-confident?   Yes   No
    f) Lacking in self-confidence?   Yes   No
    g) Accept failure as an inevitable part of
       making a vision come true?   Yes   No
    h) Find failure affects your confidence?   Yes   No

12) Which of the following *most* describes you
    (tick four only):

    Ambitious   Calm
    Obstinate   Aggressive
    Gregarious   Energetic
    Happy   Relaxed
    Driven   Pushy
    Reserved   Determined
    Independent   Responsive
    Kind   Considerate
    Ruthless   Controlling

13) Do you see yourself as (tick *one* as
    appropriate):
    a) Very tidy and organized?
    b) Untidy and somewhat disorganized?
    c) Reasonably tidy and organized?
    d) Very untidy and disorganized?

14) How much do you like meeting new people?
    (tick *one* as appropriate):
    a) A lot
    b) A fair amount
    c) Sometimes
    d) Occasionally

15) Do you enjoy talking business to someone you
    have never met before?   Yes   No

16) Do you like working in an office?   Yes   No

17) How much flair for detail have you got? (tick *one* as appropriate):

    a) A lot
    b) Some
    c) A little
    d) None

18) a) Do you drive fast?   Yes   No
      b) Do you enjoy breaking the speed limit?   Yes   No

19) How important do you consider sex to be? (tick *one* as appropriate):

    a) Very important
    b) Important
    c) Fairly important
    d) Not very important
    e) Unimportant

20) a) Do you have a partner?   Yes   No
      b) If you do not have a partner, would you like to have one?   Yes   No
      c) Do you have a lover other than your regular partner?   Yes   No
      d) Would you *like* to have a lover other than your regular partner?   Yes   No
      e) What qualities most appeal to you in a partner? (tick *four* only):

Ambitious	Calm
Obstinate	Aggressive
Gregarious	Energetic
Happy	Relaxed
Driven	Pushy
Reserved	Determined
Independent	Responsive
Kind	Considerate
Ruthless	Controlling

      f) Is your partner:
         i) Of the same ethnic origin as you?   Yes   No
        ii) Of the same religion as you?   Yes   No

21) a) How much sleep do you need in order to feel refreshed and ready for the day? (tick *one* as appropriate):

   4 hours
   5 hours
   6 hours
   7 hours
   8 hours
   9 hours
b) What is the state of your mental and
   physical health? (tick *one* as appropriate):

   i) Excellent
   ii) Reasonable
   iii)Variable
   iv)Poor

22) Are you (tick as appropriate):

   a) An only child?
   b) An eldest child?
   c) A middle child?
   d) A youngest child?
   e) Other, please state:_____

23) Were you born:

   a) Before you were expected?
   b) After you were expected?
   c) On time?

24) At what age did you:

   a) Utter your first word?
      6–9 mths
      9–12 mths
      12–15 mths
      15–18 mths
      After 18 mths
   b) Learn to walk?
      6–9 mths
      9–12 mths
      12–15 mths
      15–18 mths
      After 18 mths
   c) Learn to read?
      By 3 years
      By 4 years
      By 5 years

By 6 years
Later than 6 years
d) Learn to write?
By 3 years
By 4 years
By 5 years
By 6 years
Later than 6 years
e) Learn to do arithmetic?
By 3 years
By 4 years
By 5 years
By 6 years
Later than 6 years

25) Did you enjoy being at school?   Yes No

26) a) Did you ever trade at school?   Yes No
    b) If yes, how old were you?
      6–9 years
      9–12 years
      12–15 years
      Over 15
    c) Did you do this (tick as appropriate):
      i) For profit?
      ii) For fun?
      iii)To influence others?
      iv)Because you were bored?
      v) To stand out?

27) How many O levels/CSEs did you get?
0 1 2 3 4 5 6 7 8 9

28) How many A levels did you get?
0 1 2 3 4

29) Were you ever:
a) Expelled from school?   Yes No
b) Regarded as disruptive?   Yes No

30) Did you go to (tick as appropriate)
a) College of Further Education?
b) Technical College?
c) Polytechnic?

d) University?
e) Night school/day release?
f) None of these

31) a) Were your parents:

    i) Satisfied with their lot?   Yes No
    ii) Ambitious to improve themselves?   Yes No
    iii)Ambitious for *you* to improve yourself? Yes No

    b) Which of the following would best describe how you felt as a child towards your same-sex parent:

Dependent	Loved
Obedient	Isolated
Envious	Angry
Competitive	Neglected

Other, please state_____

32) If you were totally free, what would you really like to do? (tick *one* as apporopriate):

a) Go round the world
b) Write a book
c) Run a multi-national organization
d) Be a fireman
e) Buy a shop
f) Work in a university
g) Potter about
h) Other, please specify_____
_____
i) Run my own business

Scoring

1) Yes: 1 point

2) all 1 point for No

3) Margaret Thatcher, Jimmy Savile, Richard Branson, Anita Roddick, Andrew Lloyd-Webber, Lord Hanson, Madonna: 5 points each
Jeffrey Archer, Clive Sinclair: 4 points each
Mother Teresa, Teresa Gorman: 3 points each
Nigel Mansell, Bishop of Durham, Stephen Hawkins: 2 points each

Glenda Jackson, Harriet Harman, William Waldegrave, Paul Gascoigne, Princess of Wales: 1 point each

4) a) Yes: 1 point
   b) No: 1 point
   c) Leader: 1 point
   d) Yes: 1 point
   e) No: 1 point

5) a) Yes: 1 point
   b) Yes: 1 point

6) all 1 point for Yes

7) a) Yes: 1 point
   b) Yes: 1 point
   c) No: 1 point
   d) Yes: 1 point
   e) Yes: 1 point

8) a) No: 1 point
   b) No: 1 point
   c) Yes: 1 point
   d) No: 1 point
   e) Yes: 1 point

9) a) Yes: 1 point
   b) No: 1 point
   c) Yes: 1 point

10) Yes: 1 point

11) a) Yes: 1 point
    b) No: 1 point
    c) Yes: 1 point
    d) No: 1 point
    e) Yes: 1 point
    f) No: 1 point
    g) Yes: 1 point
    h) No: 1 point

12) 1 point each if you ticked ambitious, obstinate, gregarious, driven, independent, ruthless, aggressive, energetic, pushy, determined, responsive, considerate, controlling

13) 1 point if you ticked reasonably or untidy

14) a) 3 points
   b) 2 points
   c) 1 point

15) Yes: 1 point

16) No: 1 point

17) a) 3 points
   b) 2 points
   c) 1 point

18) Yes: 1 point for each

19) a) 4 points
   b) 3 points
   c) 2 points
   d) 1 point

20) c) 1 point
   d) 1 point
   e) 1 point each if you ticked gregarious, happy, reserved, independent, kind, calm, energetic, relaxed, determined, responsive, considerate
   f) No: 1 point for each

21) a) 4 hours: 5 points, 5 hours: 4 points, 6 hours: 3 points, 7 hours: 2 points, 8 hours: 1 point
   b) i) 2 points
   b) ii) 1 point

22) a) 1 point
   b) 2 points

23) a) 2 points
   c) 1 point

24) a) 6–9: 4 points, 9–12: 3 points, 12–15: 2 points, 15–18: 1 point
   b) 6–9: 4 points, 9–12: 3 points, 12–15: 2 points, 15–18: 1 point
   c) 3: 4 points, 4: 3 points, 5: 2 points, 6: 1 point
   d) 3: 4 points, 4: 3 points, 5: 2 points, 6: 1 point
   e) 3: 5 points, 4: 4 points, 5: 3 points, 6: 2 points, Later than 6: 1 point

25) No: 1 point

26) a) Yes: 1 point
   b) 6–9: 5 points, 9–12: 4 points, 12–15: 3 points, over 15: 2 points

　　c) 1 point for each

27) 0, 1: 5 points, 2, 3: 4 points, 3, 4, 5: 3 points, 6, 7: 2 points, 8, 9: 1 point

28) 0: 5 points, 1: 4 points, 2: 3 points, 3: 2 points, 4: 1 point

29) a) Yes: 1 point
　　b) Yes: 1 point

30) a) 4 points
　　b) 3 points
　　c) 2 points
　　d) 1 point
　　e) 5 points
　　f) 6 points

31　a) i)　No: 1 point
　　　ii) Yes: 1 point
　　　iii)Yes: 1 point
　　b) 1 point each for envious, competitive, isolated, angry, neglected

32) b) 3 points
　　c) 5 points
　　d) 2 points
　　e) 5 points
　　f) 1 point
　　i) 5 points

How You Scored

120-153 points

An outstanding entrepreneur: go and start your own business at once!

　　You will probably already be in your own business, or will at least enjoy a large degree of autonomy in the job you do, probably in a very entrepreneurial context. If you are in a strictly non-entrepreneurial situation, you will probably be very frustrated, and should do something about this. Beware of being too impatient, however, and riding roughshod other others. Don't get too carried away by the excitement of winning new business, and try not to find yourself pulled in too many different directions at once.

90-119 points

Very entrepreneurial: develop a business plan and see your merchant banker!

You may be in your own business, but if not, then this is certainly something you have thought of. There may be some risk-aversion here, an element of caution, which has stopped you. You may also need some guidance in making your one man band choice, and should not rush making the decision, or you may regret this later. Try not to be too isolated in your one man band set-up, as you may miss the corporate world a little.

60-89

You have an entrepreneurial streak, but don't go into business on your own.

You may enjoy considerable autonomy in your work and think that you could make a success of being a one man band, but you may take for granted many of the facilities and support systems that you would have to provide yourself if you were on your own. You may well be successful in a small business with partners providing complementary skills, but you may lack the all-roundedness to do it on your own. Of course, you may be an exception.

0-59

You are a very nice person, but no entrepreneur!

You have probably worked in one large company – or a number of organizations – for much of your life, and the element of risk you have encountered has been minimal. You probably don't see yourself as very entrepreneurial, and have slipped into a fairly comfortable pattern of existence. You are not in any way inferior to the more entrepreneurial types, and could probably take decisions affecting others and a wider context more successfully than they could. But you would miss the security of a large corporate and would probably worry a great deal in a less secure environment. Avoid one man band situations unless you are sure of a regular supply of business.

The One Man Band Test, Part II

These are some of the qualities and skills that many entrepreneurs and psychologists have recognized as significant, but not definitive. This is a development mechanism to help would-be entrepreneurs to cultivate strengths and weaknesses, and there are no strictly right or wrong responses.

1) Within each of the three categories put the skills and qualities listed in order of your competence in them, with number 1 being the skill or quality you have the most of.
2) Take the top four attributes from each category, and then rank these 12 in order of your competence in them.
3) Choose 12 qualities and skills from among the three lists which you consider to be the most important in running your own business; compare them with the qualities you possess now. This will show where your development needs are.

Necessary Personal Qualities
To what extent do you have the following qualities, according to a scale from one to five, with one highest?

Independence	1 2 3 4 5
Individuality	1 2 3 4 5
Creativity	1 2 3 4 5
Ability to develop conceptual ideas	1 2 3 4 5
Determination	1 2 3 4 5
Perseverance	1 2 3 4 5

Commitment	1 2 3 4 5
Vision	1 2 3 4 5
Ambition for personal growth	1 2 3 4 5
Energy	1 2 3 4 5
Stamina	1 2 3 4 5
Good health	1 2 3 4 5
Imagination	1 2 3 4 5
Discipline	1 2 3 4 5
Optimism	1 2 3 4 5
Organizational ability	1 2 3 4 5
Prioritization ability	1 2 3 4 5
Selling ability	1 2 3 4 5
Buying ability	1 2 3 4 5
Negotiating ability	1 2 3 4 5
Interpersonal skills	1 2 3 4 5
Financial control	1 2 3 4 5
Flexibility	1 2 3 4 5
Pragmatism	1 2 3 4 5
Open-mindedness	1 2 3 4 5
Liberality	1 2 3 4 5
Opportunism	1 2 3 4 5
Fairness	1 2 3 4 5
Diffidence	1 2 3 4 5
Ability to use contacts	1 2 3 4 5
Ability to network	1 2 3 4 5
Ability to cold-call	1 2 3 4 5
Openness	1 2 3 4 5
Expressiveness	1 2 3 4 5
Assertiveness	1 2 3 4 5
Single-mindedness	1 2 3 4 5
Ability to juggle with several tasks	1 2 3 4 5
Ability 'to moonlight' if necessary	1 2 3 4 5
Decisiveness	1 2 3 4 5
Ambition	1 2 3 4 5
Materialism	1 2 3 4 5
Confidence	1 2 3 4 5
Ability to think on your feet	1 2 3 4 5
Ability to convince others	1 2 3 4 5
Persuasiveness	1 2 3 4 5

Less Crucial Personal Qualities

To what extent are you *not* good at the following:

Accepting authority	1 2 3 4 5
Fitting into organizations	1 2 3 4 5
Understanding office politics	1 2 3 4 5
Being hierarchy-conscious	1 2 3 4 5
Thinking of others	1 2 3 4 5
Taking criticism	1 2 3 4 5
Delegating	1 2 3 4 5
Being tactful	1 2 3 4 5
Taking no for an answer	1 2 3 4 5
Being relaxed	1 2 3 4 5

Personal Qualities

- Self-belief/Self-confidence – The belief in your own ability and skills to achieve goals.

- Ambition/Desire to achieve – Setting goals for yourself and others, and being dissatisfied with average performance. The motivation to succeed.

- Adaptability/Flexibility – Ability to modify your approach/style to changing circumstances, priorities and demands.

- Initiative/Self-starter – Actively influencing events rather than passively accepting them. Seeing opportunities and acting on them. Originating action.

- Emotional Resilience/Ability to Handle Stress – The stability of your performance under pressure and/or opposition. Ability to make controlled responses in stressful situations.

- Integrity – The ability to maintain social, organizational and ethical norms in job-related activities.

- Independence – Keeping your actions based on your own convictions rather than on a desire to please others. Showing a willingness to question the party line.

- Resourcefulness – Originating actions and taking responsibility for making things happen.

- Tenacity – Ability to stay with a problem or line of thought until the matter is settled or the objective is no longer reasonably attainable. Perseverance.

- Enthusiasm – The ability to infect others with your own drive, purpose and energy.
- Self-awareness/Self-development – Seeking new ideas, approaches and experiences out of a keenness to learn. Taking the development of new skills and knowledge seriously.

People Skills

- Social Confidence/Social Acceptability – Confidence when dealing with people, with a personal style that is not likely to be abrasive to customers or clients.
- Impact/Authority – Ability to create a good first impression on others and to maintain that impression. Conveying confidence and credibility.
- Persuasiveness/Influence – Ability to make a persuasive, clear presentation of ideas or facts, and to convince others of the validity of your own expressed points of view, gaining their agreement or acceptance of your plans, activities or products.
- Oral Communication – Effectiveness of expression in individual or group situations.
- Written Communication – Ability to express ideas clearly and grammatically in writing.
- Listening – Ability to pick out important information in oral communications. By your questioning and general reactions you indicate to a speaker that you are 'actively' listening.
- Reliability – Ability to maintain and achieve commitments made to yourself and others.
- Networking – Building and maintaining a network of contacts in order to further business.
- 'Reading' People/Sensitivity to People – Awareness of other people and your own impact on them. Understanding others' motivations and underlying needs.
- Caring/Consideration – Actions indicating concern for the feelings and needs of others (not to be confused with sympathy).

Business Skills

- Working to Deadlines/Discipline – Ability to act reliably and consistently within time constraints.
- Preparedness to Work at all Tasks/Non-elitism – Ability to apply yourself to all endeavours.
- Pragmatism/Working Toward Realistic Solutions – Ability to work towards solutions in a practical (as opposed to an idealistic) way.
- Risk Management/Opportunism – The ability to think through and take advantage of a situation as it presents itself. Taking calculated risks.
- Attention to Detail/Routine – Tolerance for and ability to handle the details, paperwork and routine tasks associated with the job.
- Environmental and Market Awareness – Awareness of the changing economic, social, governmental and market forces that are likely to affect the job or organization. Being well-informed, with a breadth and diversity of business-related knowledge.
- Organizing/Planning/Setting Strategy – Ability to establish efficiently an appropriate course of action for yourself (and others) in order to accomplish set goals.
- Time Management/Prioritizing/Delegation – Effective allocation of time to important activities. Competent use of subordinates and other available resources, knowledge of when, how and whom to delegate.
- Problem Solving/Decision Making – The ability to analyse situations, identify problems, seek pertinent data and recognize important information. The readiness to make decisions, render judgements and take actions.
- Numerical Skills – Ability to analyse, organize and present numerical data, e.g. financial and statistical information.

One Man Band Businesses

The variety of potential one man band businesses is almost endless. Here we are concentrating on the service sector, but there is still a very wide choice. We have tried to cover a selection of the most popular and generally viable service-orientated one man band businesses, both business-to-business and business-to-consumer (as listed below). There are many others which have not been included, although many of them would be related to those listed.

Of the range of one man band businesses you could pursue according to your objectives, abilities and what market research tells you is in demand, which most appeals to you, and why? It may be a good idea to consider more than one option, or to decide from the outset that the option you have chosen might change or grow into another field. You should target either business-to-business or business-to-consumer (it is difficult to combine these two), and then decide, if you want to offer a business-to-business service, whether it will be a core or support service.

Business-to-business

Core

- Advertising
- Business and management consulting
- Compensation analysis
- Contact service
- Corporate entertaining
- International trading/importing and exporting
- Market research

- Public relations
- Recruitment research

Support

- Accounting advice
- Art sales
- Company catering
- Courier services
- Dealing in surplus stock
- DTP work
- Editing and proof-reading
- Equipment supply and maintenance
- Estate agency
- Financial services
- Foreign language teaching
- Freelance writing
- Insurance services
- Interior design
- Legal advice
- Mailing-list broking
- Organizing corporate entertainment
- Photography
- Picture framing
- Specialist printing
- Training
- Travel agency
- Video film production

Other Business-to-business Services

- Cleaning services
- Electrical maintenance
- Plants hire and care
- Pure water supply

- Soft drinks delivery

Business-to-consumer Services

- Accounting advice
- Acupuncture
- Adult education services
- Advanced driving lessons
- Art sales
- Auctioneering
- Chiropody
- Chiropractic work
- Contact service for hobbyists
- Dating agency
- Dealing in surplus stock
- Distributing leaflets
- Editing and proof-reading
- Estate agency
- Fancy dress hire
- Financial services
- Foreign language teaching
- Gift supply
- Hairdressing
- Herbalist medicine
- Holiday retailing
- Home help work
- Home minding
- Home teaching and tutoring
- Homoeopathic medicine
- Insurance services
- Interior design
- Legal advice
- Manicure
- Medicine

- Organizing parties for children
- Osteopathy
- Party entertainers (conjurers, magicians)
- Personal catering
- Photography
- Picture framing
- Psychiatry
- Repairing and refurbishing
- Retailing
- Re-upholstering furniture
- Running a disco
- Running a mobile video library in country districts
- Sandwich and snack retailing
- Sports tutoring
- Total house cleaning before moving in
- Travel agency

How to Choose an Opportunity

After you have completed your analysis of your skills and qualities, you should also bear in mind the following criteria to help you in your choice of a one man band business:

Time

This book has been written for those who see their one man band as a full-time career, but there will be some who wish to set it up first as a sideline. How much time will it take as a part-time business?

For most cases, however, it will be more than full-time, and will need an almost 24-hour commitment. Are you sure you are cut out for this?

Money

As we will discuss in the chapters on 'Defining Your Business Plan' and 'Raising Money', some businesses can start with very little capital, and this book has been written with this in mind. Yet others might need several thousand pounds, if only to provide business systems of adequate sophistication. It is often the case that the greater your investment the faster your business becomes viable and the larger it will be, but this is by no means always true. How much money can you raise?

Resources

Some one man band options require just you, your contacts, your brains and your skills. These can easily be operated from home. Other one man band opportunities need a fully-equipped office, and perhaps staff to undertake typing and support activities. What do you think you will need?

Term

Some one man band ideas could make you a substantial income in a short time. Some opportunities offer a very fast return, while others produce profits in months or years rather than weeks. Your marketing plan must accommodate projected cash flows which are short-term, medium-term and long-term. How short or long are your horizons?

The Range of One Man Bands

There are obvious one man bands and there are highly esoteric and specialist ones. It is important to be enthusiastic about your chosen area, and to feel that, for a variety of reasons, you have the special qualities necessary to make it a success. Consult the list of possible options above, and look at the case studies, which give detailed insights into what it is like to operate a specific kind of one man band business. There are many other opportunities to consider as well, some of which are outlined below.

One Man Bands within Companies

Some companies encourage a form of one man bandism in order to achieve better returns from employees while cutting costs. For example, a leading office electronics company has been very successful in this with a project involving individuals – former employees – networking to support each other. Network marketing is also very successful in financial services, such as in the selling of insurance.

Innovative One Man Bands

Some one man bands can be influenced by novel ideas of making money which do not require much labour but need a lot of thought and creativity. These include the devising and organizing of life-style holidays or theme tours, where customers with esoteric interests are catered for by highly specialist tour operators. These are especially good for accommodating cultural and hobby pursuits, and fit in with the trend towards increasing leisure time. They are quite risky, but can be very successful.

Educational One Man Bands

Other one man bands have an educational bent, and these include especially the large number of training consultancies. For example, an ex-sales director of a building society set up his own business teaching salesmanship. His services are in great demand for in-house training events, and the manner of salesmanship taught is carefully tailored to individual and company requirements.

Consultancy One Man Bands

A general consultancy business, which focused particularly on law firms, was set up by an accountant who had gained experience with two major accounting firms. He set up his one man band business advising law firms, initially with the backing of a major client known to be an especially progressive law firm.

Esoteric One Man Bands

One very specialist one man band was set up by an ex-policeman, to specialize in tracking down the perpetrators of product imitation. Many prestigious manufacturers find much damage caused by being undercut by low-priced imitators, in a form of industrial espionage. The copying of products – such as Reebok shoes, Dunhill lighters and Rolex watches to cite but a few examples – is on the increase, and few companies know how to cope with it or how to respond to it.

Personal One Man Bands

Other one man bands are based on helping in the home, especially on very particular occasions when an element of professionalism and a need to impress is required, such as preparing meals for dinner parties given by people who don't want to cook for themselves, haven't got the time to or can't do it as well as they would like to. Other one man bands within this area would include breakfast delivery and other particular food and drink items, such as hampers of fruit and cases of champagne. Other domestic-related one man bands include baby-sitters, cat-sitters (when the customers are away) and those who can keep an eye on unoccupied houses and other premises.

Other one man bands offer coaching and keep-fit activities for people who haven't got the time or don't want to go to a gym, by coming to people's homes. Certainly a lack of leisure time but increased income means there can be a demand for flexible one man band businesses, which can also include hairdressing, flower arranging and interior design. All these can be operated without an office, visiting clients' own homes. As a one man band offering such a personal service, you provide a differentiated product by being so flexible, and you also have the benefit of not having shop overheads. However, there is a danger of getting overbooked, and you can find yourself spending all your time travelling between appointments.

Celebrity One Man Bands

Many well-known TV personalities and broadcasters operate in effect as one man band businesses, selling their services to TV channels. For example, Sue Lawley was a broadcaster with the BBC, then became self-employed, and continues to offer her services on a freelance basis. The photographer David Bailey has developed a strong brand image and is effectively a one man band operation. Cliff Richard has his own business which services his fan club. These are the ultimate 'people'-branded one man bands.

Glamour, Literary and Sport One Man Bands

These would include fashion models, who are aware of the value of their assets. They can't do this type of work for very long, it is a concentrated type of job, like that of a footballer or pop star. They all provide services of a certain kind. In a certain respect they aren't necessarily one man bands, as they've joined agencies and have people who do their marketing for them, who act as their agents. But an author, for example, in spite of having a literary agent, would still be considered a one man band. Even if he or she has an agent, a model can be a one man band, as can a pop star, footballer, or a darts- or a snooker-player.

Case study 2 is an example of a core business-to-business activity, recruitment research, which can serve directly either an executive search company or a personnel department. Diane's business is typical of many in this field.

CASE STUDY 2: INDEPENDENT RESEARCH CONSULTANCY

Diane runs her own independent research consultancy, specializing in offering research services to the executive search industry. She offers assignment research in the UK, Europe and US, training through open or in-house courses, general human resources consultancy, business development approaches, and database updating. There is some fluctuation between the different services, with more demand for training when the market is good. Diane set up her one man band after working as a secretary and a researcher, and after starting a family, at which point she wanted more flexibility and independence.

Demanding More

For two and a half years Diane worked partly as a secretary and partly as a researcher, and felt that she was doing a job and a half while having only enough working hours to do one job properly. With the support of her employers she wrote to all the search firms to be a researcher. On joining another firm she found she was doing a manager's job but not getting paid for it, so after 18 months she moved to another search firm, taking up a position as research manager running a small team of researchers.

Origins of the One Man Band

She then thought of running a freelance business, as several others she knew seemed to be doing this successfully and there was a big demand for contract research. These thoughts were prompted by her having to leave her regular job to have a baby. She wanted the flexibility of being able to spend time with her child but didn't want to stop working. Only five weeks after her baby was born she received a telephone call asking her if she did freelance research. Even though her baby required constant attention, Diane decided to go to London to learn more about the opportunity, taking her mother with her to help her with the baby.

Early Success

She found that there was a big demand for freelance research, and soon discovered that she always had more work than she could handle. It got to the stage where for every one job she did she was turning three away. Her second baby was born in August 1986, and Diane thought she would have only two months off before starting seriously to develop her business. However, unfortunately her baby was very sick, and she spent the whole of the next year looking after him, during which time she helped to raise money for a special care unit for sick children. Ultimately her son's condition stabilized and she was able to return to work.

Restarting the One Man Band

It was not so easy when she re-started her freelance business, as more competitors had entered the market. She wanted to offer a better and different service but still keep a freelance, independent approach. She hired two part-time researchers who were fellow-members of the National Childbirth Trust, and all her researchers subsequently have been well-educated, professional women who have had children and are looking for rewarding work after their children are born.

All Diane's staff are part-time, working four hours a day each morning, operating in a high-quality and dedicated way. She now has five part-time researchers, and together they have 15 children between them. Now Diane is able to say 'yes' to clients and can develop more business due to maintaining a high profile through her lectures and by writing articles and speaking at conferences. These efforts have increased her credibility, and have certainly led to more business.

One Man Band Business Becomes the Breadwinner

Diane's husband has always been self-employed, as a partner in a firm of chartered surveyors. Whereas it used to be the case that Diane would be doing her business for fun and for some pocket money while her husband was the breadwinner, she now makes a more substantial contribution. Thanks to her business they have been able to continue to pay off their £150,000 mortgage and £750 per month school fees, which will soon increase to £3,000 per term.

Diane's eldest son is nearly eight years old, and his public school fees are likely to cost £45,000 over the four years he attends, at today's prices. Diane has always paid for her children entirely by herself, as well as for all her office expenses, while her husband has paid the mortgage.

Now that she is playing a greater part in providing an income for the family, her husband spends more time helping to look after the children, although Diane still contributes greatly to this and is able to juggle lots of different assignments.

Low Start-up Costs

Diane has never had a nanny and has always worked from home, and all her researchers work from home, too, each with her own fax and telephones with metering systems, which Diane owns and provides them with. The start-up costs of the business were very low, as Diane initially used the public library for textbooks, etc.

Diane owns all the equipment for her business (mostly fax machines and computers), and has bought them entirely with ready cash, never having borrowed a penny. Her bank have allowed her a £1,000 overdraft facility, which she has never used. Sometimes the business has been rather near to the bone, but she always puts her tax reserve money away so that this can be paid out of earnings. Diane is proud that she has never been a burden on her husband and has no financial commitment to anyone. Her business has been entirely self-financing and self-sufficient.

The only major payment in start-up costs was £1,000 for a word processor, which Diane borrowed from her father and paid back in four weeks. Her working-class background meant that she grew up with the belief that no one should have anything 'on tick'. When she had her year off looking after her sick baby she managed on £25 per week housekeeping.

Keeping Control of the Business

Diane wants to keep the business fairly small and to be able to keep control. Therefore, although she had ten researchers at one stage when the demand for her services was very high, she is now back to five and doesn't want this to get much larger. Diane is the only person in the company with the status of manager, carrying out all business development, and it can be too much to have ten people to control.

Diane doesn't have a grounding in running a business, but she is anxious to run her business professionally: thus she has started attending a series of seminars and courses to improve her managerial ability.

Expanding and Developing

Diane also runs her own training courses, which she began in 1985, initially training in-house researchers on an ad-hoc basis. It would often happen that she would carry out contract research for a company and then train someone to do her job. She would then return to the company when the person she had trained went on holiday or if he or she left suddenly. Diane has tried constantly to improve her training courses, and has made the most of women's networks: all her contacts are working mothers.

Advantages and Disadvantages

Diane feels that the advantage of a one man band is that she is able to remain involved with her family. The reasons for setting up a one man band came from necessity, rather than a conscious move out of employment, when she had her first child. Her work helps her retain her sanity and identity in the difficult role of being a mother, but it is also fulfilling and makes money.

She gets a kick out of bringing in new business, and feels that she is growing in her skills, especially in stress management, time management, financial management and negotiating skills. She has learned to be able to run all aspects of her own business, including the bookkeeping.

Future Prospects

Diane is essentially disinterested in big-empire building, and feels she is able to survive the downturns by having low overheads. When she started up the business she was 27, having got married at 21. She is now 35. She has found that as she has become older she has more credibility and is able to do higher-level consulting work, but she resists the idea of branching out into a partnership as she likes being in control of the business herself.

All Diane's researchers work for her on the basis that when there is work they work, and when there is not they don't. The women she hires are not tempted to join competitors, as they would not get the same perks of being able to work from home for an understanding employer who is also a mother. Diane pays her contract researchers about £10 an hour; she argues that it is important to set fees at about three times those you pay out to your employees in order to make a profit in your business, and she is able to achieve this.

Start-up Costs
- Telephone installation – £200
- Answering machine – £150
- Fax machine – £500
- Photocopier – £300
- Stationery – £500
- Brochure – £300
- Computer equipment – £3,000
- **Total start-up costs – £4,950**

Running Costs
These include telephones, stationery, and payment to outworkers of around £10/hour – all of which can be passed on to clients; Diane subsequently bought fax machines for her outworkers, but retains ownership of them.

Typical Length of Time to Become Established
One month.

Typical Rate of Growth
30 to 40 per cent p.a. There was a slight downturn during the recession, but growth has recently begun to increase again.

Typical Personal Income
£30,000–£50,000

Typical Turnover
£50,000–£75,000

Skills and Qualities Needed for Specific One Man Bands

How do you decide, from the range of possible one man bands in the service sector, which one suits you best? Here we have taken a selected list of one man band options and identified the skills and qualities necessary for each one. Professional qualifications are needed in some instances, but not all. We have also suggested corporate roles which would groom people for operating one man bands successfully in these and related specialisms.

Business-to-business

Core

Advertising
Advertising creatives need flair, vision, and an ability to see new ways of doing things and methods of fusing new ideas together. Other advertising executives must be good at handling clients sensitively; their persuasive and presentational skills must be strong, and they must excel at people management. Newspaper editors and those who sell advertising space have to be able to negotiate.

Business and Management Consulting
The key qualities here are previous experience, analytical skills, writing skills, and verbal presentation skills. You will get criticisms and objections, but you must be able to deal with them, carry on getting business, and continue to grow the business.

Compensation Analysis
Analysis skills must be very high on the agenda; would suit someone

who doesn't make mistakes with the data, who can clarify, and who is highly task-orientated.

Contact Service
This is a service that provides visiting businesspeople with contacts if they want to set up business in a new town, city, country, continent: helping them by offering a brokerage service, providing them with lists of people who are proficient in certain areas, and being able to put other clients in touch with them. This field requires good networking capability, a good memory, strong people skills, and the ability to operate within different cultures.

Corporate Entertaining
People offering this service must be sensitive to the particular styles and needs of their clients. They must be sophisticated socially and have confidence in dealing with many different kinds of people. They must also be able to arrange and manage, having good organizational skills and good taste.

International Trading/Importing and Exporting
Those in this line of business must be able to see opportunities, to work on the telephone, and to move quickly without fear. They must have a strong trading mentality, an eye for a deal, be constantly looking for an opportunity, and be eternally optimistic. They must be able to barter, and to understand the particular ways in which different markets work.

Market Research
For this service an ability to manage groups of market researchers (who may be working from home or independently, so there is a need to be able to motivate them) is key; being able to give them very precise instructions and to express their tasks clearly to them. One would also need to analyse and order the data. Good market researchers are largely data-driven.

Public Relations
Good PR work requires influence, high-level contacts (rather like recruitment research and consultancy), and being able to work long-term with clients.

Recruitment Research
You need to be able to influence and persuade people, as you're

trying to influence people's attitudes about wanting to change jobs; you will also need good analytical skills and experienced judgement.

Support

Accounting Advice
Here you need specific professional qualifications, precision and analytical skills – but you also need to have more than somebody who is working in an accounting firm, because you've got to tout around for business for yourself. If you're any good, your business as an accountant comes from banks, solicitors, other professional people: it's called a 'professional referral business'. In the main, accounting advisers don't usually have to sell themselves at all.

Art Sales
In order to sell art to a company you must have a good idea of their culture and outlook. If you know your product you will know what you are selling, who your customers are, what they want and what they might be interested in, and you will be able to offer a personalized service. You must have the ability to broke, to see something and know for which client it would be perfect, and be able to sell things forwardly.

Company Catering
You must be good at selecting and presenting food, and have an eye for detail. You would aim for consistency and for giving the same quality of product week in week out – offering what people want, at the same price, despite seasonality. Anyone can give them a great meal, but you have to do all this in a cost-effective way. You've got to be able to manage staff, who may come and go, and manage them in a way that keeps them coming back, without having to pay them so much that you lose any profits.

Courier Services
This needs good time management, a facility for managing people who don't want to be managed, the ability to look after people who are basically working for themselves, and the ability to get to places on time. It's quite a tough environment. You need to provide a tough, hard-edged, controlled structure for this business, because getting the thing there on time is what counts. If you don't get it there, it's bad. It's not the point of courier services to provide a pleasing, personal service. Results are what counts. Therefore, project management skills are key.

Dealing in Surplus Stock

You must have the ability to spot opportunities and know where you can sell equipment once you have bought it. This is bankrupt stock – you need to know where to obtain it, where to store it, who knows about it, and who wants it. You've got to be able to buy it with the prior knowledge of where you are going to sell it, so you don't have the stock left on your hands. Maybe you will be able to pre-sell it. You must be able to spot an opportunity for a quick profit, and know where the needs are.

Desk Top Publishing

This also needs flair, good knowledge of the systems side, being able to see what works and what doesn't in terms of layout and design, being able to get contracts that you can complete successfully to your clients' satisfaction. You must be able to network so that you can get some business in this competitive area, so you must be able to make contacts.

Editing and Proof-reading

You need a great attention to detail and an ability to synthesize and clarify other people's (authors') work. You need to be able to find what's good in a piece of work, and then be able to build on it. A good editor can really make an average author outstanding. For proof-reading you need an immense attention to detail, as proof-reading is not 'reading' at all, it's going over a typeset manuscript almost letter by letter, looking for typesetting errors; it's a very technical and under-rated skill.

Estate Agency

For dealing in commercial property for businesses you need a shrewd idea of what your client wants, the ability to find something appropriate in the marketplace, and the proficiency to offer them a good deal in related services. You must be a good negotiator, and have a talent for pursuing a deal to completion.

Equipment Supply and Maintenance

For providing office equipment you've got to have the technical knowledge necessary to be able to install and repair them, and the insight to know what your client's needs are. You must be able to help people save money. You've got to have engineering and electronics skills, and to know how the equipment works.

Financial Broking

In this business you need to be quite tough in order to be able make the cold calls to get the business you need. You must make people interested in something they don't really want to be interested in. This is very hard: if you can sell financial broking, you can sell most other things, especially because it is something which is so unpopular. So you need to be quite aggressive and hard: sugar-coated, but hard and tough underneath.

Foreign Language Teaching

Teaching requires patience and the ability to meet each student on his or her own level; you must also be able to instil confidence. You must be able to synthesize how things are done and to clarify how training should be undertaken. You must be sympathetic and helpful to those people who may have learning difficulties.

Freelance Writing

Good writing skills are of course essential, as well as sensitivity, being able to get things done to time, and being good at networking to gain information.

Insurance Broking

As in the case of financial broking, the same personal characteristics are required for insurance broking; you also need to know more about product information.

Interior Design

You need a great deal of flair, as well as sympathy for your client's needs. This is a very personalized business, and as you're going to get your business mainly by referrals, you must build up good client relationships. You need a good portfolio of the work you have done previously, to show new clients (as a comfort factor). You need to be a good, creative salesperson. This can be quite a hard job, as you will expect clients to pay big fees.

Legal Advice

Here you also need professional qualifications. You won't be selling necessarily, as you are going to get work referred to you from bank managers, solicitors, legal advice bureaux and other sources. It is a classic professional referral business. So, it's just professional competence that is needed, being a good chap/chappess in your local community.

Mailing List Broking

You need to be able to sell by telephone, to get and develop your lists, keep them up to date, and know how and where to invest your time and money in doing this.

Organizing Staff Entertainment

You need organizational flair, knowing what people want at all levels, meeting their aspirations, and the ability to get a deal where you offer all that is needed. If you make people satisfied, if the level desired is met or even exceeded by just 1 or 2 per cent, then you make people very happy. If you fall a bit below this then people feel unhappy. If you exceed their expectations by 50 per cent, however, they won't feel proportionally more grateful for it, so the art of providing this service is just to exceed their expectations – a point which is true for many types of service. The art is to understand the expectations and only just exceed them. You should also have an idea of the culture of the company for which you are providing the entertainment.

Photography

This requires imagination, being able to see the unusual, and technically knowing your subject: it's no good taking photographs if they don't come out. You have also got to provide a service. People are going to feel very unhappy with having their photograph taken in most cases, so you are going to have to take enough to be make sure something comes out of it they are happy with, to know what your clients require and give them that. Don't try to do otherwise, or they may feel uncomfortable. If you overdo it, you will probably spend too much time for the money they are prepared to pay. Don't do what *you* want, do what *they* want.

Picture Framing

As for art selling, you need attention to detail, quality of workmanship, sympathetic understanding, a personal service, reliability and efficiency.

Specialist Printing

You must have flair, an eye for detail, reliability, have a good sense of presentation, and the sensitivity to know what your clients want even if they can't spell it out.

Training
You have to be able to project yourself in front of other people, to get your message across. You've got to know your subject, but even more significantly you must have the ability to tell others and enthuse others about it. So you've got to have great communication skills.

Travel Agency
This is a broking business – you're going to need all the skills of making people feel comfortable, make them feel they are getting good advice; you must be knowledgeable, not just about travel but about what people might want. Having some flair and some imagination about fitting airline schedules in with their meetings programmes is a great bonus. There is a need for good people skills, as in the case of being a recruitment consultant, but at the same time you must be able to manage your business closely. You must also be ready to push those little extras, like travel insurance.

Video Film Production
This needs flair and creativity, as in advertising, but again, you are running a business so you need to acquire business acumen. You need to know how much effort to put in to gain the best rewards. You may have a lot of people working for you, so you have to be good at organizing, and be able to project manage. Corporate videos and videos of annual reports need a lot of creative imagination, but also must be well-disciplined and structured.

Other Business-to-business Services

These include people who supply plants and decorative foliage in offices, who then come round to replace, nurture, trim, tend and water the plants. There are the small service providers, who supply purified water, cans of drinks and beverages in general, washroom maintenance, stationery, and cleaning and electrical services, and those who work to maintain buildings. Even though these are business-to-business services, they are services which people who haven't worked in big companies can provide. All that is necessary is that you be reliable, proficient and competent.

Business-to-consumer

Art sales
Relatively few people spend a lot of money on art, so you must be

able to target people carefully. They will have to live with the work of art in their homes, so you must be good at matching people shrewdly with works of art.

Auctioneering
The role of an auctioneer is a particularly highly-skilled one, with a need for a lot of experience. It's quite a complicated role: you've got to be able to handle a big group, understanding its dynamics. You must know what you're doing at all times – you're in charge, and you must know how to play the moment and interpret the mood of the group and how far it can go. You must have a persona and a personality that can make people interested, get them excited even, and be able to influence them, too. There are very few people who can carry out auctioneering properly. It's a very old skill, and has often been passed down through generations of a family.

Dating Agency
In this work infinite patience is needed, and a sense of who might work out with whom; in this sense, the skills required are rather like those needed in the recruitment business. You can play it by numbers, or you can act on your instincts. The trouble with dating agency businesses are the clients who want just a fling rather than a long-term relationship, and there can be hundreds of people like this who use the agency like a cattle market. On the other hand, there are those who are looking for true love; it's all a question of matching people up correctly. Good judgement is key. As in many other services businesses, it's sugar-coated but quite tough underneath.

Estate Agency
People often come into estate agencies off the street, and you must be prepared to deal with a great variety of people. Many estate agents who like their jobs often say it's a bit like running a dating agency, because you're trying to find a house that someone is going to like and want to live with for a long time. Nevertheless, a lot of it is quite basic. Again, you also have to be able to run your business. Travel Agency and Estate Agency require the same types of skills. You have to be able to deal with people, to offer them a level of personal service and quality. You must work out where to put your time in with some people, because you will come across time-wasters, whereas others will be genuinely interested. You can get customers who come in and chat without really being keen to buy – and worse,

you can get customers who want to see 10 houses and have no intention of buying anything anyway. When you do get a serious customer, you've also got to be able to look for the opportunity to sell extra services, like financing loans, mortgages, or home/contents insurance.

Financial Broking
As for financial broking to companies, you have to be tough – perhaps even tougher when selling direct to the public, because there will be more opposition to your attempts. You have to be good at research in order to know whom to approach in the first place, or you will be wasting a lot of time.

Gift Supply
When people want to buy a present but don't really know what to buy, they need someone with special skills, someone who can make sure they're happy with what they've bought. They might be buying lots of gifts together which they might give to people they don't even know yet: the gift supplier should be able to help them with that. If somebody offers them an idea which can solve all their gift problems in one stroke, it will be much appreciated.

Holiday Retailing
In offering Bed & Breakfast, for example, you must be able to provide a very personal service. Often people will like the same, comfortable place every year; they want to stay in the same place because they know the people, it's like a home from home. You'll want to create a family atmosphere. But in a big tourist centre you of course get a passing trade. In terms of specialist holidays, like weekends for those who like detective stories, or bird-watching, there is a need for imagination and creativity, and being able weld a disparate group of people together for a period of time, making sure they all enjoy themselves. You need to have a sense of occasion, and to be able to sustain a created atmosphere.

Home Minding
You must be very reliable, trustworthy, friendly and able to be almost like a member of the family, so that your customers will be happy to leave you to look after their home and valuables while they are away.

Insurance Broking
You must be prepared to be fairly unpopular, all the while remaining

very persistent. Be very flexible in adjusting your product to your customers' needs, and to their ability to pay.

Interior Design

As with interior design for businesses, you must have a good eye for detail and know what people want. But when dealing with private clients you must be more aware of costs, and of individual as opposed to corporate tastes. You are reflecting the personal needs of an individual, not trying to put over a enterprise ethos.

Personal Catering

You must be sensitive to what is required, and to whether it is an event which the host/hostess is worried or nervous about. Is it a key dinner party function where everybody and everything has got to go well? If so you should offer a service which is at that high level, and you shouldn't be scared of charging more money to meet the client's aspirations. But when it's not so important, then you needn't charge as much or make as much of an effort. You must find out the information necessary to sell the level of service that you need to provide. If they are entertaining the boss or a very important business contact, then they can have the gold card service. If it's a dinner party for friends it doesn't need to be such a service, but will be on a different level, and you need to pitch the type of service accordingly.

Picture Framing

There is a need for detail, good taste, an artist's eye, a knowledge of wood and its properties, and for being able to make a shrewd judgement of how much your customer is able to afford.

Retailing

You must be able to make people want to buy from you, including things they wouldn't normally buy. Some people know precisely what they want, others don't.

Other Business-to-consumer Services

The potential list of business-to-consumer services is nearly endless, depending on the skills and interests of the people involved. It can include the case study examples, and others fields, such as adult education, home teaching, sports tutoring, offering advanced driving lessons, distributing leaflets, running a disco or mobile video library, total house cleaning (for those about to move into a new home), organizing parties for children, entertaining at parties (conjurers, magicians), re-upholstering furniture, and being a home help.

There are many professional one man bands, such as those practising psychiatry or medicine, and those connected with beauty, personal care and health generally, such as hairdressers, manicurists, chiropodists, chiropractors, osteopaths, herbalists, acupuncturists, homoeopaths and those practising holistic medicine. There are also one man bands who have made their hobby into their career, such as ship model makers and antiques collectors-turned-dealers. Most of these people sell their services to individuals, but they could sell them to companies as well.

One Man Bands and their Corporate Equivalents

If you are leaving a company – for whatever reason – and want to set up a one man band business, you are very likely to be attracted to a type of business which is related to what you have done before. In this case you will have the necessary type of experience and skills to match those needed for a particular one man band. It is probable that, with this background, your new activity will be a business-to-business one man band rather than a business-to-consumer operation, as your experience of working in one or more companies will enable you to be able to deal successfully with companies as your clients.

It should be realized that few companies tend to prepare people to be good one man bands, because they often move people between departments and develop them into good general workers with an overall knowledge of the company rather than specific business skills. If you are thinking of becoming a one man band and are gaining experience in a company before you do so, it is best to develop specific expertise and knowledge. Try to avoid being moved frequently, even though it may mean losing a chance at promotion. You should not mind, in any case, about losing promotion if you really want to set up your own business.

Surprisingly, most of the functions in business have to be looked at in a different light when considering a natural one man band equivalent. Even if you continue to work in the same field, you must realize that you will need to change gear considerably. It will not be an easy transition for anyone, especially because in a company there are many tasks which you take for granted, tasks that in a one man band you will have to do for yourself, or at least make sure that they are done. Also, in a company you are basically working for one person, but in a one man band situation you will have (ideally) many clients.

Typical Backgrounds for One Man Bands

Business-to-business

Accounting Advice
Ideal if your background experience is of working in an accountancy company, or being an accountant within a large company.

Company Catering
This could be the one man band for someone who was offering in-house catering facilities for companies as an employee, or who already works for a catering company.

Computer Consulting
This is an option for those who have a background in programming systems, and who know how to write bespoke software packages for clients.

Courier Services
Someone setting up a business in this could have been involved in distribution, or transport in a large company, and could have been a courier manager in a large company first.

Dealing in Surplus Stock
This would suit someone who has been working in a purchasing department, or someone who has been in marketing or has been working as a salesperson.

Desktop Publishing
To do this you may have come from the systems or graphics department of a large firm – or from anywhere in the company where they've used this facility.

Equipment Supply and Maintenance
People setting up this kind of business could be from a maintenance company or a supply company providing services. Most big companies could be involved in providing maintenance, and be training grounds for people who can then set off and do their own thing. Manufacturing companies will help one develop specialist expertise, such as repairing washing machines, televisions, and

other consumer durables. Or you could specialize in certain brands of equipment, and be taken on by a manufacturer to provide services to their customers and repairs for their equipment, but you might do it on your own as a one man band.

Estate Agents
People working in this field have often been in and around this business, or have come to it after making a career switch, knowing nothing about it before. There are property divisions of companies, but this is commercial property, and people with this experience couldn't necessarily set up one man bands in retail property work.

Foreign Language Teaching
Those entering teaching could come from any function where they have developed good communication and teaching skills in different languages.

Freelance Writing
This is also fairly ubiquitous in source, as anyone who writes as part of his or her job may feel he or she has a flair for this and can do it as a one man band. You could be a specialist journalist on computers, for example – systems analysis, computer-programming type backgrounds are a very popular area for people who want to start on their own in freelance writing.

Legal Adviser
The natural way to come to this one man band is through being in a large legal firm, or being a company lawyer.

Mailing List Broking
A background as a marketing manager, especially involving direct marketing, would be essential.

Photography
Someone setting up a one man band photography business could come from any function or company, perhaps having pursued this only as a hobby which they want now to professionalize; or they could have been an in-house photographer. This may also have been someone able to take scientific and technical pictures, who can take these types of photographs for clients as well as more general ones.

Proof-reading

Again a fairly ubiquitous skill, not depending on one's original career function or type of company. People who have specialized in writing reports, perhaps within a general consultancy, could potentially operate a one man band in this area.

Specialist Printing

A one man band in this area could be somebody who has worked in a printing department of a big company, or who has been involved in the artwork side of things. Nowadays even people coming out of a big company which has nothing to do with printing are going for this sort of activity, because, like a hobby, it's something that has fascinated them in the past.

Staff Entertainment

One man bands in this could come from a variety of backgrounds, with no corporate training at all – but it helps if they have entertained groups before.

Training

Someone practising any function could presumably have been trained to do that function, so this is also quite a ubiquitous one man band business. The skills involved are mostly concerned with whether you can get your subject across to other people, rather than which job you held or which sort of company you worked for previously. Training is increasingly in demand for improving white-collar productivity.

Video Film Production

Video skills could have been learned in-house, in a particularly large company. This is rather a specialist area, however; you probably need to have prior knowledge through working either in a company that uses videos or in a professional video company.

Business-to-consumer

Art Sales and Picture Framing

Few people are likely to have done these things in-house, unless they were working in a large gallery and then wanted to do their own thing. Similarly, people with any sort of corporate background, having done either of these things as a hobby, could turn it into a profitable one man band.

Dating Agency
Someone who has worked in personnel might excel at this, but in theory anyone could, as long as he or she has got the necessary finesse with people.

Financial Broking and Insurance Broking
People setting up one man bands in these fields are probably going to have been in that world before, or to have been somehow involved in these businesses. They could move from a big insurance company where they've been running a department, deciding to become an independent financial intermediary, in so far that this is possible.

Interior Design
People in companies who've hired interior designers, who could have had experience in helping them or even having provided them with specialist supplies, could set up in interior design. It's unlikely that someone is going to pick up real experience of interior design inside a company (unless it is directly related to this); the probability is that he or she would gain the experience necessary from within a consultancy. This could also be turned into a business-to-business one man band.

Travel Agents
Many companies have in-house travel agencies, and people having worked in these could set up on their own. Even someone who is a frequent traveller, who has observed enough and knows the business well, could run this sort of business – for example some very good, high-level secretaries. This could also work business-to-business.

Other Corporate-to-One Man Band Possibilities

Finance Function
Someone with experience in finance who's been made redundant or has decided to leave a company could go into a variety of financial advisory roles, or into selling financial products, or into strategic planning consulting. If you are a qualified finance person it can be very difficult to start on your own, because basically you're used to counting the money. Your role has always been to help control and

structure a business once it's got going, rather than actually starting one up. Finance people tend to like being given problems to solve. They know all about banking arrangements, cash flow, etc., but of course you have to have cash to have cash flow. Finance people could go into something completely different if they have a hobby and they truly want to change gear. They aren't natural one man bands, although they do well as interim managers, especially going into troubled companies for a short period and sorting them out.

Human Resource Function
Somebody from human resources could go into recruitment, training, compensation and benefits consulting, or organizational development, offering their services to a bigger organization and gaining contracts for human resource projects on a freelance basis.

Marketing Function
If you have been in marketing you can move into advertising, direct marketing, sales and sales training, buying, the media, or helping to set up a marketing department as a short-term contract.

Production and Manufacturing Functions
From these roles you could offer yourself to a company as an adviser, to improve their manufacturing or production processes. It is very difficult to set oneself up in as a one man band with these skills, however, as they are put to best use within companies.

Research and Development Function
People have moved from this role to being one man bands, even though in R & D you need facilities. The only way you might sell yourself is to become a contract R & D specialist, offering your services to companies that already have a proven need for contract R & D.

Systems and IT Function
People from this background could operate as independent computer consultants, especially in helping other companies to set up systems. However, it is likely that they would traditionally have been in a support role, and therefore they may find it difficult to operate as a one man band, unless they could come back to their old company as a consultant and get referrals to other companies through them.

General Managers

General managers have managerial skills that do not necessarily relate to one particular thing. If they are good at marketing themselves, and could offer training in leadership skills, they could be successful as independent management consultants; on the other hand they might, once on their own, find their experience to have been too varied, not focused enough. As a general rule, those who fulfilled specialist staff roles would find it easier to set up their businesses than those who had been in line roles, as the latter are used to managing others rather than working on their own, but there are many exceptions to this, and staff roles do tend to encourage specific and technical expertise rather than entrepreneurial initiative.

Market Research

How do you carry out initial market research to see if there is adequate demand for your particular services? It is all too easy to get a few clients/customers and just hope that more will emerge. Instead you must find out who could use you, draw up a target list, and then start marketing, perhaps even delaying the start of your one man band until you can see future prospects opening up.

Your business must offer your clients/customers something they did not have before: it must either save them money, provide better quality for similar money, or provide a new and differentiated service. It must be seen to add value to what they have already, and to offer clear cost-benefit advantages. Your clients/customers must feel better about themselves or their image as a result of your service, and be able to justify to themselves and others what they are paying for it.

What will be your niche speciality? Detailed market research based on your existing experience and skills will give you a range of options. The types of one man band businesses and their corporate equivalents and the corporate functions and related one man band options described in the previous chapter will help you to decide, especially when choosing a business-to-business one man band.

In choosing a speciality you must consider the following:

- Is it price-sensitive?
- Is it recession-proof?
- How many other people are doing the same thing?
- Do you know any of your would-be competitors?
  If so, how they are progressing?
- How large, potentially, could your business be in terms of the work you could get?

If you have never formally done any practical marketing, then you need to familiarize yourself with the basics. Selling is not the same thing as marketing. You must be able to research, develop and provide your services profitably for a clearly-defined target market. Marketing is key to the success of any one man band.

Using Friends and Contacts

One of the first steps before undertaking market research is to consider your contacts and friends. Have they done anything like this? That is, is there anyone you can easily talk to about it? (If you do know a lot of one man bands already, this could be indicative of your future success.)

Starting Out

It is a good idea to undertake a thorough market survey. You should identify a specific area, geographically and sectorially (depending on your service), and carry out systematic analysis. Who is offering your service in your area? How much do they charge? What quality of service do they offer? You should go around and see the people who use that service – not the competitors necessarily, but the clients – and ask them what they find good and bad about the service they already use. If you find that most people seem to be pleased with the service they are using and there doesn't seem to be much scope for new entrants, then perhaps you should think again. However, it is likely that in a specialist field some clients will welcome more choice. It is a matter of which particular niche you choose, and how you present it.

Targeting Clients for a Business-to-business One Man Band

If you are a business-to-business one man band, which sort of companies should you target? You should realize that there are many companies that use many out-of-house services, as well as those that don't. Clearly it's not much use to keep approaching companies only to find that your specialism is catered for internally and never put out to competitive tender.

There are many examples of modern organizations, however, that use outside services extensively, and give great scope to one man bands. These include well-known brand names which nevertheless don't actually manufacture anything, but design items and use third parties to make and distribute their products. Some of these organizations seem large because they are well-known, but in fact they are run with a minimal number of employees, because much of the work is farmed out. There is a potentially large market of companies like these for which one man bands can provide services; your work will be highly valued, and you will operate as an intrinsic part of the organization, gaining prestige, experience and security from this.

Such good potential clients for a one man band are very different from companies such as ICI or Unilever, which are basically traditional businesses that take on a vast number of management and technical trainees, and tend to do a lot more in-house. They were founded before it became fashionable to use out-of-house services, and they have developed a tradition of keeping a very close control on all services. However, they have been known to use outsiders for very specific tasks, when an outsider's view is needed, for example to appraise their competition and assess their position in the market. All large companies may be broken down into small units, and each of these units has its own budget. In addition, these units are often under constraints of time and cost, and one man bands are frequently used in preference to in-house staff to operate within these constraints.

There are disadvantages for companies using one man bands, and you should be aware of these. The kind of retailing one man band that provides a service selling things its clients produce is a case in point. A client company may be ill at ease with using an outside sales force to sell its products or services, fearing that the outsider may not be sufficiently motivated. If you are the producer and inventor of a product of service you are of course highly motivated to sell that product or service, whereas outsiders inevitably aren't motivated to the same degree.

As a one man band selling someone else's product or service – perhaps in a franchise operation – you must be able to convince your client that you understand thoroughly what is for sale, and that you are very keen to sell it as effectively as possible. It can be easier for a one man band to sell his or her own product or service, but there are very many successful franchise operations.

Targeting Customers for a Business-to-consumer One Man Band

This is an entirely different exercise, and marketing cannot necessarily be as closely focused. Advertising, leaflet-dropping and direct mail-outs are more important here. It is important to analyse and define the profile of your ideal customers, and then work backwards to ways of attracting their attention: through dropping leaflets through their doors or advertising in newspapers and magazines geared to their interests, or at clubs and places they may visit. You'll need more customers than a business-to-business one man band needs clients, so you should aim to hit hundreds and thousands rather than tens. You'll be able to start off with people you know, but there will be much more cold-calling and knocking on doors.

The Need to be Recession-proof

If your one man band business is going to do well over a sustained period of time, you have to thrive in both economic peaks and troughs. You have to be recession-proof. In a recession cash is king, so you'll want to ensure you are well-capitalized, with money in the bank and clients/customers able to be confident of your security and your determination to continue offering them a high-quality service.

One problem is that your clients/customers may themselves become under pressure and use you less often. One way you can overcome this is to be clear about your product, emphasizing your ability to save them money, enabling the managing director to cross out an additional expenditure and thereby enhancing his or her revenue. Does your service help the housewife to make more of a meagre housekeeping allowance? If it is merely an attractive optional extra it won't be seen as cost-effective in a recession. If you are clever you will have a product which is flexible – or alternatively you can offer a certain product for the upturn and a different one for the downturn.

Wanting to be recession-proof is a good reason for spreading your services overseas (see the chapter on 'Going Global'). If you are dependent on one market, like the UK, and that economy goes up and down, you will inevitably go up and down with it. It is a very different matter if you are operating over many countries, where hopefully the peaks and troughs will not coincide.

Differentiating Your Service

Several successful one man bands offer services which others also offer, yet their market and approach are different enough that they are more successful and are able to offer – and charge – more. It is important in setting up a one man band to segment your market accurately and to work out exactly whom you should you offer more. A successful one man band must have be practical even while it offers something unique, something that can be differentiated.

Something that is entirely new and different, however, can cause problems, especially if there is no market for it already, because it is then necessary to create a market for it, and to educate your customers or clients about it. It is perhaps better to imitate something which is going already, adapting it and adding value to it. Offer something that is different or better than what exists already, rather than going for something completely untried. Fundamentally, of course, you are only offering yourself, so it is in the area of service that you have to be able to differentiate. You should analyse what aspects of improved service you wish to offer, and initiate them. You must create a reason why someone should want to go to you, changing from the person or company they already use.

You can offer to differentiate on price while offering exactly the same service as your competitors, but this may result in very low profit margins. It is a very unsatisfactory differential to offer for a new business, because it lacks creativity. You must analyse the features and benefits of your product. Some people can get away from a 'me too' because they are better at selling. Others may have a very similar product yet not be able to explain it very effectively, and will be less successful as a result.

On the other hand, you may confuse your prospective client or customer if you offer too many supposed unique selling points. You need to pick out those features that give you the most distinguishing benefits. Think about your competitors: are they almost exactly the same as you, offering the same service? Is the only distinguishing feature the personality of the individual offering the service? Are you personally differentiable from your competitors? If so, you have to decide how to differentiate yourself. One way to do this is to imagine a potential client looking at you as well as others in your field – what is it that you can push that sets you apart from the rest?

Researching Your Competence in the Market: Do You Need More Training?

When you're a one man band, you're on your own: if you aren't sufficiently competent this is a big handicap. Training may be necessary to perfect your skills and to familiarize yourself as much as possible with the service you're selling.

You may need to acquire additional training before setting up your one man band, before you feel really competent. Once you start your one man band there's not going to be any time for training, and if you're not competent the level of service you're going to be able to offer will not be good enough. Competence is a very important factor in the success of a one man band, and you may need to work on yours more.

A lot of people don't think of training at all, they merely think of going on particular courses when they're already some way down the track, when they perceive the need to be informed on a specific topic.

It should be appreciated that courses are *not* the same as training. Courses are one- or two-day programmes that are focused on specialist topics. You can always give up some time to do that. Training, however, is a more dedicated learning process, and should be undertaken first.

Training can take months, sometimes years, during which time you are trying to develop basic competence in whatever it is you want to do. Say, for example, you want to become an advanced hairdresser, specializing in hairdressing for older customers. You would need much better depth of knowledge about the treatment of hair, so that you can really give an excellent service to the 45- to 60-year-old women who have basic hair problems. You want to be able to understand the chemistry of hair as it ages, and how to treat it, because you're going to set up in business, focusing on these aspects. Therefore, in order to provide a better service you are going to need to know a lot more than what's offered in a basic hairdressing course. You will need more competence training. You must have good training to be able to differentiate what you're offering, and this vitally important preliminary training has nothing to do with knowing how to deal with details such as how to sell the service or how to take care of your business finances more effectively.

Part-time One Man Bands

There are people who start off one man bands initially as a side-line, gradually building them up into a full-time business. This can be quite a clever approach to market research, and it doesn't really matter whether this side-line is unrelated or related to your main career.

One criticism is that you're not putting all the effort into it this way, but it can be a good way of seeing if things can work. Many people start off like this and then build the business up on the basis of success, before giving up their regular job and doing it full-time.

People who lack the confidence to set up their one man band and launch it, but who are nevertheless very interested in the idea, might find that starting a part-time business is a good way to begin. The types of one man band businesses discussed in this book include many that could be established in this way, especially those that you can run from your own home, with start-up costs that are usually fairly minimal.

But, strictly speaking, our definition of a one man band is a full-time occupation which a person pursues entirely on his or her own, which he or she has set up solo.

Continuous Market Research

Market research should not take place only at the outset of your one man band venture, but continually. With each piece of work you do, you follow it through and see how it progresses. If it interests you and seems worthwhile and profitable, you should seek feedback from the customer or client as to how useful it was to them. Then you can start to look at other people who might be interested in this service, and consider if they will pay similar rates for it. Ask yourself: are there other things I can do that are adjacent to this, that are spin-offs? This is a very pragmatic way of finding out what people need, simply by doing. Inevitably the market for your services will change over time, which is another good reason for maintaining a constant market research effort.

Defining Your Business Plan

Once you have chosen your one man band specialism, there are several questions you should ask yourself when planning the setting-up of your business, even before you sit down to write your business plan:

1) What **input** is required, especially in terms of **money** for equipment and for premises?
   a) How much **time** is required?
   Most one man bands, and those for whom this book is written, are running their business full-time, but there are examples – including some quoted in the case studies – of people who first start their one man bands part-time, and then become full-time once the business takes off.

2) What do you need to **start** your business?
   a) Where will your first piece of business come from?
   b) How will you get it?
   These points will be discussed at length in the chapter on 'Getting Started', but it is important to think about them at this stage. As a service business, items to get you started will be minimal, but will include:

   - a telephone

   - some basic office systems

   - perhaps a series of announcement advertisements in the national or local press, depending on your perceived market

3) If your business needs regular **supplies** of certain items, such as top quality stationery, photographic films and copier paper, do you know where to get the supplies?
   a) Can you be sure that you will get reliable supplies at the right

prices? This can affect your own reliability and lead to fluctuations in your income

4) Who are your **clients/customers**?
   a) What markets are you going to address?
   b) Do your clients/customers exist in sufficient numbers in your business area?
   c) How will you draw up your target list?
   d) Have you already appraised the demand for your service among potential clients/customers?

5) Who is serving your market now, or is your service entirely new?
   a) Are others already working in your projected area?
   b) If so, will you be in competition with them?
   c) Can you give convincing reasons why you will be as successful or more so than they are?

6) Can you **market and sell** your product or service effectively?
   a) By what method?
   b) How will you go about targeting your potential clients/customers?:
   • With advertising?
   • With a mail-shot of brochures or flyers?
   • With a launch event?
   • Will this promotion drive be on a small or large scale?

7) Approximately, what do you expect your **income** to be likely to be in the first six months to one year?
   a) Is it possible to test this in some small way before starting in business full-time?
   b) Do you have a few assignments in hand, or a few long-term clients/customers whom you know you can fall back on?
   c) How much financial risk is at stake?

8) If you assume the lowest possible income, will having set up your one man band still be worth your while?
   a) What do you consider to be the **minimum revenues** needed in the first few months to keep you going?

Contents of a Typical Business Plan

Overview

At the beginning of a business plan, it is important to take an overview of the market for your particular service:

- Does a real opportunity exist to enter this market?
- Is the market in its infancy, or is it well-developed?
- How favourable are the economic and business conditions for entry into the market?
- How will you differentiate yourself from your existing competitors?
- Will this be in terms of your speed of response, your fee structure, or will it be in terms of the specific service you are offering and its style and approach?
- Are you convinced that your entry will be profitable?

Business Objective

It is then necessary to decide upon and define your business objective and the manner of your service to your clients or customers: What are you offering them? You must be able to state this in a short phrase which you can explain easily and readily to potential clients/customers – and anyone who may be able to help you in your marketing efforts.

Scope

You must define how far you wish to extend your business in the foreseeable future. If you anticipate that it might diversify into related areas, you should define these up front. If you expect to develop business overseas, you should mention this in your business plan. You should analyse time phases for the expansion:

- How long do you expect it will take before you've established a foothold in your chosen market?
- How rapid do you expect expansion to be?
- What are the restrictions of your initial scope?

You must ensure that you have the resources to match this scope, that you are neither over-stretching yourself nor under-using your capacity. The resources relate to both capacity to do the work and marketing.

Market Summary

In drawing up your business plan and making a presentation for funding, you must be prepared to answer many questions. Your bank manager might not know anything about your business, and you must explain it for his or her benefit, and to show that you know what you are talking about and that you are enthusiastic about it.

- What is the history of your business?
- Is it old/established or new?
- Did it begin in Britain or in other countries?
- What is the size of this business worldwide, in terms of total revenues (if it is possible to calculate this)?
- Does your business take away from other businesses, or will it create a new market?
- Will it draw business from related markets?

If you are entering a relatively new business, will you have to do much of the pioneering yourself, or are there others in the field who have already created an awareness of it in the market? You should beware of the difficulties of entering a totally new business which no one has heard of or understands, because it will be an uphill struggle to create market awareness and primary demand. The best time to enter a business sector is perhaps when it has already been shown to yield profitable business but it still has relatively few players, so that demand exceeds supply.

- To what extent do current business and economic factors support your entry into this business?
- What has been happening to the companies you see as your clients, and/or to the individuals you see as your customers?
- Which aspects of their business or personal needs are they now emphasizing?
- What have been the changes in the attitudes of individual managers among your potential clients, and among your individual customers?
- Will they be more prepared to use your services than before?
- Is your business able to benefit from specific economic events, such as the creation of a single market in Europe and the opening up of Eastern Europe?

You must make sure your new business idea fits in with these and related trends within the business environment in which you will be operating. You will need to address carefully the matter of entry point, in terms of coming in during a recession or a growth situation, and determining the extent to which your business will be recession-proof. Whatever the climate, your business must help your clients to be more competitive.

The Service

You must define the exact nature of your service and the different variants you have to offer, specifically in terms of whether your clients/customers will need your work. Rather than just offering a list of services, it can be helpful to identify scenarios in which your clients/customers have a clearly defined need for you. You should make your service seem as unique and essential as possible.

In some cases your clients/customers may not have experienced a need for your service, but will be able to see that should this need arise then your service fits the bill. They may remember instances in the past when they had this need and it was fulfilled unsatisfactorily. Your service must be need-based and client-/customer-driven, so you should set it out according to their requirements, and not according to the way that you may see it. Where you offer a differentiator, in terms of speed, effectiveness and personal service, you should make this clear.

Service Differentiators

- What are the advantages which you offer clients/customers?
- Do you offer them access to new information, new techniques, new and improved quality?
- Do you offer them sufficient flexibility in your arrangements with them?
- Can your service be used with other, related services offered by others?
- How cost-effective is your service, and why is it different from anything they may already have in-house?
- In what way do you offer new ideas to the company?
- How is your service better than the one they are using already?
- To what extent can you offer them an uncomplicated and straightforward service, without unknowns?
- To what extent is your client/customer able to review the progress of your work while it is underway?

- What do you say in the outline of your service about your personal approach, so that clients can see if you will fit in with their approach, and customers can see if it fits in with their particular needs?

Potential Clients/Customers

- What is your source of potential clients/customers?
- Are there constraints in terms of industrial sector, geography or size of population?
- Will you appeal most to small, medium or large companies, or solely to individuals?
- Do you think you have an ability to appeal to all of these?
- In business-to-business one man bands, whom in particular, within a given company, will you be targeting?
- Will you also be approaching individuals? If so, how will you reach them?
- Will you be prepared to adjust your fees according to the ability of your clients or customers to pay, or have you decided to charge a flat fee, or at least a minimum fee, to all, rejecting those who will not pay your minimum?
- For business-to-business one man bands, will you be targeting just industrial and manufacturing companies, or companies in the service sector too?
- Will you be targeting professional advisers?
- Could you work for banks and investment trusts?
- Could you envisage working in the public sector?

It is important to define your desired client/customer base, and target those areas where you are familiar with the business or with your customers' requirements. It is important not to be too ambitious at the beginning, and not to put yourself into situations where you do not understand the client's or customer's exact requirements because of your lack of knowledge of a sector.

Competition

How many others are working in your field? Do you know anyone else who is considering entry into it? Are your competitors of good quality? What do you feel your competition lacks, and how are you

different? It can be difficult to break into a field where your
competitors may have earned a bad reputation. This can be a
difficult hurdle, because potential users of your service may tar you
with the same brush. Having good competition is not a problem if
the market has room for expansion. It can be an additional source
of satisfaction to win against good competitors, and this can also give
you a marketing feature for the future, i.e. that you beat a well-known
person in competition for a particular piece of work.

If possible, in your business plan you should identify your known
competitors and how they are positioning themselves, and why your
business is different. You should show an awareness of what you will
be up against:

- What do you feel is wrong and ineffective about what your
  competitors are offering?
- How would you be able to answer a question asked by potential
  clients/customers about why they should come to you and not
  go elsewhere?

In your business plan, it may be an idea to enclose short sketches
of the history and current profitability of your main competitors:

- Who are your competitors, why did they set up and how are they
  doing?
- Are they in their early stages, or already well-established?
- To what extent do they fail to cater for the needs of specific clients,
  in terms of fitting in with their style and approach?

You should also define potential entrants into the market, and the
implications of their entry on your business.

Facing Up to Competitors

How will your business differentiate itself? Will speed, quality work
or top-level service play an important part? How can you prohibit
others from offering the same things? To what extent are you
uniquely committed and qualified? How will your resources and
contacts be able to help you differentiate yourself?

You must also make the point that as you are a one man band,
what you see is what you get, and in this way you may win against
those big-company competitors who tend to send in juniors to

undertake work. It can be helpful to draw up a chart showing what differentiates your service, comparing it directly with what your competition offers, including fee structure and unique services – although the comparison should not rest on price alone.

Success Factors

You must define exactly the reasons why you think you will be successful. The first will probably be your individual commitment and skills. Others will include your determination to adhere to your service differentiation. You should also emphasize your aim to establish close and open working relationships with your clients, and how much you can benefit them according to their particular requirements. You must underline your commitment to continuous marketing of your service, because in most cases this is essential in setting up a successful business. You should also point out that your suppliers and resources (when this is appropriate) will be of the very best quality.

Financial Forecast

You should draw up a table forecasting your income against your costs for the first three years. Your income should be estimated realistically, and your costs should include everything you can think of, including marketing costs as well as the cost of executing your business. You should include your salary in your costs. You should calculate your profit and analyse your stages of growth through break-even, profitable expansion and unit optimization. You should include depreciation and interest charges on any money raised. You should calculate your forecasted possible return on your investment, and your percentage of total profit according to your turnover. You should think about leaving money in the business to invest for the future.

You must allow for the first few months of your business being spent on establishing your premises, equipment, space, stationery, brochures and administration, and of course marketing. It is best to focus on known or warm contacts to start with and then move into mailings to cold contacts. It can be worthwhile to establish a programme for marketing approaches. Much of your first year will be spent gaining market exposure among your targeted clients, and acquiring experience in undertaking assignments.

By the end of your first year you should have ironed out any administrative glitches and be operating smoothly, dependent only on the market demand you can create for your services. By your second year you should plan to be more profitable and on a sound footing, and it may be that you achieve optimization of profit within your chosen scope by your third year. Then it is a question of whether you wish to expand beyond your one man band status and enlarge your business by taking on a partner. These timings are approximate, and are offered here as a guide only.

Marketing

Your marketing programme must be defined strictly in terms of creating an increased awareness of your business, gaining opportunities to pitch directly for work, and ensuring you win and complete the work when it comes. You should promote yourself as a cost-effective and viable alternative to competitors with your own special differentiation, i.e. you. You may do this through advertisements, leaflets, by designing a brochure and carrying out an extensive mail shot, through articles appearing in the press (which will appeal to a wide readership among your target client group), and through direct contacts gained through your own research and intelligence.

Some of your contacts will be warm, and every effort should be made to effect a warm introduction in preference to a cold one. Cold contacts should be the last resort, and in these cases a letter (as personalized as possible) followed by a telephone call should be your course of action. In business-to-business one man bands you can ask for advice on a new business in your approaches, and offer some way of benefiting your potential clients, to make them feel you are giving and not just taking. You should research your approaches carefully and show them that you know what they need. You may find that to generate around 50 genuine enquiries that you may need to arrange some 150 face-to-face meetings. For each face-to-face meeting you will need to make many more telephone calls or send out many more letters. That is why constant marketing and mail shots are very important.

All of these marketing efforts will help you to build up a marketing database for the future. This will, of course, vary according to the type of service you are offering, but all one man bands need to know as much about their clients/customers as possible.

Presenting Your Business Plan

When approaching a bank for a loan, it is well to modify your style and approach. You'll want to appear fairly modest and not too pushy – don't act as though you assume you're going to get what you want. Their forms and enquiries may seem trivial, but they must be paid attention to. Some would-be one man bands are more advanced in their thinking than many bank managers, but if you want to borrow money from such a bank manager you should not make this too obvious.

Be prepared to explain and defend all points of your business plan in a straightforward and convincing way. It can be a good idea to find someone to practise on first.

The banks will judge you on how well you make your presentation, so you must pay attention to detail, and consider how you come over to a customer or client. Bank managers are trained in analysing people as a good or bad risk.

Advice from the High Street Banks

Here we include short summaries of the sort of information the main high street banks are looking for before they will lend you money. They are prepared to send copious quantities of literature, but are equally cautious of lending to start-up businesses unless they are convinced that your advance thinking and planning is sound. What will they ask a potential one man band preparing a business plan?

Barclays

Barclays emphasize the importance of detailed planning, of defining your objectives and how you will achieve them. They argue that this calls for a certain amount of time and discipline, and suggest that you follow precise stages in approaching them with a considered and professional business plan, including a projected annual profit and loss account, monthly budgets and cash-flow forecasts. Barclays ask would-be one man bands to see the whole issue from the perspective of the bank manager. The bank manager will ask him- or herself why you need Barclays to lend you money, how much you will need and when, how you are going to pay it back, and whether you have any security you can offer them.

Barclays ask that you establish what the cost of borrowing money is, when and how you will pay for this, and the period during which the principal amount will have to be repaid. Barclays' prime consideration is your ability to service the loan, mindful of the risk factor in starting up a one man band business. They ask that before you prepare your formal business plan you should analyse the nature of your product or service, the target market for it, your own personal skills and experience, how much cash you are going to need and when, and what your personal position will be should the business fail, in terms of how much you stand to lose.

Barclays ask that you gather together a series of answers to specific questions before you prepare your business plan, concerning objectives, management, market, products, pricing, supplies, physical resources, personnel, profit and loss account, cash-flow forecasts, budgets and finance. Barclays suggest that you show your plan to an independent adviser, such as your local enterprise agency or accountant, before visiting the bank manager, and that this adviser accompany you when you go to discuss your business plan with your Barclays manager.

When you fill in your business plan form and present this to your bank manager, you should be able to give a good introduction to your business and its market, and be able to communicate the positioning of your particular business. You should present your business plan as professionally as possible.

The *Barclays Business Plan Form* asks for comprehensive details of the business and its product or service, as well as personal details about yourself. It also asks about your market and the marketing activities of your competitors, and asks about your premises and any necessary capital goods. It inquires about your records system and finance, and especially about any business you have already developed. It inquires about your personal objectives in running the business in the short, medium and long term, the security you are personally putting up, and details of your accountant and solicitor.

Midland

Midland Bank also emphasize the need for planning. In drawing up your business plan you need to know where you are now, where you are going, whether you have the ability to get there, how you are going to do it, how much it will cost, how much you will get out of it, and whether it is all worth while. A business plan is not required to simply open a bank account, but if you require financial assistance, Midland emphasize that you will need a plan and a cash-flow forecast to show your bank manager.

In approaching a Midland manager for finance, this manager will be considering a range of questions, summarized by the word *PARSER*. *P* stands for *person*, including his or her character, competence, capital and financial capacity; *A* is *amount*, in terms of the purpose a given amount of money will be used for and how it will benefit your business; *R* stands for *repayment*, requiring an analysis of expected profits and cash-flow forecast; *S* is *security*, according to the risk involved; *E* stands for *expediency*, i.e. when an external factor may influence Midland's decision to lend, such as a family connection between you and another Midland customer from whom support might be available, your other business interests, and the local economic environment; and *R* is *remuneration*, estimated according to the risk involved. It may be necessary for you to pay an arrangement fee to cover the costs of the bank's monitoring the advance, based on how long it takes to assess your proposal.

When the Midland are considering amounts to lend, they need to review cash-flow forecasts and how much you are personally investing in the business. Usually they are looking for an equal commitment from you as an investor. They need to know if you have made allowance for any additional working capital to fund the growth of the business, if there is a contingency plan for setbacks, if full costing and pricing have been carried out, and what level of sales are needed to break even.

The Midland then provide examples to help in the completion of the financial projections part of their business plan form, including the calculation of gross profit, gross profit margin, overheads, actual turnover required to break even, the monthly target that needs to be met in order to break even, and accumulated profits. They ask that would-be borrowers complete cash-flow forecast forms, as part of their business plan, for at least six months. The Midland's Business Plan Form, as in the case of other banks, asks about you, your business, your products and services, your market and the arrangement of financial considerations, projections and requirements. In the Midland Cash Forecast Form there are columns for budgets and actuals, with space for commenting on details about capital expenditure, asset disposals, and significant fluctuations between periods.

NatWest

National Westminster also emphasizes 'profit by planning', and explains precisely why you need a detailed business plan, arguing that it's basic common sense. They have a detailed checklist for you to complete, and suggest you make full use of your accountant, your solicitor and your local enterprise agency. They ask about your aims, your confidence of your family's full support, your awareness of the risks as well as the opportunities, whether you have the personal qualities necessary to run your own business, if you are ready for hard work and long hours, if you enjoy good health, if you have enough experience in your field, and if you have thought everything through before committing yourself to a specific project or location.

National Westminster also asks about markets and marketing, the law and your business, basic bookkeeping and money matters, and employing people, if necessary. The NatWest emphasizes that the information your bank manager will require is that which you should already have at hand in order to run your business efficiently. They ask that you put yourself in the bank manager's shoes. Would you lend money on the strength of your presentation? You should be as clear and as brief as you can, and not leave everything to the last minute. Give yourself lots of time, and send the bank manager a copy of your plan in advance of your meeting. You should not be overly optimistic, instead looking at things realistically and considering the need to cover contingencies. You should be prepared to answer searching questions about the information you have prepared.

The NatWest business plan also asks about the business, key personnel, premises and assets, the product or service and the market place, assets available as security, and financial requirements. Their cash-flow forecast sheet has separate columns for the following: budgets and actuals for each month, receipts and payments, and VAT. This bank also requires the completion of an Operating Budget Form, looking at sales, direct costs, gross profit, gross profit as a percentage of sales, overheads, net profit before tax and sales required to break even. National Westminster is very much concerned with monitoring your performance, and provides examples of actual trading figures, analysing the reasons for fluctuations. They suggest remedies to problems in performance, providing comments on how to maximize profits, especially on how to ensure prompt invoicing and credit control.

NatWest's business plans, and those of most other banks, are geared more to manufacturing than to service businesses, and especially to business-to-consumer rather than business-to-business one man bands. It will be important to emphasize from the outset that yours is a service business, and to define your target clients or customers so that the bank understands that your requirements may not be the standard ones outlined in their brochures.

Case study 3 underlines the importance of the business plan in starting up your one man band . . .

CASE STUDY 3: BUSINESS CARD DESIGN AND PRINTING

William had a variety of corporate experience before setting up his one man band in business card design and printing. He had been thinking about starting his own company soon after he left university. Ironically, one lunchtime he went to the bank to pay in the first investment in the company which he had just formed only to be told that afternoon that he'd been made redundant from the company where he'd been working. His business card printing company has been going for just over a year, and he is very seriously trying to grow it into a major business in due course.

Deciding on the One Man Band

As early as 1982 William had considered setting up a one man band making business cards. When he joined the sales department at his first job and was given his business cards he was amazed at how expensive they were and how long it took for them to be made. William now produces business cards the same day, if this is what a client wants.

William started producing business cards before he was really ready, as a friend had recommended him to a buyer and he could not turn down the chance of his first order, even though he knew it would actually cost him a lot of money because he had to sub-contract everything. He only had a telephone – no equipment – but he wanted to get the business started. Then he looked around at the printing market, and got to know a printing press operator. He watched his own stationery being printed, and that was his first lesson in printing training! So then he bought his own printing press and set up in business, at home in the first instance. It is possible to spend up to £1 million on printing equipment, but you can get a good secondhand printing press for between £3,000 and £10,000.

Redundancy and Launching the One Man Band

When William was made redundant he was sent by his former employers to an out-placement company. The psychometric test showed him as being quite entrepreneurial: out of 50 people being out-placed at the same time he was the only one who didn't want a job exactly like the one he'd just come from. He wasn't gloomy or shocked at losing his job, but couldn't understand the rationale behind some of the redundancies made by his employers, because they'd got rid of some people who were good fee-earners and marketers. Many of these people subsequently went back to the company on a sub-contracted basis! William took advantage of all the services offered by the out-placement company even though he already had the mechanism in place to launch his own business. He was interested in the out-placement company's analysis of his capabilities, and he also wanted some free advice.

Early Marketing Strategy

Initially William decided to target professional firms, so he consulted a directory of lawyers, looking for medium-sized firms, and telephoned to find out who their print-buyer was. Some told him, others wouldn't. He approached only six at first, and had a good response because he'd pre-selected them carefully. He couldn't cope with big companies, but thought it a waste of time doing anything for very small ones.

He analysed the competition in detail, and spent hours telephoning them to ask how much they charged and what their delivery times were. He also did a lot of networking among people he knew, and often just went into print shops and nosed about.

William's early successes in getting business came from being faster than anyone else. One of his clients had been waiting a month for his cards: upon ringing up his printer he was told that not only had the work not been done but that the originals had been lost. William said he could do it in a day, and did. Another possible reason for his success, he considers, is because he's one of the few specialist printers who is well-educated. Most businesspeople like to deal with someone who has a ready understanding of quite sophisticated needs. He's selling to businesspeople all the time, and in medium-sized companies these people have wide responsibilities, and they like to talk to someone on their level.

He has since gained more business from further mail shots and by making thousands of telephone calls. William emphasizes that spending money on marketing is clearly worthwhile, but also that having a clear target in mind is vital.

His main idea was to differentiate on service more than on price. He has started off as a top-quality printer, and aims to stay that way. He spends as little as possible on materials and capital goods, yet adds value in terms of personal service and special extras, like two- or three-colour printing and thermography, and speedy and reliable delivery.

Managing and Operating the One Man Band

William believes that capital equipment must be made to work for you. There is no need to be extravagant to achieve good quality. For example, you don't actually need to have a full-colour Visual Display Unit screen, as you can work just as effectively with a black-and-white screen. The difference is spending £3,000 for the former or only £400 for the latter. It all prints out exactly the same. Why spend this money when you don't need to? It's just a luxury.

In his business you also have to be very clever at picking suppliers, nurturing the good ones and abandoning the bad. William admits to having sometimes nurtured some bad suppliers out of misguided benevolence, as he tends to give people a second chance. But his business is at stake if he does. He finds sub-contracting very frustrating, especially because he came out of a professional environment and not out of industry. He wasn't used to getting poor-quality work, or to dealing with suppliers who weren't prepared to accommodate his needs.

William did a lot of research, including finding out where to get his printing machine from. He considered a Japanese printing machine, and tracked down manufacturers via the Japanese Trade Federation in London. Then he spent time setting up his other systems. Because he is quite computer literate, his business started off being highly automated. He has tried to get a type-setting agency to accept a modem link to his computer, which he would pay for and install, but they have said they won't do it.

William's print-buyer clients seem to vary a lot: in some companies buyers are dedicated to buying for quality, and it's hard to prove the quality of your goods over the phone. Cold-calling is emotionally the hardest thing to do for William, but he has always targeted it carefully, and has always been well-prepared. He has telephoned so many buyers now that he knows what they are looking for. In large companies the print-buyers tend to be dedicated, but in other companies they are office managers with countless other duties.

Banking and Accounting Problems

William has found that in terms of which bank you should go to, and how you should deal with your bank manager, as a consumer you don't have a great deal of choice, and you may also find that they are not as sophisticated as you are. He prepared a very detailed business plan, and feels that this was really important. You might not stick to it but it is essential to have one, and it's a good discipline because otherwise you can forget something really key.

At the first bank he went to, William paid in his £5,000 redundancy money. Nevertheless, he soon required an overdraft. He saw the manager and gave him very detailed cash-flow predictions, spread sheets and profit and loss (P & L) plans, prepared on sophisticated computer-based systems. However, he was still asked to fill out in handwriting a rather scrappy form which they had designed. Their attitude was that they were doing William a favour, and their charges were very high. So he went to another bank (these were both high street clearing banks), which had a different attitude and seemed to understand what he was trying to do; their charges were also considerably cheaper. It is important to have a bank manager who understands your problems and has confidence in you, and doesn't think of you only as someone who ticks boxes.

William considers the administration of running your own business horrendous. He has a computerized accounting package which seems simple enough but is actually quite difficult to use correctly. Yet because he has started his business on the basis that it will become a big company, he wants the administration to be squeaky clean, with everything right from day one. This has meant a big learning curve, as double entry bookkeeping doesn't come naturally to most people. There have been many anomalies in the accounting package which have had to be sorted out, but at the end of the day the company accounts will be in good shape.

William's first expansion move has been to hire an enthusiastic woman trainee from a government training course. Dealing with government agencies is difficult and depressing, but the people can be very good, and William says he will probably hire more trainees in due course.

Future Plans

William wants to build his company quite quickly, and it is possible that in the end he may well sell out. He will diversify ultimately, but not yet. He hasn't got the slightest idea of what he might be doing in 10 years' time, and thinks it will be difficult keeping to a business plan long term. William would like a partner, but if someone wanted a stake in the business he knows he would be reluctant to give it away.

In setting up his business, the pull factors have been:

- independence
- being able to make his own decisions
- variety
- empire-building
- control

Of these advantages the last has been most important to him. William likes working on his own and doing things when he likes, the way he likes. The major disadvantages have been the heavy load of administration and also the need to be constantly self-motivated, which he finds can sometimes be tricky. People in Britain are very sceptical about success, and people still ask him what he knows about printing. He feels you can't know everything about something before you start. He doesn't know all the jargon yet, but can explain what he wants.

He is not yet making as much money as he did when working in the corporate sector, and he is still juggling overdrafts. The capital value of the business is hard to assess, but he set it up for well under £15,000. Return on sales, not assets, is vital for one man bands.

The business has been going for just over a year now, and it is difficult for William to say exactly how successful it is; nevertheless he feels he has made a good start, having done extensive market research, put in good systems, and achieved a reputation for high-quality work. His review of his first year was totally different from what he'd expected. He thought he would see big volumes and low margins, but he has actually got better margins than he thought. And above all, he has a good feeling about having his own company at last.

Start-up Costs
- Telephone installation – £200
- Answering machine – £150
- Fax machine – £500
- Computer equipment – £2,000
- Purchase of specialist equipment – £8,000
- Setting up of company – £250
- **Total start-up costs – £11,100**

Running Costs
These include rent on his office, the telephone, printing inks, card, and his assistant (not all of which can be passed onto clients)

Typical Length of Time to Become Established
Three months

Typical Rate of Growth
20 to 30 per cent p.a.

Typical Personal Income
£35,000 – £45,000

Typical Turnover
£50,000 – £75,000

Raising Money

Some one man bands don't need money to start up (and therefore don't necessarily need a business plan, although it is still a worthwhile exercise). If you do need to raise money for your one man band, however, you need not only a well-thought-out and viable business plan (with the help of your accountant), but you must be convincing in your case for raising money, not generally but specifically. You must know how much you want, and *why*. You may have to modify your business plan later, but you must not compromise at the fundraising stage.

Sources of Financing

Once you have a good and complete business plan worked out – as discussed in the previous chapter – you will be in a position to raise money to start your venture. Get your accountant to help you.

Again, the one man bands we are discussing in this book require fairly minimal financing. It must be emphasized that the idea of running a small-scale service business is that you should not need very much money. Your initial financing may come from members of your family or even from a second job, which you might do in the evenings or at weekends. It may be necessary to remortgage your house, and this option is more and more commonly used.

However, if you require a modest loan of between £5,000 and £15,000 to invest in office equipment to get yourself started, an obvious source is the high street banks; if this doesn't work it can be worth applying to the Government's Loan Guarantee Scheme (if you live in the UK), which is designed to help small businesses that haven't got access to conventional financing. It's not possible to try this avenue first, because it is designed for those who cannot attract bank funding.

Three Principal Ways of Raising Finance

The main ways of raising finance, in order of preference for most one man bands, are:

1) Your **own capital** and savings, which may already be invested – perhaps in a bank, building society, in Unit Trusts or other forms of investments. Such savings may not all be realizable immediately, nor may it be a good time in the market to sell them. But you don't need all the capital at once: a cash-flow analysis will show how much you'll need in the future.

2) Additional capital can be borrowed from any **friends and relatives** who are particularly keen that your one man band business should prosper. They may even be prepared to lend it to you at very low rates of interest, or **interest-free**, hopefully over a longer period than the banks would.

3) A loan from a **bank** or **financial institution**

You may also be able to find enthusiastic supporters of your business who are prepared to become outside investors, to inject capital into your business venture in return for a share of the profits. These may be friends or contacts, but they may also be formal venture capital companies. Sometimes you may even see 'venture capital available' advertisements in newspapers. However, before borrowing money in this or any other way you should always consult an accountant and a solicitor, because there could be hidden constraints, and the rates of interest may be very high.

Banking

When you have arranged the finance for your one man band, you need to arrange separate banking facilities to handle your business finances. You will need a personal account and a business account, and perhaps high-interest reserve accounts with each. It is usually practical to do your business banking at the same branch as you do your personal banking, but this is not always necessary, and you may even prefer to go to a different bank altogether. You may need to approach another bank when specialist financial transactions occur, for example, in import-export businesses, but this all depends on the activities of your one man band operation. For this a major city branch is essential. You can ask your bank manager, accountant or solicitor for an introduction to a new bank if necessary.

Banks will apply charges to business accounts, and you should ask for details of these in writing. Managers may negotiate a reduced-charge or no-charge period for new business customers.

It can be useful to open up a line of credit by way of an overdraft. Again, charges could be negotiable. For an overdraft you may have to pay an arrangement fee, in addition to the interest. Security may be required such as assets or a first or second mortgage on your home.

The Loan Guarantee Scheme

The Loan Guarantee Scheme exists – according to its well-explained literature – to provide finance to those small firms with good business proposals that are none the less unable to obtain finance by conventional methods. It is essentially a Government guarantee to banks and financiers to lend up to £100,000 to new or existing eligible businesses. Since its inception the Scheme has guaranteed in excess of £700 million to some 21,000 small firms, including retailing, manufacturing and service businesses.

The scheme is intended to supplement normal commercial finance, but will not be unavailable if a conventional loan is obtained. A borrower should present a business plan, incorporating the amount needed and the purpose to which the loan will be put. Once eligibility has been confirmed by a lender, the borrower can then apply to the Department of Employment for a guarantee, which is issued guaranteeing 70 per cent of the total loan, for which the borrower will pay the DoE a premium of 2.5 per cent p.a. on the guaranteed amount.

A loan application for up to £15,000 can be granted without the lender referring to the Department's Loan Guarantee Unit, and a further incentive to new businesses in some areas is a guarantee of up to 85 per cent.

The lender makes commercial decisions affecting the loan, whereas the Department only checks the eligibility of the borrower and his or her business.

When applying for any form of finance a borrower should make a detailed calculation of his or her business needs, monies being allocated for working or fixed capital, project development, and all the forms of finance and related costs available – a business plan. Loan finance is usually repaid by regular capital and interest instalments to the lender; is leasing or hire purchase a good idea, or maybe a fixed-term loan is preferable to an overdraft? How soon will your business generate sufficient funds to make the relevant repayments?

You may also consider equity finance, whereby a risk-bearing investment is provided by shareholders or partners in the enterprise, since equity capital usually carries no fixed charges – a plus when flow is tight. The UK Government encourages such investment, available through the Business Expansion Scheme (see below) or specialist financial bodies, by providing tax relief on equity investment made by independent investors in unquoted companies.

Eligibility

The Loan Guarantee Scheme is appropriate to one man bands, as eligibility extends to sole traders, partnerships, franchises, co-operatives and limited companies who are trading or are about to commence trading soon, and excludes businesses with over 200 employees, although groups of companies/businesses with broadly similar ownership or control will be considered as one unit. Business plans will of course be scrutinized carefully before any grants are issued. A borrower previously involved in a business which has failed under the Scheme should declare this on the application form, but this will not automatically provoke rejection.

As discussed in the previous chapter, a business plan is essential if the borrower is to convince a potential lender that his or her business is viable. It is a good idea to use an enterprise agency or a qualified accountant to prepare a plan, although the advisory offices of many lenders and small firms publish advice on planning and monitoring a business. It goes without saying that the borrower must also convince the lender of his or her personal commitment to the venture.

The application form requires the following information:

- personnel details: their experience, knowledge of the industry, education, age and training
- product or service details: development, intellectual property rights, follow-up products or services
- market details: size, type, planned penetration, sales estimates
- information about your competitors, and how you intend to succeed against them
- your results to date (if the business is already established), borrowing history, existing commitments, current bankers

- your business objectives, detailed short and long-term business and financial projections including typical accounts and risks
- total funding required, based on the projections, application of such funds, and repayment predictions
- what security for collateral is available
- which accounting systems are used, and their likely ability to produce regular management accounts
- the most likely risk areas, such as personnel sickness or injury, and how these will be coped with.

Eligible business activities are primarily those involving tradeable goods and services. Eligible purposes encompass only business purposes, such as improving and developing a project or business, or starting up trading – a detailed description of which should be given on the application form and even in the business plan. It is not permitted to use the Scheme to buy any type of shares in another company, to buy out members of a partnership, or to replace current loans, overdrafts or finance interest payments.

Terms and Conditions

There are several terms and conditions to the Scheme, the first of which applies to the Loan Agreement itself. The Agreement is a legal contract binding upon the borrower and lender only, and its terms are variable as they are negotiable between the borrower and the lender.

A lender could agree to a capital repayment holiday, i.e. a period during which the borrower need not repay the loan itself but only the interest and premium. The lender must consider the viability of the business, even though he or she has the benefit of the Government guarantee, and will fix the interest rates accordingly; an arrangement fee may also be charged.

A Guarantee can cover loans with no lower limit, although there are simplified arrangements for those of up to £15,000. The upper limit is £100,000 available to any one borrower. A borrower may have more than one loan, but all loans together must not exceed a total of £100,000; associated companies and partnerships will count as one borrower. Having reached the limit, a borrower will not be entitled to a further loan under the Scheme unless interest in the business that received the loan is less than 10 per cent.

Guarantees are only available on medium-term loans given for a period of between two and seven years. In guaranteeing 70 per cent of the loan the Department of Employment is liable for this to the lender if the business fails; the borrower will also be liable for the full 30 per cent of the debt in the event of the business failing.

These terms and conditions apply equally to businesses in the Inner City Task Force areas, which are eligible for an 85 per cent guarantee irrespective of where the lender is situated.

On being granted a loan, the borrower is required to pay quarterly – in advance and by direct debit – a premium of 2.5 per cent p.a. on the guaranteed part of the loan outstanding to the Department of Employment. The amount to be repaid will of course decrease as the total is paid off (these premiums in turn help fund the Scheme). If a loan is up to £15,000 the premiums are paid in advance as a lump sum, and may be incorporated into the loan itself; the loans can only be made in multiples of £500 and cannot qualify as part of any capital repayment holidays.

The actual loan is usually paid to the borrower in a lump sum, or paid in up to four stages within two years, each stage being a minimum of 25 per cent of the total loan. The dates of these stage payments should be specified on the application form.

A lender will always consider carefully whether a prospective borrower has used all personal assets for a conventional loan, since neither they nor personal guarantees can be used as security for the Scheme. The borrower may, however, need to use premises, machinery and other business possessions as collateral, which collateral will apply to the whole loan amount.

The Department and lender will of course want every business they support to succeed, but it is in the borrower's interest to keep good, detailed accounts, including cash flow, budgeted and actual profit and loss figures – especially as this information must be provided quarterly in accordance with the Scheme – together with a Progress Report, if requested. The Department uses reports and accounts to judge the Scheme's effectiveness, so not every borrower will be contacted for such information.

Failure

Having accepted an offer of a Guaranteed Loan and a loan contract with the lender, should the borrower fail to comply with any conditions the lender has the right to demand full repayment of the loan. Do remember that in such an event, despite the Guarantee and having paid the Scheme's premiums, the borrower is still liable for the full amount of the loan. The lender can of course claim the collateral to off-set any remaining debt, and will reduce its claim on the Department's Guarantee accordingly.

How to Apply

Applications for the Scheme can be made to local branches of the large high street banks. Further details on the Scheme can be obtained from:

Department of Employment
Loan Guarantee Unit
Room 221
Steel House
11 Tothill Street
London SW1H 9NF

Department of Employment
Small Firms Centres
Dial 100 and ask the operator for Freefone Enterprise

Local Enterprise Agencies
Contacting Small Firms Centres (see above) or
Business in the Community
227A City Road
London EC1V 1LX
Tel. 071-253 3716

Scottish Business in the Community
Romano House
43 Station Road
Corstorphine
Edinburgh EH12 7ES
Tel. 031-334 9876

or qualified accountants.

Further Financial Help from the Government

There are numerous schemes providing financial help to small firms. Most high street bank managers can provide you with further details.

The Business Expansion Scheme

The Business Expansion Scheme helps small firms by making shares in small companies more attractive to outside investors. It does this by offering investors tax relief; an investor who buys shares in an unquoted company can often obtain tax relief on investments worth up to £40,000. Accountants and local Tax Inspectors (Inland Revenue) can fill you in on the details of this scheme. Recent changes in UK law have made it possible for small business owners to sell shares to outside investors and make an agreement with them that the company will buy back the shares after a certain time. This benefits small firms, including one man bands, who want to raise capital but who do not want to part with equity permanently.

Enterprise Allowance Scheme

There is also the Enterprise Allowance Scheme, which helps unemployed people set up their own business providing they have £1,000 available to invest in it. They are paid a weekly allowance of £40 for their first year to help compensate them for loss of unemployment benefit while their business gets underway. Job Centres can provide more details.

Investing in Equipment

Nearly all service-orientated one man bands, whatever their line of business, need at least a telephone and fax machine (which can share their existing telephone line), a typewriter and probably a word-processing package and computer system.

Setting Up an Office

You should take time to set up your office, thinking about all the items you will require and how they will be organized in the space available. Whether you are using a spare bedroom or a prestige office suite, you will probably need some if not all of the following:

- a telephone or two (especially so that one incoming line is free at all times). Contact British Telecom or Mercury for a system appropriate to your needs, considering their range of services including 'Call Waiting'
- a fax
- a typewriter or computer for word-processing. You could buy one second-hand system via classified advertisements. Alternatively you could use a typing service, but this is rather inflexible, and expensive in the long run
- access to services like photocopying, printing and binding (you could use a local business services bureau)
- files – ring binders and lever arch files for storing documents and to act as ledgers, and at least one lockable and fire-proof filing cabinet

Computer Systems

Service is key, so you must get everything you require quickly. From high-level strategic consulting to providing a personal catering service, all one man bands need to keep track of projects, clients, potential clients and accounts, besides day-to-day word-processing of correspondence and reports.

What sort of office systems are your competitors using? Do you need a lot or a little? Do you really need very extensive systems to set up your own business, bearing in mind that they will represent a substantial proportion of your start-up costs? Many people become obsessed with their systems, but many – if they are honest – play with them as much as work with them. *Need* rather than *desire* should be the operative word. You must not get carried away at first, but you must not be so mean that your work suffers because of poor presentation, inadequate equipment or tools, or inefficient storage of data.

Using good equipment can save you time and money, and can make you appear more professional. But you must be able to use it to its full potential, to leverage the efficiency of your business. As a one man band, as your work expands in volume you will need good systems to save increasingly valuable time and effort.

Systems and equipment generally are a crucial aspect of your preparation. You must buy the best that you can afford, in terms of offering capacity for future expansion. If you will need to be working with computers, and if using computers is appropriate to your one man band, it might be worth attending a short computer course so that you are not afraid of computers before you start. You certainly won't have time to do this once you begin.

Flexible systems with potential for add-ons will also help you to leverage your time more effectively. Setting up a parallel system between a portable lap-top computer and your main office machine will enable you to take your work with you when you travel.

You don't even need two or more processing units, as it is possible to cater for all your needs with a lap-top (or even notebook) computer which you can plug into a large screen and printer at home.

It can take a long time to set up your systems for your individual requirements: it is a good idea to see if there are any good software packages available which can help you work smarter an save time and effort.

Using Business Services Bureaux

There are basic requirements in setting up an office which can be expanded as necessary. The best rule is to start out using the services of a nearby print shop or business bureau. When you find yourself going there every day, and suffering inconvenience when they are closed, this is the time to acquire your own equipment. Yet this needs careful consideration. The best equipment producing the best results is very costly, and usually bulky. It would take a lot of usage to justify buying a full-colour photocopying machine costing several thousands of pounds, for example. Even a binding machine for binding reports and presentations to clients, etc., costing £150–£200 may be too big an investment for a one man band until it becomes absolutely essential.

Setting Up Your Own Company/Sole Trader Operation

Legislation affecting companies and sole trader businesses is constantly changing, but there are general principles relating to the legal and accounting requirements of running your own business in the UK which need to be understood.

Forming a Company/Sole Trader Business

In the UK, there is no need to seek permission to start in business. Any individual or group of people is allowed to trade as a business. However, every business must have a formal structure. People trading on their own account are considered sole traders, or sole proprietors. A sole trader has full personal liability for his or her business and any debts incurred, but also has full control over the running of the business. There may be problems if you've previously declared bankruptcy; if this is the case you should check first with your solicitor.

Types of Business Organizations

Individuals trading together can be formed into a partnership, sharing the liabilities and control. A partnership agreement (made through a solicitor) is advisable; it should lay down how disputes between partners are to be resolved.

Those starting in business may also apply for limited liability status. The limited company is a legal body which offers those who set it up limited liability against some debts. The Registrar of Companies (Crown Way, Maindy, Cardiff CF4 3UZ) is the place to register, but an accountant can handle the procedure. Rather than setting up a new business from scratch, a common and cost-effective technique is to buy a defunct or non-trading company with similar aims and simply change its name. This can be achieved for around £100–£150.

Most new businesses start out on a sole trader or partnership basis, but you should always get the advice of a solicitor and an accountant. Some advise that company status is only worth having where turnover is expected to exceed £100,000, but this is not always the case. Some people like the idea of being a company for the status and aura of long-term commitment and professionalism this brings.

English Law and Setting Up Your Own Business

English law is based on settling disputes rather than on the Continental concept of rights and duties in society. Procedures such as 'due process' and 'fair trial', based on case law, are most significant, and although great changes have taken place over time, a high degree of significance still attaches, under English law, to these procedures. Scottish law is different again. The common law was developed in England by the courts; case law emerges in instances where legal rules and certain procedures are linked with the facts of a particular case.

The law in the United Kingdom allows for a range of different business organizations. All of the following forms can be one man bands, although there is a need for other partners or directors, if only in name. At one end of the spectrum there are the sole proprietorships and small partnerships, and at the other the large public limited companies. Sole traders and partnerships are the principal forms of business entities in the United Kingdom, followed by limited liability companies.

Sole Traders

The sole trader is the smallest and simplest legal entity within which to conduct business in the UK. Most one man bands start off as sole traders, and often find it convenient and cost-effective to carry on in this form. A sole proprietorship consists of one person carrying on business. He or she may employ other persons, but the sole trader is entirely responsible for the conduct of the business and has unlimited liability for the debts the business incurs. Usually there is no requirement for registration or for the independent auditing of accounts, but the latter is often recommended, especially by the banks.

Partnerships

Partnerships have been defined under the 1890 Partnership Act as '[relationships] . . .which subsist between persons carrying on a business in common with a view to profit.' Although the partners may be referred to collectively as a firm, the firm does not have the legal status of a company. This situation is slightly different under Scottish law, where a partnership does have a legal status separate from that of the partners. But the partners in a Scottish firm are ultimately, like those in an English firm, personally responsible to creditors for the debts and obligations of the firm.

Most partnerships are fairly small, and there are official limits to their size. One of the few regulatory controls affecting partnerships stipulates that a partnership may not consist of more than 20 persons unless they are lawyers, accountants, or members of a recognized stock exchange. A partnership often evolves from a sole proprietorship, and can still be to all intents and purposes a one man band, if only one of the partners works and the other(s) do(es) not take an active interest in the running of the company.

The **1907 Limited Partnership Act** allows the creation of a general partnership with one or more general partners who conduct the firm's business and have unlimited liability, and one or more limited partners with liability limited to their capital contribution. The limited partners must not take part in the management of the firm lest their limited liability status be lost; because of this stipulation limited partnerships have not proved to be popular forms of business entities. Either a conventional partnership or limited liability company is seen as preferable.

Limited Liability Companies

The limited liability company is the dominant form of business entity in the UK, although in sheer numbers sole proprietorships and partnerships are more common. Limited by shares, the members' liability for a limited company's debts is restricted to the amount paid or unpaid on their shares. Limited companies may be public or private. Only a public company may offer shares or debentures to the public, but they need not be quoted or traded. A public company – plc – must have an allotted share capital of a minimum of £50,000, of which one-quarter of the shares' par value must be paid up. Clearly, relatively few one man bands reach this status, but some particularly ambitious ones do, including a number of those quoted in the case studies.

The company's memorandum of association specifies its authorized share capital and the division of the capital into shares, which may have different voting, dividend and other rights. One man band limited companies tend to keep the vast majority of the shares to themselves, except those which must statutorily be apportioned to another director. Public companies must maintain a register of shareholders with an interest of 5 per cent or more of the company's voting shares. Bankers and those from whom capital might be sought will want to see copies of the memorandum of association.

Every company must hold an Annual General Meeting (AGM) every year, and at least 21 days' notice of the meeting must be given. Business at AGMs include the accounts of the most recent financial year, including the directors' report, the auditors' report on the accounts, approval of the dividend proposed by the directors, the election or re-election of directors, and the appointment of auditors and the fixing of their remuneration. For a one man band limited company the AGM is a very straightforward matter, although there is a question of how much dividend should be kept in the company and how much taken out.

1992 may herald differences in the way companies can be set up and run. With the stated objective of the EC's industrial policy, i.e. 'creating a unified business environment involving the harmonization of company law, and the creation of a community capital market', and the advent of the single market, existing company law in the UK could be affected profoundly, bringing it away from the US model and more in line with systems practised in mainland Europe.

Being a One Man Band Director

The directors responsible for conducting a company's business need not be shareholders in that company, although articles of association sometimes require share qualifications. It is possible to have one director working in and running the company while other directors play a more passive role. The directors appoint one or more of their number to executive positions, such as managing director and chairperson, each of which may or may not hold a full-time executive position. It is possible to create a private limited company

with one director who appoints him- or herself managing director
and then designates a person outside the company to be a fellow
director and company secretary.

The company's articles of association define the powers and duties
of directors. These include ensuring that company information is
divulged to potential and existing investors, if there are any.
Directors must take into consideration the interests of employees as
well as shareholders (again, if these exist). Every company must
appoint a secretary (who may also be a director) who is usually the
person responsible for ensuring that the company complies with the
requirements of company law. A company may have only one
director, but this person cannot be the company secretary as well.
The directors also decide on the dividend, which may be ratified or
reduced by the shareholders. No dividend can exceed the amount
recommended by the directors.

A public company must have at least two directors; a private
company need only have one. The largest British plc's have an
average of 12 directors, decreasing to nine in smaller public
companies and five or six in private companies.

Private Limited Companies

All other companies are regarded as private companies. There is no
authorized minimum share capital for a private company, but such
a company must include as the last part of its name either the word
'limited' or the abbreviation 'Ltd', or their Welsh equivalents. Unlike
a public company, a private company need not acquire a trading
certificate and can do business or borrow as soon as it is registered.
There are other legal requirements from which private companies
are exempt, but they must file annual accounts, which are thus made
available for public inspection. This ruling applies to all limited
companies. If the company is only small or medium-sized, it may
file modified accounts, though these accounts must contain all the
information specified by the 1985 Companies Act.

Private companies are also incorporated by a memorandum of
association. This provides details of the company's name, the
country in which its registered office is to be located, the limited
liability of its members, and its authorized share capital, subscribers
and objects. The objects clause is normally so widely drafted that
it gives the company the powers necessary to conduct any business
it may wish. It is important when drafting the objects clause to allow
plenty of scope for expansion and diversification. Usually the articles

of association are drawn up by lawyers at the same time as the memorandum of association. The articles lay down the internal rules for a company and its members, setting out provisions on voting rights, transfer of shares, the powers of directors and many other items. In fact, Table A in the Companies Regulations 1985 may be adopted as the articles, with or without modification, and this is what many start-up small companies do.

Share Capital

A company's authorized share capital and the division of the capital into shares are specified in the memorandum of association. Issued share capital is held to be that part of the authorized share capital which has actually been issued to members. It may not exceed the authorized share capital. Shares may be of any fixed amount – usually £1 or less. Shares of no par value are not allowed. They may be of different classes, having different voting, dividend and other rights. Issued shares may be full or partly paid. Shares may not be issued at a discount in relation to their par value, but may be issued at a premium. Each company is required to keep a register of members, recording details of the shareholders and the quantities of shares they hold. Companies may issue debentures as well as share capital. Debentures are normally issued as security for a loan. They usually bear rights to interest at a specified, often fixed rate, and repayment at some future date.

Choosing a Business Name

Every business must have a trading name. Sometimes this has been decided upon at a very early stage. This might be your own name or a special business name. Do you want the business to revolve totally around you, or do you see it as a possibly separate entity which you might sell in the future? This consideration does play a part in selecting your business' name. You must also choose it with an eye to future marketing: it must convey the essence of what you are trying to do.

The name of your business must also be different from that of your competitors, and there is a legal provision that it must be unique in the case of a limited company. A superficial check can be made through telephone directories, but a solicitor will undertake a search for you at Companies House.

It is necessary to justify the choice of certain words in a name. If you want to call your business 'International', then you must prove that a substantial proportion of your income is derived overseas. Names may not include terms such as 'National', which implies national ownership, or that you are representing the whole country in what you do, or that you pioneered the development of your line of business, as in the case of a name such as 'British Bio-technology'. For sole traders, however, there is no need to register a name, nor any central register of names to consult.

If the business name you have chosen to use is a general name and not related specifically to your own, then your name and official business address (even if it is your home address as well) must be displayed on business documents and at the business premises by means of a small but prominent notice. A booklet (C469) advising on choice of company business names is available from the Registrar of Companies (address above).

Licences and Permissions

In setting up a business in the UK no general business licence is required, but a few businesses may need official permission because of the nature of the products and services they sell. For example, businesses handling food – such as personal and company catering, and some elements of corporate entertaining which include meals – require environmental health clearance from the local council. You must be careful not to expose yourself to potentially disastrous liabilities.

You should check licence needs with a solicitor or business adviser before starting any business. The small business advisers appointed by the high street banks can be helpful and may save your time in this matter. If licences are needed the local council is usually the appropriate body, but you may have to contact HM Customs & Excise or some other public authority.

Value Added Tax

This is a tax payable on sales by businesses with a turnover above a certain limit. Such businesses can also reclaim the tax they pay on most purchases. Registration once you reach the limit is compulsory; below the limit it is voluntary.

Ask HM Customs & Excise for the booklet *Should I be Registered for VAT?* and for details of the current registration limit. For your local office, look under Customs & Excise in the telephone directory. If you are in doubt as to whether or not you must register they will advise you impartially; alternatively you can consult an accountant.

Getting Started

What do you have to do to start a simple sole trader operation? How do you go about buying a company 'off-the-shelf'; how do you register the name, once you have chosen it? How do you justify being 'international', 'national', or any other title? Where should you have your registered office: at the place where you actually work or at your solicitors? Who should you have as your fellow director(s), even if it is only you who is actually working? Who should be company secretary?

How do you go about preparing a simple advertisement/announcement of the formation of your company? You must select and design attractive stationery, a logo, and develop a house-style and format. How do these compare with those of your competitors? It can be a good idea to look at their literature and ways of presentation, to get some inspiration for how to present yourself.

Right from the beginning you must keep up-to-date and accurate accounting records, whether you are operating as a sole trader, as a limited company, or as a partnership.

What help might you be able to get from the Government in getting started? What sort of assistance is available? How can you find out more?

Another important aspect of setting up your business is its physical environment, i.e. your office and your business premises. The main question here is, will you work from home or rent an office? There are important pros and cons in each instance.

Types of Companies

In the previous chapter the various types of companies and business organization were described. In most cases it is appropriate for a one man band to be a sole trader, as it is certainly easier and cheaper, requiring only simple accounts and minimal official declarations. A partnership is also relatively uncomplicated. A limited liability company involves much more work and expense, involving complete annual auditing for which a qualified accountant and auditor are absolutely necessary. A limited liability company is only really justified by a conviction that this is the only way to attract the amount and nature of business that you want.

Starting a Sole Trader Operation

Starting a simple sole trader operation is merely a question of opening a business bank account, keeping your accounts for your business separate from your personal accounts, and contacting the Inland Revenue with regard to your self-employed tax status. Then the question of VAT registration must be considered, especially with regard to expected income.

Starting a Limited Company

It is important to take the advice of a good accountant before taking this step, so that you understand fully the extra expense and effort involved. You should meet with a number of different accountants before you choose one, as chemistry is important. Then, if you are sure you want to proceed, you should contact a law firm that specializes in company law. They should have access to companies that are being sold for the purposes of being set up as new companies. You will need to find a company with goals and aims similar to yours, and then change its name. You will need to check first if anyone else has already registered the name you want to use (the law firm will be able to carry out a search for you, or you can do this yourself by contacting Companies House, 55–61 City Road, London EC1Y 1BB, tel. 071–253 9393).

When the company is officially incorporated, you will receive a large package of documentation, including a minute book, articles of association and certificates of incorporation and change of name, as well as your company seal, with which to seal share certificates and to use for other official purposes. You will then need to appoint officially an accountant, auditors and solicitors, unless you have done so already. You may decide to make your company's registered office your law firm's address; this is the usual practice.

Launching the Company

You will need to produce a small brochure containing brief information about your company's services, or even just a simple flyer: the main idea is to have some literature to mail out to potential clients and to leave with people you have met in your business development work.

You will also need a complete set of stationery. Find a good print shop, and cultivate the staff there for your future needs. They may be able to help you find and choose a logo if you'd like to have one, and will show you an array of typefaces. Take a while to choose the one you feel most comfortable with, one which goes with your style and image. Ask a close friend to go with you to help. It's like buying a house or making a similar major decision which you will have to live with for a long time; you don't want to keep changing your typeface and logo, as this will negate your attempts to build recognition and familiarity value for your company. Don't go for anything too zany as it may go out of fashion and lose you credibility; similarly, there's no need to go for the same boring style as everyone else.

Among stationery items, you will need: business cards, headed notepaper, compliments slips, fax headers and perhaps printed labels and small cards for less formal notes such as thank-you messages. You may also like to have a sign for your door or wall!

Smart Accounting

Once you have launched your company, you must start as you mean to go on, keeping an accurate record of all your financial transactions. You must always have a record of your business activity, whether you are a sole trader, partnership or limited company. It is recommended that you use one of three basic methods of record-keeping, relative to the type and size of your business. You may decide to employ a bookkeeper to handle this for you, but you should still understand the basic principles of how your business' books are kept.

There are three basic types of record-keeping:

1) Where cash transactions are prominent a proprietary system, using a daily record and a weekly sheet proprietary type book, will be enough; in the case of retail outlets, if you are selling goods this system must be backed up by a cash till and a till roll.

2) An analysed cash book system and maybe a sales invoice summary book for ease of VAT information are necessary if you are selling primarily on credit with some cash sales, with up to 200 sales invoices per month; the cash book should be backed up with two temporary folders and two arch files as a permanent store of original records. Standard petty-cash forms and VAT summary sheets can simplify the whole operation.

3) Especially for service-type businesses, a full double-entry system suits the larger business. Special training is required to keep a double-entry book, case book, bought and sales ledgers, day books, wages book, and nominal/private ledgers, and it can be best to employ a bookkeeper here.

Why Keep Business Accounts?

To survive and progress, your business must have sufficient cash when needed, and make a profit, and it is your accounts that should give you the information required to judge the state of your cash flow and profits, and summarize which parts of your business have scope for improvement or need to be abandoned.

You should, ideally, be using your accounting for managing your business and making decisions as well as for keeping a record of the results of your past decisions; this is strictly 'management accounting'.

The Main Purpose of Keeping Records

Accurate financial records assist in the making of management decisions, providing information for the assessment of relevant taxes which must be submitted on time, providing evidence to support applications for finance, and providing a valuation of the business if up for sale. They also assist you in complying with the laws regarding partnership agreements, the Companies Act and the Insolvency Act.

You should be able to assess your VAT ingoings and outgoings by yourself – although a bookkeeper can be useful here – but all other functions should be dealt with by a qualified accountant, and especially by one with experience in small businesses. One of the best reasons for keeping good records as you go along is the fact that an accountant's fees will, of course, be minimized if your books are up-to-date and accurate.

Proprietary Systems

Systemized books are available from many stationers, but you should take advice on which to choose. It is important to keep records (in whichever type of book you select) as up-to-date as possible, with each page carefully balanced: you will then know your cash, bank and unpaid bills position, although not in terms of stock – if this is appropriate – as this is usually estimated monthly and checked bi-annually. Complete the book's summary forms and you will be able to ascertain your profit position at any given time.

The Analysed Cash Book System

Accounts should show the following:

- monthly sales
- running expenses
- direct sales cost, e.g. labour, materials, etc., as relevant
- overheads (in detail)
- how much money is tied up in stock
- how old the stock is
- net profit (after expenses)
- your cash or overdraft position at the end of each month
- the value of money owing to you and how much is overdue
- how much money you owe your creditors.

The purpose of your accounting discipline is to monitor constantly the quality of your service or product, and your ability to sell it. Good accounts enable you to analyse continually your sales and the number and value of assignments coming in, and how other factors can affect sales and level of activity.

Business management is therefore making profit happen by overcoming circumstances that could cause adverse variations in sales or expenses. There are of course further considerations.

Accounting for the Limited Company: Income

If your business is set up as a Limited Company you and any other directors can include a reasonable salary and DHSS contributions, which are then allowable for tax, since you are technically company employees. If you are a sole trader or a partnership, DHSS contributions and any monies drawn from the business are ignored for tax purposes. Tax will be calculated on net trading profit. After all business calculations, your net profit will be treated as personal income and have the benefit of normal personal tax allowance, quite separate from the business. You should allow in your Profit and Loss budget for expected drawings and DHSS contributions.

Budgeting

Your budget should then be broken down into 12 months; your business may have a seasonal element in its sales and activity, you may make a loss in some months and profit in others, but when you calculate all the months your budget should equal your annual profit.

As time progresses you will be able to check whether you have achieved what you set out to do, what needs attention or a management decision. If your action is to be positive and effective you must be able to understand the reasons why your results vary from your original plan.

Cash Flow

A cash-flow forecast is an important part of your annual budget. It pre-empts how much cash you will have in the bank, or the cash deficit – usually an overdraft – which you will need to meet. You should prepare what action you will take with a large surplus, such as investing it either back into or outside of the business. If you have a deficit you should ensure that you make provisions to have sufficient cash to meet it. Again, you should divide your cash forecast into 12 months. In your accounting book, use two columns, the first for your forecast and second for actual results. Next, calculate the income from each item sold or assignment undertaken in your Profit and Loss budget. You should not see this in terms of when you will sell items or complete assignments each month, but when you believe payment will be in the bank – there is often a difference of some considerable time.

Outgoings

Similarly, you should prepare details of your expenses and as far as possible make monthly projections. You cannot always make exact monthly projections, however, as many regular bills such as those for electricity, gas and telephone tend to appear every three months, whereas car tax and insurance will be annual.

In the income section of your forecast you will need to make headings for loans received, capital raised, capital items sold, etc., and on the payments side make headings for loans repaid, capital items purchased, etc., entering each in the relevant month. This is especially important during the start-up period, when you will be buying equipment and setting up your office and other parts of your establishment.

Rolling Cash-flow Forecasting

Finally, once you have completed your budgeting you can add up all your monthly income and outgoings; the difference will either be a cash surplus or a cash deficit. Once your business has been established for a while you will be able to work your way progressively through the months, and you will probably see that the cumulative total at the end of each month will fluctuate up or down.

The point of a cash-flow forecast is to enable you to be prepared to meet any cash deficits as they arise, or to make arrangements to do so, in terms of borrowings. At the end of each month you will enter the actual figures, with which you will be able to revise your forecast for the three months ahead; this is called a 'rolling cash-flow forecast'. This will give you time to make special arrangements or make management decisions, based on sound information.

For those in small businesses with expensive stock items, even high-grade stationery for making presentations and reports, an important element of cash control is stock control. You should carefully design a good stock control system, whereby you're not stuck with too much surplus stock for which you will have paid and because of which you cannot cover your outgoings.

Overall, don't think of Profit and Loss and cash-flow budgets as existing just to keep the bank manager happy, they are essential for you to run your business properly.

Recording Transactions: Business Account

You should open a specific business bank account – in addition to your personal account – and use it for business only. Some items, such as your telephone and car, which fulfil both business and personal functions, can be entered into the business account and paid for through your business bank account; subsequently you and your tax adviser will agree on an apportionment. You may wish to enter your living expenses and then demonstrate to the tax inspector that they are reasonable business expenses. In this case, private expenditure must be entered gross (including VAT), and only in the 'drawings' column, as even if you are registered for VAT you cannot claim it back on personal expenditure.

Your business account will supply you with a paying-in book and cheque book to use in business transactions; you should always complete any counterfoils carefully as they will serve as records. It is important to remember that all cash received must be properly banked and not used for petty-cash purposes; in this way you will avoid complications with Income Tax and VAT, and the 'true' gross contribution percentages for management decisions will be demonstrated.

Petty Cash

Petty cash is necessary as you don't want to have to buy small items with a cheque. Obtain receipts for all payments (except coin purchases) for which you make out a standard petty cash slip (available from stationers). If you are registered for VAT, do the VAT calculations on each slip to take account of VAT at 17.5 per cent (not for postage costs, however, as they're exempt from VAT). It is useful to use a monthly petty cash form, whereby you enter the expenditure as it occurs and attach the slip or receipt with a paper clip. At the end of the month, staple the receipts to the form, draw a cheque from the bank for the total amount, and enter this transaction in your cash book with the full analysis in the normal way, using the petty cash form as a voucher.

If you start using petty cash you need a 'float'; draw a cheque for a round amount which will cover the expected month's total, and keep the cash in a separate safe box for use; the balance of the petty cash form at the end of the month should equal what has been taken from the box.

Banking Income

A Bank Analysis Cash Book is coded with a double code e.g. 4/10; the first figure being the number of 'receipts' columns, printed in blue, and the second figure indicating the number of 'payments' columns, printed in red. The most common are 5/14, 5/16 and 5/18, depending on the analysis required.

Banked monies may be from different product groups, from capital introduced into the business, or from the sale of non-trading items such as surplus office equipment; on the payment side you will have extra columns for capital equipment, e.g. cars, machinery, furniture, and capital withdrawn, including your own drawings.

Dealing With Expenses

In the expenses part of your Profit and Loss budget you have a list of headings against which expenditure is to be incurred, e.g. rent, telephone, postage, etc. Add up each of the actual columns and compare these with the corresponding budgeted columns: these actual figures will be your Profit and Loss control budget. Incidentally, the end column is normally used for non-trading expenditure, e.g. capital items, which are not part of the Profit and Loss account. You will also need columns for 'direct' material purchases and 'direct' wages, such as costs of manufacture or the purchase of material and goods for sale. This may include items not directly for sale as such but which you need in presenting your work to your clients.

When deciding your analysis column headings, remember that the objective is to control the business, so you could group some together, such as rent, rates and insurance, and consider some columns annually rather than monthly.

Filing and Organizing

Do set up a simple system for your accounting paperwork or you could waste hours searching for it. This includes invoices sent out to clients as well as invoices you receive for goods and services you have bought. These invoices should always be numbered in the order in which you send them out.

When you receive invoices requesting payment for your purchases, fasten the 'goods received' note to them, check quantities and price, and collect them in a manila file marked 'Purchase and Services'. Keep them until you are ready to make payment, then draw a cheque for payment, enter this transaction in the Bank Analysis Cash Book in the 'payments column' with the cheque number, giving each item a sequential number, then enter it on the invoice and write 'paid'; finally, file the invoices sequentially in a permanent file. Remember to enter VAT and net column, and then enter the net amount under the appropriate heading as desired for your analysis of the accounts.

At the End of the Month

When things are up and running, there are other things to do at the end of the month, like arranging the figures to give an accurate picture of the business. It is a good time to examine the situation with your debtors and decide on appropriate action, particularly as they adversely affect your cash flow. A diary reminder system can be helpful to remind you of when you wish to chase your debtors, as well as when you are prepared to pay your creditors.

You should now also enter all the direct debit payments, standing order and bank charges, etc. which appear on your bank statement and for which cheques or cash have not been drawn into the Bank Analysis Cash Book. Finally, rule off, total and agree analysis book totals, agree columns relating to banking with your bank statement, taking uncollected and unpresented cheques into account.

A good analysed cash book system will produce all figures necessary to reconcile your bank balance, establish VAT figures, show total sales, the cost of sales and progression of expenses at any time by adding in outstanding items, and form a basis for your Profit and Loss account and balance sheet.

Basic Requirements

The accounting system described here is very detailed, but not everyone will think so much effort necessary. Nevertheless, everyone must at least keep:

- a record of all invoices issued
- lists of sales and purchases
- a record of wages or amounts for services paid
- records of cash position using cheque book and paying-in book stubs, not forgetting standing orders, direct debits and bank charges.

This may seem easy, but doing no more than the basics could mean that your business will suffer from lack of foresight, and that preparing for the Tax Inspector becomes a time-consuming headache at the end of the year.

If you are registered for VAT then you must calculate the figures for your VAT Return, which will be fairly easy to do if you have kept up a good detailed accounting system. Modified arrangements apply to VAT special retail schemes, so if you are involved in one of these you should take specialist advice. It might be useful to keep an invoice register for VAT purposes.

Use of Annual Accounts for Control and Pricing

Separate from your Management Accounts are your Annual Accounts for Inland Revenue purposes, which should be done by a good accountant who will be able to use your accounting figures to produce an annual consolidated Profit and Loss account and a balance sheet. Using annual accounts as a control is no substitute for good monthly management accounting, although they can be a very useful check because the figures should now be audited and error-free. You can do this yourself and handle your own tax affairs, but make sure you understand the rules and get it right.

Most Annual Accounts are drawn up by auditors or accountants in a conventional form for their own convenience and to suit the Tax Inspector, so are often useless for the control and management of the business. You should therefore insist that your accountant presents figures in a way most useful to you, and that he or she provides an explanation for anything you don't understand.

Annual Accounts Presentation

The layout of an essential statement, the Profit and Loss account, should show the value of sales less the cost of materials, labour, etc. as appropriate, i.e. the amount sales have contributed to the general expenses and profit of the business, or your 'gross profit'. The remaining expenses should be grouped and set against the total, to portray the cost of each category of expense, from which you examine your performance. Reproducing information in graph form provides a ready and easily understood means of control. Remember, though, that figures do nothing on their own, it is action that improves the business.

In the formative years of your business you must remember to

consider its broader aspects. Failing to reach expected sales will lose
you profits and fail to cover your overheads, while exceeding sales
will gain you not only more actual profits but extra money in that
you will recover more overheads than you'd incurred; do ensure
your overheads present value for money, too.

Finally, maintaining accurate records and carrying out smart
accounting procedures can only help your business to prosper and
be successful. It may seem time-consuming, but incomplete or false
records will only fool you and cause huge complications later.

Government Assistance

The UK Government has sought to improve the opportunities for
small firms to win new business by giving them new incentives.
Monopoly power has been reduced, such as the slackening controls
on the bus and telecommunication services, and the Government
has challenged a number of anti-competitive practices, e.g. by
introducing laws requiring local authorities to put certain services
out to tender; and by opening up Government purchasing, whereby
Government departments are given greater freedom to choose
suppliers of goods and services.

The Small Firms Service

Increasingly the Government has attempted to provide a variety of
services, e.g. information, advice and finance, to meet the needs of
small firms. There is now a Small Firms Service, providing a free
telephone enquiries facility and in-depth counselling throughout the
UK. The enquiry service will give you basic information and will
put you in touch with sources of detailed advice on any business
query, as well as making an appointment for you to use the
counselling service. The counsellors are experienced businesspeople who have all had experience running companies. Their
advice is confidential and impartial, and can even take place at your
business premises.

The Enterprise Initiative

The Enterprise Initiative, available through the Department of Trade
and Industry, was created specifically to provide practical help and
guidance for small firms. Financial assistance is available for
consultancy projects in independent groups/firms with fewer than
500 employees, whereby the DTI pays half the cost of 5–15 days'

consultancy in marketing, business planning, financial and information systems, design, quality and manufacturing systems. Applicants first receive a free Business Review from an experienced business counsellor, who will then advise on the most appropriate form of assistance. Practical information and advice on the management of design, quality, manufacturing and purchasing and supply through the 'Managing into the 90s' programme is also available.

Special Projects

In some cases there is help for small companies employing fewer than 25 people, in the form of investment projects for which the DTI will pay 15 per cent of expenditure on fixed assets up to a maximum grant of £15,000, and for innovation projects, for which the DTI will pay 50 per cent of eligible costs up to a maximum of £25,000. Finally, the DTI can also provide assistance under the Research and Technology Initiative, including grants towards collaborative research projects, funding under the Small Firms Merit Award for Research and Technology, and access to existing technology through case studies, seminars and information on current research in higher education.

Specialist Fields: Inner Cities

The Action for Cities programme provides special help in inner cities, using Inner City Task Forces to help small businesses with grants and loans through their Task Force Development Funds, the City Action Teams who co-ordinate Government programmes and can offer extra support to individual projects which are not eligible for main programme funding, and Urban Development Corporations and the Government's Urban Programme (run through local authorities), which can help with renting premises and training.

Other Sources of Help and Advice

Many local authorities offer services to businesses in their area, providing advice, information and help with marketing, premises, training and raising money. Look under Local Government in your telephone directory to inquire of your city, district or county council.

Local Enterprise Agencies

There is also a UK network of over 400 independent, privately run Local Enterprise Agencies (known in Scotland as Enterprise Trusts), offering business advice, counselling and often additional services such as access to loan funds, managed workspace, business clubs and information services; some specialize in advising local minorities.

Young One Man Bands

Specialist business counselling is available for young people wanting to start a business, such as the Prince's Youth Business Trust (071-262 1340) and the Prince's Scottish Youth Business Trust (041-223 3711), which provide grants and low-interest loans to disadvantaged young people starting a business. Livewire (091-261 5584), sponsored by Shell (UK) Ltd, offers advice and assistance to young entrepreneurs (enquire about the age limit).

Training

There is a wide range of training to meet the needs of small business owner/managers (and their employees, when appropriate). Most notable is the Business Growth Training programme, offering free kits to aid better business plans and identify training needs.

Backed by expert advice, this programme puts on low-cost seminars on business planning and skills, e.g. marketing and accounting, and offers concentrated help for selected businesses with the potential to expand quickly. The programme includes a consultancy to help firms review business strategy and devise and implement plans for employee training and development. It offers specialist advice and financial help for projects produced jointly with other businesses aiming to meet future skill needs, and specialist financial advice and help for firms that wish to introduce innovative training projects in order to improve their business performance.

The Business Enterprise Programme offers short courses and an open learning package on basic business training and on starting a business. Contact Training Agency Area Offices.

Colleges, polytechnics and universities are increasingly able to meet the professional, industrial and commercial (PICKUP) training needs of small to medium-sized firms, and to provide advice.

Business Resource Centres

In many local authorities in Britain, local Business Resource Centres have been set up to provide business consultancy services and low-priced facilities for small start-up businesses, for the benefit of residents of each borough or local authority. For example, in Kensington and Chelsea in London, residents can visit their Business Resource Centre for general business and accountancy advice, sales and marketing help, use of micro-computers, desk-top publishing (dtp) and fax machines, and to examine registers of information on premises for rent and for sale. This Centre also provides information useful to people running a business in the area, as well as details of available grants and loans. The Centre also offers liaison services between banks and their business clients, helping prepare business plans and cash-flow forecasts, and also helps run business training courses. Further assistance is given with problems of importing and exporting, with PR, and even with business stationery.

This particular Centre is used by 4,000 people per year, with demand greatest for their dtp facilities. Users of the Centre include a fruit-stall holder, a freelance graphic designer, a seller of printed fabrics, a number of specialty clothing shops, a small café proprietor, an art gallery, an exporting business, a freelance photographer and a gardening adviser.

Getting Further Help

Further information is available from the following books and organizations:

The Department of Employment's *Accounting for a Small Firm* guide.

The Department of Trade and Industry's *Your Guide to Government Help for Small Firms*.

The Small Firms Service, operated by the Department of Trade and Industry. Offers (initially free) business advice. Dial 100 and ask the operator for Freefone 2444.

The Training Commission, which offers training (and sometimes finance) for small businesses. Contact via Job Centres.

Business in the Community, a useful enterprise agency for local help. Tel.: 071–253 3716.

Local councils: many have a Business Officer or a Development Agency. They can help you deal with regulations and find premises and sometimes finance.

COSIRA (Council for Small Industries in Rural Areas) can help with advice for those living and working in the country or small towns. Tel.: 0722 336 255.

More telephone numbers:

Freefone Enterprise 0800 222 999
Freefone Enterprise Initiative 0800 500 200
Inner Cities Unit, DTI 071-214 4330
Action for Cities Unit, DoE 071-276 3053
Government's Urban Programme 071-276 4488
Department of Education and Science 071-934 0888

Premises

Working from Home

Working from home is a good, low-cost way of testing a new business idea, and many one man bands start off this way. Strictly speaking, though, residential properties do not have planning consent for business use. While a discreet business, like one conducted by telephone, rarely causes trouble, officially you do need 'change of use' planning consent for anything more, especially anything involving the storage of perishable goods or toxic substances, etc.

If working from home you should check with the following:

- the local council planning department, to see if you need any planning consent;
- your building society, if the property is mortgaged;
- your insurance company, to clear insurance problems;
- a solicitor, to check house deeds for restrictive covenants;
- your neighbours, to prevent possible future complaints!

Working from Premises

By their very nature some businesses (some forms of retailing, for instance) need special premises. In others, premises are optional but provide many benefits over home operations, such as extra space and 'site' advertising. However, premises-based businesses do require a higher capital investment.

Go through the following checks when looking for premises:

1) Take your accountant's advice on renting or buying
2) Find out the going rate for the type of premises you require
3) Use commercial estate agents to find a property for you
4) Don't agree to lease or purchase without a valuation and survey from a surveyor and advice from a solicitor
5) Make sure you have 6 months' rent (or mortgage repayments) in cash before starting, plus capital to cover insurance, rates, electricity, water, and decoration and furnishing costs.
6) For flexibility, don't sign a lease/commit yourself to anything for longer than 5 years.

Much business accommodation is provided by private firms, but local authorities can assist you in finding premises. Industrial and commercial premises in Assisted Areas are available on flexible terms and often simple tenancy agreements; English Estates (091-487 8941) builds or alters premises to meet firms' specific needs, and provides financial and business advice.

There are more than 25 Enterprise Zones in the UK which are totally exempt from rates and almost free of planning controls. 100 per cent Capital Allowances are available on the construction or extension of property within these Zones.

The Rural Development Commission (0722 336 255) builds workshop developments for rent or purchase at commercial rates through English Estates, and offers grants for converting redundant buildings, loan facilities for general premises, and advice on general planning matters.

Managing
Your Money

To operate a one man band effectively it is very important to be good at managing your money, not just to keep your costs down (although these should in any case be small), but to make your money work for you. It is important to control your budget. Once you have identified your business, you need to consider your income requirements? You must find ways of protecting yourself against various contingencies that probably did not apply when you were safely under a corporate umbrella. For example, what if you got sick? What about your pension? Do you need disability cover? How can you provide for holidays?

Do you ever lose money unconsciously? Do you wonder where your money goes to? Some people are extremely lax about managing their personal financial affairs. But, even if you are bad at managing your money, you should definitely be able to find a good financial adviser. You need an accountant (who becomes a friend), depending on the nature of your business, to assess whether your business will have a fairly regular level of income, to prepare profit and loss returns, and to help you with all aspects of tax.

Banking

- Set up a separate business account
- Declare yourself to the Inland Revenue and DSS as self-employed
- Make a cash-flow prediction of how much you expect your business to expand (you should already have done this as part of your business plan).

Everybody will have limits on their time and abilities. You can only double your income by doubling your fees, but this brings its own limitations. It can therefore be very difficult to build earnings once you are working alone.

Are you prepared to sacrifice the earnings of the first year (or two or more) in the anticipation that you may well be earning considerably more in subsequent years?

Taxation and National Insurance

Since 1979, both the rates and structure of tax have been simplified considerably. The basic rate of income tax was cut from 33 per cent to 25 per cent, the nine higher rates of income tax, ranging from 40 to 83 per cent, were replaced by a single higher rate of 40 per cent, the 15 per cent surcharge on investment income and the National Insurance surcharge were abolished, and the small companies rate of corporation tax was cut from 42 to 25 per cent, as well as the profit limit for this rate being increased to £150,000. There were wide-ranging reforms in taxes, the reform of the inheritance tax, simpler arrangements for paying VAT, the reduction of controls and cutting of a lot of red tape.

All income is liable to tax. The Inland Revenue have a booklet (IR28) giving basic details. It contains a form you can use to advise them that you have started in business. The address of your local office can be found under Inland Revenue in the telephone directory.

If you are full-time self-employed you will pay tax by annual assessment. If you are a limited company you will draw a monthly payment (salary), subject to Pay-as-You-Earn (PAYE) taxation.

If you are part-time self-employed, perhaps with a full-time job, make this clear to the Inland Revenue. It pays to consult an accountant at the outset, and ideally retain him or her to deal with all taxation matters.

National Insurance contributions are payable by those in business, except those with only very small part-time earnings. Ask the Department of Social Security for booklets NP15, NP18, NI27A, NI41, and N208. For your local office look under Social Security in the telephone directory. National Insurance contributions are based on your profits, and work out at 6.3 per cent of your annual pre-tax profits within annually adjusted parameters. For the current tax year, profits between £5,900 and £20,280 are charged at 6.3 per cent by the DSS; 50 per cent of this is allowable for Income Tax. The difference between £5,900 and £20,280 is £14,380, which means a maximum liability of £905.94, of which 50 per cent is allowable for Income Tax. Therefore, net profits above the level of £20,280 will not be subject to further N.I. contributions. These parameters may be subject to change.

Tax Planning

You are advised to have a one-year tax window if you expect/predict your income to be fairly irregular. If you believe your income will escalate fairly dramatically in the first three years then you should have a three-year window. Opt for the three-year accounting period with the Inland Revenue, as this allows for your annual tax liability, in the first three years, to be based on Year 1 Assessment. Check with the Inland Revenue and your accountant.

Your accountant will help guide you and advise the DSS of your position as self-employed, whereby you will go on Schedule D for tax purposes, and will be classed under the DSS in such a way that allows you to pay your liability on a monthly basis, which also helps your cash flow, rather than on an annual basis.

Discuss with your accountant the most suitable end-of-year date for the nature of your business – i.e. avoid December 31 if you are involved in retailing and expect a Christmas peak. Agree the first trading period, which can be in excess of one year and perhaps as long as 12–21 months. This need not be decided upon until you have actually traded for 15–16 months. Indeed, the more facts you have accumulated about your actual trading, on which to access your trading year, the better.

If you believe your gross income will escalate fairly dramatically in the first 3–4 years of trading, ask your accountant if you can elect prior-year assessment. This means that for the first three years your tax can be based on your first year accounts. If you think your gross income will increase steadily in line with inflation, opt for regular annual assessment. Check with your local tax office as well, for remember that although your accountant is working for you responsibility for any mistakes is yours alone. So check, as accountants are unaccountable to the Inland Revenue.

Remember that if you are married and your spouse is not working, your accountant may advise that he or she assists you in running the business; you are then able to pay him or her a salary, to a maximum (currently) of £2,400, without he or she incurring National Insurance liability. Alternatively, dependent on the cash-flow profit forecast of the business, your accountant may recommend you form a partnership with your spouse; thus net profits can be apportioned between yourself and your spouse, commensurate on the amount of input from both of you.

For example, if you pay your spouse £200 per month, this means another £2,400 which you can claim as a deductible expense. Inland Revenue have to be satisfied, however, that your spouse is making an acceptable contribution to the running of the business.

Main Income Tax Allowances and Reliefs

Allowances	1990-91	1991-92	1990-91	1991-92
	Personal		Married	
Age at 5 April 1992	£	£	£	£
Under 64 years (basic)	3,005	3,295	1,720	1,720
65-74 years*	3,670	4,020	2,145	2,355
75 years and over*	3,820	4,180	2,185	2,395
* Excess reduced by 50% of income over			12,300	13,500
Single parents etc., and maintenance relief			1,720	1,720
Business Expansion Scheme relief			40,000	40,000
Mortgage interest relief on loans			30,000	30,000
(relief limited to 25% 1991-92)				
Occupational pensions - new entrants				
Maximum pensional earnings			64,800	71,400
Maximum employee contribution (15%)			9,720	10,710

Pension Planning

Pension planning has to be considered, recognizing that the sooner contributions are made the bigger the fund at the end, and also acknowledging the tax advantages of pensions. It is important to note that many loans or mortgages for large amounts of money could be supported by a personal pension plan, using the tax-free lump sum as the repayment vehicle. Make sure, though, that you do not mortgage your retirement! All contributions to personal pensions, within Inland Revenue limits, are subject to tax relief at the highest rate at which the individual is taxed. Pension Funds themselves are exempt from UK Capital and Income Taxes, and therefore the returns are naturally higher and more beneficial.

Current legislation allows increased contributions at different age levels (your age being calculated on how old you are on 6th April of a given tax year):

- Up to 35 years of age: 17.5 per cent of your net relevant earnings
- 36-45 years: 20 per cent

- 46–50 years: 25 per cent
- 51–55 years: 30 per cent
- 56–60 years: 35 per cent
- 61–74 years: 40 per cent

There are financial limitations on each category, however.

Personal pensions effected under current legislation allow both a lump sum free of tax, to a maximum of 25 per cent of the fund, and a pension to be drawn from age 50 onwards.

Anyone employed in a company with a contributory Pension Scheme has an average 5 per cent deducted from their salary and put towards the Company Pension Scheme. Therefore, the self-employed person must be financially disciplined enough to put aside for the future, otherwise the only pension benefit will be that provided by the state – and you cannot rely on the state pension as it is so minimal.

Some people have been very successful one man bands, with such trappings as a Rolls Royce and two homes, only to come to pension age with little actual income because they failed to plan for the future by putting money by and planning with a pension. Perhaps such people were brought up to enjoy money while they had it, they may have got used to a way of life, and when they suddenly can't afford it it can be a great shock, and very frightening. Do you want, on retirement, a better, same or poorer quality of life than the one you now enjoy?

Some people think that they can sell their business when they retire and live off the proceeds – forgetting that by definition they are the one man business; if they want to give it up they will not be satisfied working for someone else, and the good will they have built up may be a personal good will and hence unsalable at the price they think it is worth.

You must realize at the very beginning that you should not put all your money into either the business, your home or personal spending, but put it into a pension which will at the same time help reduce your tax liability.

For one man bands who are coming out of companies and have built up previous pension benefits in a company scheme, you can now transfer these benefits into your own personal pension plans, even being able to claw-back on the benefits gained many years hence. However, prior to transferring it is important to seek professional advice to ensure the viability of the transfers.

Income and Health Protection (Plans)

These are essential for a one man business, and often for employed people as well, as there are limitations on company health/accident scheme benefits. State aid here again is limited, and therefore an Income Protection Plan (IPP) can be taken out that will provide an income in the event of any disablement, which could be caused by accident or sickness. The IPP should at least assist in covering personal expenses such as your mortgage and general living expenses, as an inability to work invariably means an inability to receive an income. The banks will look more sympathetically on a recently disabled individual with an IPP than one without. These plans can be tailored to suit your individual requirements and provide a income after as little as one week, although the longer the deferred period the cheaper the premium. Rates are based on age, sex, whether or not you smoke or drink, the nature of your occupation and the level of benefit required. Here again there are Inland Revenue restrictions. These limit benefit to a maximum of 75 per cent of earnings after state benefit has been deducted, and tax is payable if the benefit continues into a second fiscal year.

You *may* wish to take out special insurance to pay for private hospitalization in case you fall sick, not only in cases of emergency treatment but to ensure that medical attention can be arranged at your convenience to fit in with your business needs. Also, private medical care can minimize the amount of disruption to your work, as you can be provided with a private telephone and other necessities while you are in hospital.

Life Assurance

An individual leaving a company and a company life assurance scheme no longer has the benefit of what is termed 'Death in Service'. This normally pays out between two and four times one's annual salary to a nominated beneficiary. Therefore, adequate provision for your dependents must be made in the event of your death, to ensure that your family does not suffer extreme financial hardship. A suitable life assurance policy can be effected to provide for this contingency. Similarly, banks or other lending institutions may require that you have adequate life assurance, to protect their interests against any loans you have been granted.

Additional insurance may be required for expensive equipment, and certain occupations may also require contingent and professional liability cover. If you are utilizing your home or part of it for your business, professional advice should be sought from both the local authority for any permissions that may be required and from your accountant with regard to claiming for the use of home on your taxes.

Motor insurance is a well-known requirement, but a special policy may be needed for business use of vehicles. If you operate from premises, both buildings and contents insurance may be required. Public liability insurance (should a customer be injured on your premises) is advisable. It is also possible to insure for product liability (should injury be caused by a faulty product or service). You should also consider permanent health insurance, to cover loss of income due to illness.

At the outset consult at least three insurance brokers. Tell them of your plans and ask them to advise and quote for any compulsory insurance as well as for any useful but non-compulsory insurance.

Savings and Investments

Additional investment plans can be taken out to provide capital sums for the future by utilizing unit trusts, savings plans (including the TESSA plan) and personal equity plans. Although tax relief is not allowable on contributions to these plans, efficient tax planning will ensure there is no tax liability when the proceeds are drawn. You need to be able to put money away, to earn interest on it, and to build it up without it then being reduced by tax liabilities.

These savings and investment plans are extremely efficient ways of assisting your retirement funding, for although a pension is very tax efficient, pensions paid in retirement are taxable. Therefore, savings plans can supplement your income on retirement without incurring further tax liabilities. All these plans are very complex, and professional financial advice should be sought to ensure that policies are tailored and structured to suit your individual requirements.

Pitching for Business

In developing business for your one man band once you have set it up, if you have not had previous experience of pitching for work you should try to get an idea of what others are doing and learn the tricks of the trade from them. Your market research work will help you with this. How are your competitors going about it? How should you position yourself comparatively? Are there some you would like to see yourself closely linked to, and others you want to keep a clear distance from? Be aware of your competitors, but not paranoid about them. And remember that you don't need to rubbish the opposition to sell yourself.

In your pitches, you must clearly differentiate your quality of service and your attention to customer care. You must not be too pushy, but neither must you allow yourself to miss opportunities. You can start off by using your existing contacts and networking among them to lead to other clients, but you will also have to do a great deal of cold-calling. In pitching for business, you must above all not be afraid to hustle. Remember, your livelihood is at stake.

In a business-to-business one man band you can pitch for work to your old company, and by approaching new potential clients in other companies. How do you convince them to engage your services rather than anyone else's? How do you deal with negatives and objections? In this chapter we will also look at advertising for both business-to-business and business-to-consumer one man bands; how to sell (including how to develop a good sales pitch), and how to write a good business letter.

Your Former Employers

As discussed previously, it is possible to become a business-to-business one man band by continuing to do work with your old company, but your status and focus will be different, and you will have to be proactive about getting work for yourself. This can a very good way of making the transition from a corporate life to a one man band, as you will always know your worth, because if the company really accepts what you're going to do and rates you they will always want to give you work. But you must work out clearly how you are going to go about doing this.

There are three basic ways:

1) You can become a consultant with your old company, in the sense that they want you to work on projects and you get your one man band business going in parallel; this is a form of parallel working.

2) Better still, your new enterprise is contracted to work for this company for a number of projects.

3) Perhaps not so good, it could be that your old company has asked you to leave, but has said that they can offer you two days a week work. So you're employed two days a week by your old employer, but then at other times you do what you can do on your own. This may be a way in which your old employer might get more work out of you for less money, but it does give you a good base from which to start.

Many people find pitching for work with new clients very difficult, so this form of transitional period between corporate life and self-employment is very popular. It has been made a lot easier by a number of companies, who provide contract work for a large number of people who are leaving.

Work from New Clients

Approaching Potential Clients

There are two ways to get work out of an organization:

1) Find out whom you should talk to and write to them or telephone them with the object of getting a meeting to tell them all about yourself and what you can do for them. This is the cold call approach, which is not ideal but might be all you are in a position to do.

2) Get yourself referred by someone else. This second approach can be much more effective. Buyers of services are very strongly

influenced by third-party referrals because they seem trustworthy and objective. Trust is vital.

To Whom Are You Selling?

Are you selling to a particular department in a company, or just to its chief executive? You've got to know at whom you should be aiming your sales pitch. You must be talking to people who have the influence to agree to employ you and who can sign off your invoices.

Getting Referrals

You must take the trouble to cultivate potential referees, people who will take an interest in you and promote your services. You should always gain opportunities from all contacts with future clients in whatever context. This provides you with a referral base for the future. This also means, of course, doing your best work at all times, otherwise you cannot hope to get a good reference.

Gather early sponsors who will take a chance on you, people who like you personally, perhaps more than your service, and will want to recommend you. It can be useful to have a corporate 'sugar daddy' (or 'sugar mama'!) in your early days. He or she will give you a chance, and hopefully give you referrals to others.

Similarities to Gaining Job Interviews

To be a successful one man band, you must be able, essentially, to sell yourself and your skills; most one man bands are people businesses. One way of seeing the job of pitching for business for your one man band is to compare it with selling yourself and getting work for yourself, in terms of what you would do going for an interview for a regular job. Think about the problem of how you get work for your one man band business from a client and compare it with how you might go about getting a full-time job. There are important parallels. Every time you pitch for business for your company, imagine you are at a job interview and that you really want the job. You might think that you are not that good at selling your services, but you might be quite good in a job interview.

You can take the parallels further than this. The best plan may be to go along for a job interview, and when they offer you the job, say that although you are attracted to the idea of working for the company you feel that you would rather work on a consultancy basis, and tell them about your daily rate or any other way in which you charge out your services.

In a wider context, getting new business can be seen to be like job-hunting. As if you were looking for a new job, you can draw off some of the self-marketing ideas discussed in *Career Turnaround* and other self-help career books, in terms of finding out about enhancing your image and developing your personal brand.

Similarities to Interim Management

In selling a service business to clients, you can also see your work in the context of being an interim manager, an executive who takes on freelance assignments for a limited period of time. Your potential client has a problem, but cannot afford to employ someone full-time – or hasn't the time to find someone to work full-time – yet he or she wants results. So, you can offer yourself and your skills, like a temporary executive, to solve the problem, from the point of view of this being a service of your business. The important thing is to provide solutions to your clients' problems that appeal to them yet suit you and the way you want to run your one man band.

Countering Negatives

In pitching for business to a company you will inevitably meet with criticism and opposition to the idea of using one man band services. There are difficulties for the company in using one man bands, and you must be prepared to present arguments against these in advance.

Confidentiality

There can be a concern about confidentiality, as information is inevitably being passed outside the company. Using out-workers means that company secrets can be revealed. A company can be reluctant to fire a one man band because he or she has gained so much inside knowledge which could be dangerous on the outside. This is not the best reason for getting repeat business. Emphasize to the client the importance of confidentiality and discretion as regards your relationships with them; stress that this a fundamental aspect of your attitude to your business.

Loyalty

Clients can worry that out-workers, who after all have a number of other clients, will lack loyalty. They may fear it will be difficult to control the work you do, unless they feel they know you well, since you will not be working in the office all the time. You must demonstrate to your client that you are prepared to show them great loyalty in return for their support. You may even be prepared to give up other opportunities for business out of loyalty to them, if it means a threat to their interests.

There is a whole area of difficulty about what should be kept on the inside and what should be let out. Some areas of work may be too politically risky to involve an outsider, although on the other hand the converse might be true whereby the task is too politically risky to let an insider do it.

Subjectivity

Many clients may suggest that it can also be difficult to influence the development of a person who is not in the office all the time. That person comes in periodically to help them with a specific task, and then goes away again. They cannot make him or her be as sympathetic to the organization as are those within the organization. In response, you can argue that your value rests precisely in being outside the organization, that you are providing an objective input which could not come from within.

Allegiance

It may seem to the client that most of the benefits of being a one man band go to the person doing the work rather than to the company. There may be a feeling that the company has invested so much time and money into you that they then feel obliged to carry on using your services, almost out of inertia. You should avoid your client feeling in any way resentful or ripped off. They should feel privileged that you will spend your valuable time helping them, and that they are competing against other potential clients for your services.

How to Advertise

No business – whether it be business-to-business or (especially) business-to-consumer – can exist without advertising or PR in some form. There are surprisingly few different types, but an important business skill is to identify the best forms of advertising for your particular project.

Newspapers and Magazines

These are always the first choice for advertising. Local and regional newspapers are cost-effective and easy to use, though only really suitable for local and regional businesses. Advertising in national publications can be expensive, so should only be used for products and services you can sell nationally. You should also consider specialist media relating to your specific business. *Benn's Media Directory* and similar guides, which are available at libraries, list all the publications you can use. Ask each for a rate card. Most newspapers have specialist sales staff who will help you.

Yellow Pages

Advertising in the Yellow Pages is a must for all new regular businesses as it prompts unsolicited enquiries, and because one advertisement lasts a full year. Take the largest space your budget will allow, possibly advertising in more than one section. There are other similar local directories; they are quite expensive but quite cost-effective. They are only published annually, so reserve space in the next issue as soon as you start up your business.

TV and Radio

These are rarely used, as they are quite expensive. TV is only for major projects, although it can be suited to some regional businesses. Radio is more localized, but really is only suitable for certain types of well-known products or services. It is best to consult an advertising agency for advice.

Leaflets

These are suitable for local 'town-wide' businesses. They are a good, cheap way of launching a new business quickly. Consult a specialist printer and leaflet distributor.

Mailshots

Mailshots are a good advertising method when you are selling to other businesses (not so good when you are selling to the public).

A mailing list can be complied from telephone directories, and an attractive mailing piece sent out. It can be expensive, so is suitable only for products and services of high value (£100 or more). Consult a specialist writer and/or mailing agency for advice.

Direct Canvassing

Personal or telephone calls on prospective customers should be considered an advertising technique. Direct canvassing is suitable for both trade and retail customers (e.g. door-to-door selling). It is very cheap, though sometimes a great deal of 'cold canvassing' has to be done to get some worthwhile prospects. There are marketing agencies or freelance representatives who will do this sort of work, sometimes on commission.

Buses, Hoardings

Advertising on buses and hoardings can be a good method for local businesses, though it is really only suitable as a supplement to other techniques. Consult your local bus company or the hoarding agency (as shown on the hoarding itself).

Other methods

There are other methods of advertising, but they should be considered minor and only suitable to support major methods. Use them only when you have surplus advertising capital left after using the major methods. Advertising in local tourist guides, on street maps, parking meters and sandwich boards can be worthwhile. But test their potential as it relates to your particular business first.

Advertising Agencies

An advertising agency can look after your entire advertising requirements for a particular project for a set fee. Find one in the Yellow Pages (look under Advertising Agencies). However, most agencies will only be interested maintaining a certain annual turnover of advertising business, so may not be of help to small concerns.

If you want or need to do your own advertising *The Creative Handbook* is an essential publication. It gives contacts for consultants, designers, illustrators, printers, publishers, etc. that you can use to produce professional advertising material. It is published by Thomas Skinner Directories, and is available at major libraries.

How to Sell

Selling is distinct from advertising. Advertising gets you a business lead; your sales effort converts client prospects into income. Selling is a mixture of information, explanation and persuasion. Any business owner with commitment usually makes an excellent salesperson, even if he or she does not consider him- or herself good at selling. The following tips will help:

- Be highly informed about your product or service
- Get to know competing products or services
- Always have professional sales literature to hand, whether manufacturers' brochures or your own.
- Prepare a sales presentation for the customer
- Don't hesitate to meet the customer person to person, but always make an appointment first.
- Explain the nature of the product fully. Mentioning both its advantages and disadvantages usually goes down well.
- Tell the customer what the product or service can do for him or her.
- If possible, offer sale-or-return terms, or a free sample.

Considerable effort should be made to get initial sales. These can be used as 'testers' for future sales efforts.

Canvassing can be undertaken initially by mail, which establishes the contact and makes personal selling easier. Assume, for example, that you have identified a possible new customer and want to approach him or her to offer your services. A well-written letter could be valuable in creating a sales opportunity.

If you really don't feel you can sell personally, then employ sales staff. Advertise through Job Centres or in the 'sales staff' column of the newspapers.

Developing Your Sales Pitch

You must consider the following points and prepare your answers to each one:

- How the service or product can help you (the client) gain a competitive advantage
- How it can help you (the client) bring in more business
- How it can help you (the client/customer) cut costs
- How it can help you (the client/customer) get a better service
- What you (the one man band) have to offer
- Why what you have to offer is different
- Why it is better than anything the client has in-house
- Why it is better than similar out-housed services
- Why it is better than what your competitors can offer
- Why it is more cost-effective in the short/medium/long term
- Why the client/customer will be missing out if he or she doesn't take advantage of this opportunity
- When you will deliver (faster and more efficiently)
- Where there are differences in your product

You will need to refer to the market research work you have done on your competitors and your marketplace in order to perfect your answers. Do not make claims you cannot substantiate.

Writing Business Letters

Despite the increasing use of telecommunications in business, letter writing is still a key skill. A well-written letter will sell you effectively to some customers. It can have great value in getting you new business contacts and in selling. It is a very good idea to follow up potential clients/customers with a polite yet sales-y letter which shows you mean business. Not everyone thinks of doing this, so it can mark you out from your competitors.

Many one man bands learned good letter-writing skills at college or in companies, but the following tips will be useful for those unused to writing business letters:

- Good business stationery and a typewriter or word-processor with good-quality printing are essential
- Always quote the name and address of the person you're writing to at the top of the letter
- Start 'Dear Mr or Ms . . .' (ideally you will have found out the person's name)
- Most letters should have a heading for quick reference explaining the subject to be discussed ('with reference to . . .')
- The first paragraph should always refer to any previous contact you have had with this person or company
- The second paragraph should launch immediately into the subject. Ask clearly for what you want
- Keep any non-essential information very brief
- The final paragraph should instruct the reader as to what to do next
- After the final paragraph finish with 'Yours sincerely' (if you began the letter 'Dear Mr . . . .') or 'Yours faithfully' (if you used 'Dear Sir or Madam'), and nothing else. Always sign letters personally, typing your name and/or position underneath
- Add a 'PS' to highlight important items, especially in a sales letter
- Keep it concise – no more than one page if possible
- Good grammar/spelling/syntax are important

Final Points

Pitching for business is a difficult art. Practise makes perfect, and it can be a good idea to go on a sales course. If you are too discreet and laid-back in your approach it will be assumed that you're not really interested. On the other hand, if you are too pushy you can put people off. It's a difficult balance to achieve and, of course, your style and tone will vary according to the person or company you are approaching. It is only really learned by experience. But you must remember that even fairly mediocre services can be sold effectively if pitched well, whereas even an exemplary service may be a flop if it is not sold well. When meeting potential clients you should be as smartly dressed as possible in order to present the sort of image you want to present and give the sort of impression you want to give. What does the potential client remember? 60 per cent how you look, 30 per cent your body language, and only 10 per cent what you say. Clients/customers rarely go to a lot of trouble to find out about the availability of certain services, and are more likely to be so swamped by different sales pitches that it is enough to choose between them without investigating those who haven't even approached them. And certainly, clients/customers aren't psychic. You must tell them about yourself and your services, through a variety of methods. You must build relationships with clients, through being helpful and approachable.

Your First Project and Beyond

It is particularly important make a good job of your first assignment or first commission, because this will give you confidence and will also give you an example of your work which you can show to other clients/customers in the future. But don't forget the importance of constant business development even while you're in the middle of working on your first assignment or job.

Just because you have your first piece of work you can't stop looking for new business, hoping that something convenient will turn up as soon as you've finished it. It should not be assumed that a particular client/customer will always come back to you with more work. You have to make him or her form a conscious decision not to go to anyone else, that you are the best.

Your First New Client/Customer

Your first client or customer should not necessarily know that he or she is the first. He or she should think you've been going for ages. Your first client/customer may think that buying your services is nothing exceptional, but you will provide something special because it's your first assignment. It's worth thinking of all your subsequent assignments in the same way. Every client/customer should be made to feel special.

Gaining Custom by Accident

In many of the case studies it's happened that somebody has heard on the grapevine that a certain one man band is in business, even if the owner wasn't actually embarked on it but was only thinking of it. In these instances the soon-to-be-formed one man band receives a telephone call from a would-be client saying, 'I hear you're doing such-and-such an activity'. The one man band can't help but say 'yes', and before he or she knows it he or she has agreed to start work for the client. It almost always happens by accident. This may be the boost you need to actually get started when you've been planning your one man band for some time.

The Hard Way

In the worst case, your first client/customer is the result of your having had to send out lots of marketing letters, coming as a result of a marketing letter and a pitch, or even of knocking on doors. This is not the best way to get yourself your first piece of business, but for some people it will be the only way. It's too random, however, and too slow in coming, and you can easily get downhearted in the process.

The Importance of Your First Client/Customer

Your first client or customer is so important because he or she can be a useful influence on subsequent clients, and because through working for him or her you've got something to show other people. You will remember him or her forever. He or she will give you a new confidence: you're getting paid for your work, you're in business, you're doing some work and so you're busy, and, obviously, you're getting some money in to help offset your start-up costs.

How long you keep your first client/customer and how much repeat business you get is a sign of the success of your first assignment and subsequent work, but clearly this will depend on the nature of your work and on how long you can reasonably expect to gain repeat business.

A First Client from Your Old Company

Your first client might be somebody whom you've worked with in the past, who knew you were setting up your own business, who actually had some work for you and was pleased to be your first client because he or she rates you, and almost gets some kick and pleasure out of being your first client. So, your first client may easily be from the company you have come from.

But it's a different issue to take clients away from your old employers, to their loss. If you are setting up on your own and its something related to what you did before, in some cases you're not allowed to take clients with you and you may have had to sign various contracts against this possibility.

The Importance of Your First Assignment

Obviously, the quality of your first project is very, very important. If you've done a good piece of work the first time, the way to really develop it further is to try and do reference sales from that first one. Ask the client if he or she knows if any other people who need that service. Also, if the satisfied client/customer can telephone a contact and say that you were very good, then you're more than likely to win over this new potential client/customer.

Getting the Work vs. Doing the Work

Before getting your first assignment you may have thought that the hardest part would be bringing in the business, but this may not be the case. Getting the business in some instances isn't the main problem. For example, receiving a recruitment brief in an agency is not very hard because there is no exchange of money: the agency has to complete the assignment, and only then can they get paid. There are other instances of jobs where you've got to put the effort into the process rather than into the getting of the business. Also, a travel or estate agent only gets paid once they've signed up a client/customer, as is also true in insurance and finance broking.

There are many instances where gaining your first assignment is very difficult indeed, and you may heave a huge sigh of relief once you've achieved this – but you should always remember that if you don't complete the business, or if you haven't made a good impression, then you won't get asked back. So even if you were paid up front, not completing a job well can mean not only no repeat business but that the client/customer may start spreading negative criticisms about you, which can be hugely detrimental. So, for a new one man band, completing your first piece of business well is just as important as winning it in the first place.

Handling Objections

In closing a deal to carry out work for your first client or customer, and for others in the future, you are at the stage where objections may arise, where the client/customer is not entirely convinced whether to use you or not. Is your fee structure being questioned, or your timescale, or your previous experience and ability to do the work?

In dealing with objections knowledge is power, and having knowledge ahead of time is often seen as perceptive and imaginative. Objections to what you are saying can occur at anytime throughout the sales process. Rather than being worried or concerned about them, they are in fact the best thing that can happen to you. The reasoning behind this is that these objections bring out into the open for the first time what the client or customer is really thinking. The process of selling, especially in terms of agreeing your fees, has much to do with removing objections. If you think you will be forced to give on your fee level, fix it at a high rate to begin with (many potential clients like to bargain in any case); that way you can come down a bit and still not hurt profits.

Objections come in two styles and types. There are surface objections, i.e. objections that are very obvious ('I think your fees are too expensive'). Some examples of surface objections are:

- Why should I (the client/customer) use you in particular?
- How do I know that you are the best person for this work?
- How can you make me confident in the relevance of your experience?
- Can you give me an assessment of your competitors?
- How can you do a faster-than-normal piece of work without sacrificing quality?
- What guarantee can you give me that you will complete this work satisfactorily? What if your solution or work is not what I wanted?
- Tell me about an assignment or project that did not work out.
- How do I know I will get personal service from you and no one else?
- What if I discover I am able to do the work on my own? (in the case of business-to-business one man bands in particular)
- How do I know you're not working for my competitors? And that there isn't a conflict?
- How do I know you're going to do the necessary research and preparation well enough?
- What flexibility do you have in your fees?

- How much will expenses be?
- What questions should I have asked you that I haven't?

These objections are the easiest to deal with, providing you know your service well.

The second area of objections are those that are more hidden and below the surface. The client may be saying one thing, but actually means another. For example, 'You and those like you come along and tell me all this good news and then never really live up to your promises.' This may be what he says, but it may be that in truth he doesn't like you very much and rather than say so directly he is making broad points about your activities to conceal and camouflage his true feelings. In cases like this you have to decide whether it's worth persevering, whether you've got a chance of overcoming the client's doubts.

Closing a Deal

One mistake that is often made in the art of selling your service is that you try to close too early. So when *should* you close? If you are unsure, we should try out a few 'test closes'. For example:

- How do you feel about the service I have described?
- How does my approach strike you?
- Are there any other aspects of your requirements that you feel we should cover at this stage?

Subsequent Client/Customer Relationships

After you have completed your first assignment/commission and gained new clients/customers, how do you make each individual one of them think that they're the most important to you, above any of the others? How do you keep them interested in you and wanting to go on giving you work? How do you maintain close contact with them and make yourself available for several opportunities, without seeming too desperate for business? How do you keep all your different clients' interests separate, and maintain Chinese Walls in your organization?

You must be able to adopt a different approach to suit different clients. The aim here is to develop strong client relationships and show loyalty to your clients, hoping they will show loyalty to you in return.

Using Clients/Customers to Get More Business

Developing good client/customer relationships means keeping your contacts warm and using them to attract more business. There are three ways in which you could use your early clients or customers for gaining more business:

1) By asking them to be referees for other work you might get
2) Through reference sales, or asking them if they know other people who might want your service
3) By gaining further work from them as a spin-off from your previous projects.

Keeping Clients on a Long-term Basis

In most businesses you probably do want to achieve this, as this is part of building up the assets of the business, principally goodwill. (Goodwill technically is the assurance of future profits, or future income based on the value that people put on your service. If someone is buying your business, they're very interested in what the goodwill is, so that they can evaluate whether people will still use the business when they take over.) It is therefore very important to build up long-term relationships, especially as this saves you time in marketing for new clients all the time.

Keeping Existing Clients while Looking for New Opportunities

You must continue to look after the interests of your clients rather than looking to the new too much. This is particularly true if you are on your own; on the one hand you want to try and look out for new work, to come from new projects, but at the same time you have to continue to offer your service to the clients that you have at the moment. This can be very difficult. In fact it is the single hardest thing you have to do in a one man band business: to continue to look after the clients that are there and have been using you while you continue to stake out new work.

It is inevitable that successful one man band businesses have this great problem, and that is why they often get to the point where they feel they must expand, because they have too much to do and feel a bit overwhelmed – they can't cope with the combined pressure of the people who want the continued level of service they have provided in the past and at the same time look out for new business and tackle it when it comes in. They feel pulled in too many directions. This is the single great reason why one man bands become two, three and four man bands, and start to face new problems, especially that of clients wanting the person they originally paid for – you – when there is more than just you (this will be discussed further later on).

Keeping Your Client-base Small

To prevent this problem, you can limit your client-base to three or four clients for whom you work very significantly, and basically tell them that this is what you are going to do, and agree with them financially that they will offer you a secure income for the work you are going to do. You agree a relationship which makes both sides happy, but you don't go on looking for others. It's a key and critical decision for the one man band business. Otherwise, if you go down the road of making your one man band much bigger, then that brings a separate set of problems, such as the problems of managing staff. Few people running a one man band necessarily have project management skills. You would need to work with someone, introduce him or her to existing clients, do joint work together, test ideas together, and when this all works out push this new person forward. Meanwhile you are able to keep the relationship with your clients, whatever happens. This can be difficult, but if you choose instead to keep your business small and singular this can limit the amount of business you can do, and for some people this can be very frustrating.

Providing Personal Service

You must offer your clients/customers a service, and you should always be, above all, service-minded in your attitude. This does not mean being servile or just doing what you are told, but genuinely caring about the interests of your clients/customers and anticipating their needs.

Keeping Clients Sweet

Every client or customer wants to feel special. Your clients/customers must never be made to feel, as in the song, that 'you don't bring me flowers any more', that you don't rate them or care about them as much as you rate some other clients/customers. It's very difficult when you're building a one man band business to share out your attention equally.

You should never say to a client or customer that you've been working for others, and that you've got ten other assignments or commissions going at the same time. If you say you're busy it sounds very bad, not least because it can be interpreted as an indication that you do not really want work from him or her.

You must of course be honest if you can't do something, in which case it is better not to take it, and even to suggest someone else who could. Doing too much work puts a lot of pressure not only on other work, but on your home life, too. If you have a one man band business and you have the type of work that means you have to work all night to get it done, then something has to give, and it's usually your personal relationships. The appalling rows and tension are going on while you are trying to fulfil a client's or customer's expectations and needs. The knowledgeable client or customer with whom you have worked for a long time knows the sort of pressure you might be under and will be sympathetic. He or she will appreciate your efforts, and may be prepared to be flexible and considerate. This is one reason why long-term clients can be best, and are certainly well worth cultivating.

Building and Maintaining an Effective Network of Relationships

As a one man band, especially one offering a business-to-business service, you should build relationships with clients in the same way that executives in companies do. Current research shows that a distinguishing characteristic between effective and less effective managers, particularly at senior level, is the network of relationships that they use to achieve their objectives. When moving into a new managerial position effective managers place a high priority on and devote considerable time and effort to building a network of co-operative and collaborative relationships among those people they feel they need to help them towards making an initial successful impact in their new position. Even once established this activity will continue to take up a considerable amount of their time, but generally the amount of effort needed will be most intense during their first few months in a new position.

The nature of relationships in a manager's network can vary immensely in intensity and type. For instance, there will be relationships that are interdependent, often involving trading and negotiating; others may be dependent, wherein the relationships are absolutely vital for the continuing performance of the job.

Some relationships are much stronger than others and some are much more personal than others. Indeed, to some degree, every relationship in a network is different because it has a unique history, it exists between unique individuals.

Effective managers are quick to perceive gaps in their networks that can adversely affect job performance, such as the movement of people both inside the organization and in the organization's wider environment. Consequently they give a high priority to identifying and building new key relationships. Moreover they are not slow to weaken or sever a relationship that is no longer of productive value in the short or long term.

Shaping the network process is common among effective managers: they will endeavour to create certain types of relationships among the people in various parts of the network. In essence they try to establish the appropriate 'environment' or climate (norms and values) necessary to achieve their objectives.

Typically, the best performers among managers in an organization tend to mobilize more people to get more things done, and they do so by using a wider range of influencing tactics. They will ask, encourage, cajole, praise, reward, demand, manipulate and generally motivate others with great skill in face-to-face situations.

The effective manager may of course be in a reporting relationship to someone who is a 'skilled networker', and he or she may therefore have opportunities to use a modelling approach in developing, maintaining and effectively using his or her own network.

An understanding of these types of networks and attitudes to networking can be helpful to one man bands working for companies from the outside. By targeting the most well-networked people they can make sure that their work is utilized as much as possible.

Presenting Results

Good presentation is very important indeed. You might be a one man band, but there is nothing to say that you shouldn't produce work which *looks* as good (and *is* as good) as something produced by a large corporate. Good presentation also means using top-quality equipment cost-effectively, and presenting material or your service in an unusual way for further added value. Your work must also be presented in a way which is unmistakably yours, so that everyone who sees it will recognize instantly the value of your work and, if they are not already your clients, will want to have you do some work for them.

Personal Presentation

In presenting results to your clients or customers, and in packaging your product/service, you need a clarity and quality that reflect your personal image and style. In personally turning up with the work you've done for the clients or customers your own confidence and well-planned introduction can make the work increasingly acceptable; your enthusiasm for your work will be infectious. Your belief in its success will be transmitted to them, and give you an enhanced value in their eyes. You must work on your presentation skills, your analysis and packaging of your work, to get the best reception.

The Format of Your Work

In terms of the work itself, your format and the way it looks are very important in leveraging its value. If you're a business-to-business one man band and your work involves presenting information, whether it's a short project, or a long-term, detailed assignment you must know the agendas and have a strong political nous of how an organization works and how it wants to be seen by the outside world. You must be in tune with the organization's culture and problems, and be sensitive to these elements. You must match the format of your work to your client or customer, with sympathy to their style and approach.

Consistency

The format must have consistency, a unique feature of your own as regards the way you present your work. If you're running a catering service, for example, your logo or design feature (if you have one) should be evident. You should have a hallmark which is related to quality and service. When presenting food your consistency must be apparent, particularly in terms of attention to detail. Don't just put a sprig of parsley on top of the sandwiches, but come up with something attractive and original, like napkins with pleasing designs; things that make people come to value your special touch. These features make your service interesting and different, and when your customers don't receive these extras from somebody else they will find they miss it, they'll miss your distinct approach.

Your hallmark must be memorable so that your work is identifiable. It can be that special finishing touch which shows you care and take trouble with your work.

Anticipating Your Clients' Needs

In presenting your work you should show that you have anticipated your clients' requirements. You should aim to give your clients more than what they asked for, so that when they get it they're really pleased. You will have understood their needs so well that they will have got that important bit extra, which they'd really wanted but had not defined entirely beforehand, and had not asked for specifically. If you keep telephoning them and asking whether they want something or not, this is not necessarily helpful. You should know in advance what they want, by research and sensitivity, so that when it comes to presenting the results you are able to show that you have anticipated their needs, without ever losing professionalism. You should try to do work which always exceeds your clients' expectations. This is very difficult to achieve, and not all one man bands realize its importance, but it is key to success.

Qualities in Good Presentation:
A Checklist

Your presentation should always be:

- Attractive
- Top-quality
- Creative
- Imaginative
- Thoughtful
- Accurate
- The result of extensive market research
- Efficient
- Anticipatory of requirements
- Explained clearly
- Stylish
- Sensitive
- Tasteful
- Caring
- Well-organized
- On time
- Reliable

Invoicing and Getting Paid

You should always invoice you clients or customers promptly and thoroughly in line with your agreement with them, itemizing your expenses, including receipts, and making clear how each expense was incurred in serving the client. It is important not to exceed the overall budget previously agreed, unless there was a very good reason for doing so. The end of a job is not when you finish the work or supply the goods, but when their cheque is in your bank account. You should also discuss stages of being paid, because you may see it as appropriate that you should receive payments in advance and during the work. A further very important aspect of invoicing is how much to charge, and you should be sure neither to under- nor overcharge for yourself and your service.

Deciding on Terms

Following up unpaid invoices is not pleasant and wastes time (unless it can be tactfully mentioned during your usual client or customer contact), but it has to be done, although hopefully the majority of your clients will not need reminding. It is worth while stating your terms on each invoice, i.e. the period in which you expect to be paid. This can be 7, 14, or 21 days, or longer. Some clients will insist on 30-day terms.

You will want to be paid as soon as possible, but you must be realistic. It's not necessarily true that your clients are dragging out the time before they pay you, that they are hoarding their money and deciding how much longer they can avoid paying you; in many cases they'll just have a slow, overworked accounts person who might only work part-time and who is under a lot of pressure. However, some companies – especially those seen as large and respectable, and therefore bound to pay up in the end – will often take the longest to actually come up with a cheque, and will insist on terms like 90 days, which are tough on a one man band.

You will soon learn that some clients pay faster than others. A constant problem for every one man band is receiving payment, and this can seriously affect cash flow if it is not closely monitored. You must agree with the client up-front as to when you will be paid.

It is important always to discuss your terms before starting work, not waiting until you put them on the invoice. Once you have come to an amicable agreement with your client about the work and the payment you expect, ask him or her about when your invoices will go through for payment, and how long it will take from then. Make it clear from the start that you want to know when you will get paid.

It can be a good idea to draw up a schedule of payments, such as monthly in the case of a long project/major order, so that the clients pay as they go along, and get results for each stage of payment. Meanwhile you get paid as you work, and if for some reason you don't get paid, you haven't wasted time unnecessarily on work which may go unremunerated.

Invoicing Procedure

When you've prepared a sales/services invoice, immediately send out the client's/customer's copy and put the file copy in a folder marked 'Unpaid Invoices'; as a client/customer pays, retrieve your file copy of their invoice, enter the amount paid, invoice number and details on the left hand side of your Bank Analysis Cash Book, and file the copy invoice in an 'Invoices Paid' file, in payment order. Always bank cash and cheques received as soon as possible. Enter items in the Bank Analysis Cash Book for each banking, and then rule off and enter the total to be banked in the receipts column. Finally, complete the slip in the paying-in book and pay the money into your bank account.

The following month you should start another file, labelling it with masking tape, and deal with the items as in previous months. When you have three 'Invoices Paid' files you can at the end of the third month transfer any unpaid items to a special file marked 'Urgent Action' for particular attention to the collection of the money owed to you, i.e. debt-collecting. Re-use the files (changing the masking tape) for the subsequent three months. Obviously if the payment terms are not monthly, or you don't issue many invoices, you can modify this system accordingly.

Costing Your Services

It can be useful to find out what your competitors charge for similar work, but in any case your fees must be profitable to you. Remember, profitable sales and making good margins on your assignments are what keep you in business. You sell to your customer not only a product/service but also the time you spend on your product/service, therefore you should take into account the total value of your work – which can be a service as well as a manufactured or value-added item – including the time and expense spent preparing, marketing and finally selling it.

The method of calculating costs and selling prices is to divide your total annual expenses by your expected saleable hours for the year, not forgetting materials used per product and due allowance for scrap, labour costs and expenses spent to make the product or provide the service. Add to this total the required profit margin, and decide whether delivery costs are to be included or an extra. This procedure should be carried out for each product/service to ascertain just how much each is contributing to your profits and so that you can reassess which products need to be discontinued, which methods or prices altered, whether to increase or decrease marketing, and whether to re-tune your prices in order to maintain your offer of 'value for money' to clients/customers.

This all applies to services, especially regarding your own work in serving the client/customer; you should calculate your time at an hourly rate that is at least three or four times higher than that you would pay an employee.

Many one man bands who use part-time labour claim that you must charge out to your clients three times what you pay employees, to account for your time in supervising them and directing the successful completion of the work. Always remember the importance of your particular value added to the product in the end.

Differential Pricing

This can be the best tool for the one man band. If you are very busy, but further work is offered to you, what is your fee? You can make it more than usual, upping it say 150 per cent, to make your clients or customers think. If you are not busy, and need work, you may take a reduction in your normal fee to ensure you get the work. In this way you can exercise some control on the flow of work coming in. If the project is in a new area for you, and you have to do new preparatory work for it, you might decide to charge more for it. If the project is well within your area of knowledge you can do the job more cheaply, because it won't take you long; you can pass the savings on to your client or customer.

Fees

One of the things that people starting up a one man band often feel very unhappy about is arranging their fee. They have to negotiate a fee, and they don't know what to include in the amount they charge.

You must be straightforward about fees. You're always going to get objections – people object because they want to test your reaction. You must know how to handle objections to your fees, and be able to work out the right rate for a job.

If you're doing longer pieces of work you must be prepared to offer your clients a more innovative deal. Be flexible. If you receive retainers, or pieces of work in big blocks, as you're a one man band you will want to break up the blocks, to stretch the work out as much as possible so that you can fit in the odd smaller assignment or piece of work as it comes in. Don't leave yourself a timescale so drawn that you can't fit in other assignments. You are going to have to balance time, and then in instances where you're pricing for a bigger piece of work and they want it done very quickly, you can charge twice your normal rate. Especially if the work is something very esoteric which only you can do. Thus your fees are differential.

You've also got to have something up your sleeve, because clients will say 'How much would you charge for doing that?' and you think, 'Oh . . .'. You've really got to think how long it's going to take, how much you want the work, how difficult it is going to be – and you've got to think on your feet.

What you've got to do is talk your customer through, at least in your mind. Say, 'I don't know about this yet, let's talk about it, look, I think this work would take me about three or four days at the moment, and you want me to fit that in within the next ten days, so you want four out the next ten days of my time.' You want the customer to feel special, but you also want him or her to know that you have many other demands on your time, so you could say, 'This is clearly very important, and I would like to help you with it very much.' He or she can then ask what your other commitments are at the moment. Clients want to know how busy you are; it's not that they're interested in what you are doing for other people, they're only interested in how it will affect them.

So this is why you should talk things through with the customer. 'You want this work, which will take three or four days, done within the next ten days. OK, we need to do x and y. It might even take me slightly longer than four days, but must it be done within the next ten days?' The client will say, 'Yes, it's got to be done because so-and-so wants it.' So then you say, 'I think I can get it done within four, four-and-a-half days. So I think the timing can be about four-and-a-half-days, does that seem about right to you?' The client will say yes, probably. Then you specify your rate for the amount of time plus expenses, and ask how it sounds.

Therefore, talk it through with clients. Don't say that you have to think about it, always make a decision, there on the spot. You don't want to lose the opportunity of discussing it. Therefore, discussing it through with them tells them how you're thinking and at the same time builds confidence. They will be concerned that as a one man band business you haven't got the time, that your other clients are more important than they are, so you need to convince them that you can get the job done.

Managing Multiple Assignments and Avoiding Conflicts of Interest

It is of course important not to take on too much work, but you will be amazed at how much you can accomplish with the adrenalin that flows from having your own business. You must learn the effective juggling of many balls in the air at the same time; the ability to do this is one of the true tests of being a good one man band. You will need to spread your interests to attract enough business, while keeping within your specialisms, but you must not spread yourself too thin or too wide. You will quickly learn to make the most of synergies between different assignments, applying knowledge gained in one assignment to another. You must also keep Chinese Walls between your clients or customers, never betraying confidences and avoiding conflicts of interest. You should always discuss a potential conflict of interest with an existing client or customer before taking on new work.

Time Management

A vital aspect of being able to manage multiple assignments is being good at time management, a very important feature in managing a one man band successfully, and it can be worth investing in a specialist course to learn how better to do this. Some people are naturally good at time management and organizing their day, week, month and year. Others, especially those who have spent a long time in a big corporation, almost accept as a matter of course that at the end of a given day they will have achieved very little.

Good time management also helps to relieve stress. Too much emphasis on time management can make a person appear ruthlessly practical and tough. Life is a question of priorities, but these should be assigned subtly. Above all, you should make every client feel that you work exclusively for him or her and that, although you are very busy, you can always make time for his or her assignment. But you must not work so hard or so quickly that the quality of your work deteriorates. You must allow yourself some time for relaxing, and for holidays, otherwise you can suffer a breakdown.

The time management question raises the point of whether your business life should be welded around your personal life, or the other way around. Those running a one man band (both men and women) have to be good at structuring their personal lives to suit their business, however difficult this might be. The wider view of good time management is good career management and life management.

Managing Concurrent Assignments

You may find that it's famine or feast: either you have lots of work or none at all and no prospects of any. There is a frightening gap between having been thoroughly over-extended and coming into a period when you have no work. One of the ways you can get round this is to have some lower-paid work, in the form of long-term work and projects for example, in the background, work that you can pick up in quiet times. There is the work that spans over years at a time, which is your lowest paid work, your 'base line' work, that you can drop, pick up, drop, pick up, but can always have going. You can then be free to complete another project which is more highly concentrated, as short-term work, without leaving yourself nothing to do afterwards.

Managing Work According to its Income Value

In managing several assignments at the same time you must apportion your time according to what you can get paid for it and how urgent it is, achieving a balance between highly-paid, urgent, short-term work and more poorly-paid, long-term work which can be in the background. Say your highest rate is £1,000 a day, and that you work 30 days a year at this rate. Then you have your middle-level work, which costs £500 a day, of which you have 100 days. Lastly you have your base line work, at £300 a day, which you can add and fit in around the other two types of work.

You can use this system to decide your rates and total annual income. Then you try to see whether you can organize the most highly-paid work better. There is a problem of optimization, because if you get rid of your base line work in favour of more highly-paid work, then if the highly-paid work falls through you may be left with nothing. You may also wish to allow yourself days for holidays and for marketing and business development, days on which you don't expect to earn anything.

The idea ultimately is to optimize the high-paying jobs. This may mean that you have to choose between jobs. You could say, 'I am not going to do base line work, I am going to be here when clients or customers need me for the higher-rate value.' Or, 'I am not going to worry when that work doesn't come in.' So you have 50 days a year of that work, which brings in £50,000, but that will be all you get. You can certainly survive on that. Or perhaps you decide not to take base line work but to take only big projects and some middle-sized ones. So you do 35 days of the very high work at £1,000 a day and another 10 days at £500, giving you £40,000. If you do half the number of assignments at the higher rate and twice as many at the lower, you will probably come to the same total amount, but there is an optimization element there.

It all depends on how much work is available, and how busy you like to be, and how ambitious you are. You could attempt to do 25 days at £1,000, 100 days at £500, and another 100 days of base line work at £300 per day: this gives you a lot more, i.e. £105,000. It depends how you want to organize the work, and whether your chief aim is to optimize money or job satisfaction.

The outcome of all this is that you should keep your base costs quite low, so that in good months and years you get a very large amount of money which you can put into a pension plan or other means of saving, while in bad months or years you will have your costs under control.

Avoiding Conflicts of Interest

There are certain types of service businesses, especially in business-to-business one man bands, where conflict of interest can be a problem. You need to be careful about taking on new work, making sure that this new work does not compromise you in any way. In running a one man band, as in any other form of business, you must keep your integrity intact. Before you even get started you must decide on your own personal standards and stick to them. You must turn down work if necessary, while perhaps letting your existing clients know that you are making such sacrifices.

In business-to-business one man bands in particular you must consider very carefully before you take on certain clients. You must think through the strategy of working with certain clients in combination with other clients. You should decide which clients you would like to work for and which ones you would certainly not work for.

However, you should not be so opportunistic that you get boxed in; turning away business when you are trying to expand is not a welcome thing to do. If there are potential conflicts of interest you should discuss these with your major clients, making them aware of what you are giving up in terms of other income by continuing to work for them. The answer can be to get more work from existing clients and customers, and to have only one client from within each business sector.

Conflict of interest needn't be a problem, however. It depends on how close you are to your clients' organizations. Different clients will have different views, and as long as you are up-front there should be no ill-feeling.

The main point is that having ethics and standards is very important. In a service business trust is absolutely vital, and loss of trust simply means loss of business.

Keeping Costs Down

You must always keep an eye on costs, otherwise you will find your profits substantially and needlessly eroded. You should be careful to avoid expense on unnecessary equipment, and should charge as many expenses as possible to clients or customers. Every bill must be paid by somebody: preferably *not* you.

One big expense is premises: you may be able to work from home, as long as you have suitable space to meet clients, and live in a good, central location; alternatively you can rent economical office space (see Case Study 4, below). Meanwhile, efficient bookkeeping enables you to monitor your expenses, and helps you to continue to work smart with costs. From the outset it is wise to make use of any Government schemes that can help reduce your costs if possible, and then be cost-conscious in running your operation itself, especially in terms of your relationship with suppliers.

Keeping costs down is vital for a successful one man band. One of the major decisions you'll have to make is whether to use premises or work from home, as this is such a major cost to a one man band.

Working from home immediately saves you major expenditure. Dealing with suppliers from whom you need equipment or material for your business can be a problem, as you need to get a good deal from them and you often can't if you're not giving them volume work. You have to accept that. You may be told that you will get 10 per cent off, but they probably give their other, bigger clients 12 per cent.

You need to find suppliers who will provide you with good services and are keen to do so, and who may be a little more flexible on payment because you are willing to pay a little more in return for this flexibility. Say you need some work for a client or customer done by a print shop, then it might pay to get the print shop's credit card, which allows you a more flexible way of payment. You won't get much discount from them, but what you are really keen about is more flexibility about when you have to pay them, and the quality of service they provide. One thing that can always be a big advantage to a one man band is that whatever you are doing you should get economies of scale. Keep in mind that if you do lots of things in different sectors, your economies of scale are less.

How to Deal with Suppliers

All businesses have suppliers, whether they be the printer who does your letterheads or the manufacturer of the product you sell. For those not used to dealing with suppliers a few tips might help.

It is important to realize that most suppliers want new customers, even small buyers. No matter how new or small your business, don't under-estimate your value to a supplier. Give a professional image and they will be interested in doing business. When choosing suppliers the general rule it to track down at least three, tell them your needs and ask them for a quote. The Yellow Pages are always the first place to look for suppliers if you have no prior knowledge of a given trade; alternatively you can ask for references from other people whom you rate.

Dealing with suppliers usually involves negotiating in some way. Rarely pay 'list price' without negotiating first. A good way of operating is to put your requirements out to tender. This makes it clear to suppliers that you are asking others for quotations, and that therefore they must be competitive.

Try to make personal contact with suppliers. Go to see them or ask their representative to call. In this way you can often negotiate reductions on their initial price. Once you have several quotes for supplies cost them carefully to ensure that they fit your plans and budget. Don't order until you are convinced.

When ordering, get all details in writing – not only price, but also quantity, type of product, delivery and payment terms. Subsequent problems can ruin the profitability of your project. It is good business practice to use a standard order form for all orders. Finally, most suppliers are used to handling all sorts of enquiries, so you don't have to be 'in the trade' to canvass them with a view to starting a business that will make use of their products.

How to Get Credit

Some suppliers are very willing to give new customers credit. Never offer payment without asking for the standard 30 days' credit. If payment has to be made in advance a discount of 2.5–5 per cent should be requested. This can help with reducing costs, because if you are waiting for clients or customers to pay, having credit helps with your cash-flow situation and minimizes the need to borrow.

A simple letter requesting credit can be sent to all new suppliers. State your business address, names of the owners, and references. References should include a bank and two of your trade suppliers (if you don't have any suppliers yet give the name of your accountant or of anyone who may have given you credit in the past).

On receiving an application which is professional in approach the majority of suppliers will grant credit, or a least seriously consider it. If a supplier does not offer this standard business facility it may be better to buy elsewhere. When applying for credit, estimate the amount you can afford and do *not* exceed it.

Being Cost-effective

Minding the pennies is not only good for your business, it's good for your clients' businesses, and for your customers, because you are being careful with their money, too. People want to see control of costs, because this indicates professionalism and care. And the more you can control costs, the more there will be for you in the end.

CASE STUDY 4: FOREIGN LANGUAGE TEACHING

Françoise started her own business in partnership with her husband in October 1984, but she is now a sole trader. Before then she taught English in her native France and in the UK, for language schools on contracts as a freelancer. Her husband is a Mauritian Chinese whom she had met in London. She was dissatisfied with her job as a language teacher, and her husband was also frustrated with his job as an accountant in a company. The two set up the language school business seven years ago and it continues to go well: demand is increasingly steadily and she has more and more corporate clients, rather than individuals.

Training and Company Experience

Françoise came to England as an assistant teacher; in 1975 she decided to stay. First of all she worked in a number of high street shops, and eventually applied to be a teacher with a famous international language school. She had a full-time contract with them, but then wanted to go freelance, because she had a number of private clients.

Impetus

One night when Françoise and her husband were both very fed up with their jobs and couldn't sleep very well, he woke her up at 2 a.m. and said she should definitely set up her own language school, and that he would be her partner. This was in June of 1984.

Françoise had always wanted to be her own boss. She knew there was a market out there for language teaching, and she knew the product inside out.

Setting Up

Language teaching is a business where capital is minimal. Françoise knew of a friend who had started his language school from his flat in Islington, but she lives in the suburbs and therefore had to have an office in town. Right from the beginning she wanted to have an office and not work from home, as she welcomed the discipline a separate office would enforce.

Her brother-in-law had a small office in the City of London which he sub-let to Françoise and her husband. It was very small but very cheap. She did give some lessons there, but it was too small to do much teaching. She did not then have a listing in the Yellow Pages (it is necessary to book in January to get in the Yellow Pages printed six months later). It is extremely important to be in the Yellow Pages for a language school. In the mean time she did mailings, building on the small nucleus of students which she had already made contact with while working freelance. At the beginning it was difficult to know what to charge people, so she telephoned around and found out what other people were charging. When she finally got a small ad in the Yellow Pages she was able to get more clients, and ultimately to hire extra people on a freelance basis to offer instruction in other languages.

Expanding

Location

Françoise and her husband stayed in their first premises for two years, but found they needed more space. They rented a building in another City area, which had a licence for a year. It had a basement, reception room, and rooms on three floors. The rent was quite high, however, and the turnover of the business was just not enough at this stage. The business broke even in terms of balancing income and expenditure, but made practically no overall profits, so the decision was made to find somewhere cheaper. The City is very expensive, but Françoise wanted to continue being able to call the business 'City Language Services', and by this point many of her clients were in this area. She wanted to keep a City address.

In language teaching you need to have small rooms for individual tuition; open-plan office space is not such a good idea. However, Françoise found a place which had 200 square feet, with two rooms. It was in quite a bad state of neglect, with windows you couldn't see through, but it was very cheap. Françoise and her husband put in partitions and did all the decorating themselves, dividing the space up into a number of rooms. The lease runs out in 1993, but Françoise is hoping that she will be able to renegotiate it, depending upon how much money the freehold owner wants. It doesn't matter too much about the lack of really extensive offices, because 90 per cent of the tuition she offers is done on the premises of the companies concerned. Most of her clients are big companies in arenas such as banking and insurance; of her individual clients, most want to learn a language for business purposes.

Service

Françoise has written her own language-learning manual, and has her own unique method of teaching French. Her manual has not been published, but this has been her choice: she wants to keep it to herself. She is still learning all the time she is teaching, and is continually trying to improve her service to clients.

The nature of her client base has changed, because a few years ago most of her clients were learning individually, but now she finds that more and more companies want her to run group sessions for them, as more people have to learn foreign languages now. The margins are higher on group sessions, but she still provides private tuition. Most people like to be in a group, but she discourages big groups, keeping most classes to five people or so. Its OK to teach subjects like mathematics to a big group, but languages have to be spoken; if you have too many people in a group it is hard to involve everyone.

Françoise's school has a large number of clients now, and teaches 120 hours of French a week as well as offering English, German, Spanish, Italian, Japanese and sometimes Chinese and Portuguese. She doesn't want the business to get too big, however. She wants it to be smallish yet solid, strong and progressing steadily, keeping expenses as low as possible and investing in new equipment when feasible.

Françoise thinks it is important to give people personal service, and adapts her service to give people whatever they want. For example, she would give lessons by telephone if people wanted them, and this is mentioned in the school's brochure. An eight-hour intensive course is on offer, since other language schools offer this option and she feels she must do the same, but she recommends the four-to-six-hour course to her clients as better value for money. Because her school is small and doesn't have big overheads she can offer not only a more personal service, but one which works out quite cheaply. She feels that her business is high-quality yet competitive, and offers courses tailored to her students' needs. She offers a free assessment test to advise students of their level. The school also keeps in touch with its former students, and offers flexible lesson schedules for those who need them.

Future Prospects

In terms of investing and equipment Françoise didn't need very much at first, just a photocopier. She now has a word processor and a fax. In theory she could open another office in the future and this would lead to more capital costs, but this would depend on how the market expands, especially after 1992. She could expand the business also by offering overseas trips and intensive courses in France, but this seems too expensive at the moment.

Françoise doesn't want to invest big amounts, and feels it is better to stay small, believe in your product, and sell it well. If you have doubts about your product then you cannot sell it. She never lost confidence, because she has always had a well-defined product, and although she has made mistakes she has always been prepared to learn from them. She used to think that if she failed to convince someone to buy her services then she was no good, but she doesn't feel this way any more.

Françoise insists that she doesn't want to be a slave of the business. She feels that her business is going into a new phase, during which she won't have to worry so much any more. However, she's very careful about money and concerned about credit control. She now tries to get payments in advance, before lessons, but this isn't always necessary as most companies are reliable about payment, although individuals have sometimes caused problems over this. Nevertheless, only twice in seven years have people not paid their bills, and this has meant that the business has been about £500 out of pocket. She thought it wasn't worth going to the Small Claims Court for this, but she will always take care that it doesn't happen again.

Advantages and Disadvantages

Having her own business has caused Françoise to change in lots of ways: she is more confident and responsible, more independent, self-contained and self-reliant. She has also become much more business-minded, doing a large part of the bookkeeping herself and making financial decisions. She is much more conscious of money now.

She likes the fact that it is not a 9–5 job, although she admits that at the beginning she had to give it her all. Françoise feels that running a business is a bit like having a child. You have to nurture it and help it to grow. It is always with you and it has to be treated with respect, even love. She is not desperate to make a huge amount of money, but is ambitious for a certain lifestyle and wants to get it herself, liking the security that this brings with it.

Françoise is now 39; she began her business at the age of 32. She worries ten times more than she used to, but argues that she gets ten times as much joy. She likes the challenge, is never bored, and there is no routine. She felt a bit lonely when her husband left the business, having to make decisions on her own, but she's able to cope with this now, and has never regretted having started up her one man band.

Start-up Costs
- Telephone installation – £200
- Answering machine – £150
- Fax machine – £300
- Computer equipment – £2,000
- Photocopier – £300
- Rental on premises (most of teaching carried out on clients' premises) – £1,000
- Advertising – £1,000
- Brochure – £1,000
- **Total start-up costs – £5,950**

Running Costs
These include a secretary (paid about £12 an hour), rental costs on the premises, the telephone, photocopier, and on-going advertising costs

Typical Length of Time to Become Established
Two months

Typical Rate of Growth
30 to 50 per cent p.a.

Typical Personal Income
£30,000–£40,000

Typical Turnover
£50,000–£65,000

Reviewing
Your Progress

Your should review your progress constantly. At the end of the first few months, how does what you've achieved compare with your original objectives? Are you surprised or disappointed? Do you feel you need more time to decide if things are going well or not? What assignments are you most/least proud of? Are you satisfied with the opportunities you won, the income you made, the reputation you are building? How can you be even better in the next few months to come? How can you further refine your service? Are you making the most of advertising opportunities? Is your cash flow satisfactory? Do you have friends to talk to about this?

Meanwhile, how are you managing the balance between work and your home and social life? It is, of course, easier to run a one man band with a stable home environment as a base. Do you find that you are working harder than ever? If so, are you enjoying work more than ever? What set-backs have occurred so far, and how can these be overcome? How do you feel about your original marketing plan? What adjustments need to be made?

As you continue running your one man band, you will find that your motivations change over time, as do the goals you have in mind for your business. You start off with a 'wish' list of what you want to achieve: once you have achieved these wishes you can become interested in other things. After the first few months you will still be working to achieve your 'wish' list, but you should bear in mind that your ambitions could change over the next few years.

If you are successful immediately, within the first few months, you will find that your basic needs for money and independence will have been fulfilled, and that some of your early motivations may no longer apply. You may find that you are not so hungry for the same sort of success. Ultimately (although this may still be a long way off when you've only been in business for a few months) you should be able to cherry-pick whom you want to work for, and what you want to do, and then work only for these more favoured clients and pet projects, weeding out those who don't really deserve you.

Continuing to Focus

To set up a one man business successfully, you have obviously got to focus your services sharply. Whereas the skills you develop in a corporation are often broad, you've got to concentrate them in running your one man band, and be careful not to be diverted. You will find, if you have come out of a large corporate, that many things which you did before are of no use any more, and you've got to become very, very proficient in a narrow area. That's why successful people in service businesses offer a quite specific service. They certainly can't do anything over-extensive, particularly as they won't be able to match the service differentiators of those who can offer a range of businesses.

After the first few months, you must resist the temptation to broaden too much, because you may become overstretched and unable to maintain quality of service, and because you can't compete against more wide-ranging businesses. Your distinction lies in being focused.

Networking

After being in business for a short time a client may ask you to deal with a specific project which you don't know anything about, something that is, however, within the sphere of your knowledge generally and which you could in theory take on and work out. Many people find that they hate saying they can't do something. This is the time when a network of other people who can give you their necessary skills (which you may have to pay for) will help you out.

The greater your need for cash, the broader the service you've got to provide. So you may have to be able to do everything before you get to what you do best; after that you can specialize.

If you're offering a very focused service and you want to be a purist about it, it might take you longer to get it up and running than it is for somebody who is diversifying more. If you have spare cash you can afford to specialize, but sometimes you do need to diversify more if it's a matter of making or losing money. Above all, don't get a reputation for inflexibility, because you are, after all, in the client service industry. If you help someone out in a big way, even if it's outside your usual area, then he or she will remember you in the future.

Some people can be snobbish about assignments which they think are inferior in level or status or fee, but this attitude is a luxury few can afford. You may risk being accused of being *too* flexible, but you should always put a priority on client service. And if you know what it's like not to have any business, it probably makes you a better, hungrier salesperson.

It all comes down to the immediacy of your need for money, and the nature of your long-term plan for developing your business. If the business plan which you present to your bank doesn't call for any revenue, or any money back for a year, then of course you're going to take a different view than if you've only got one month's money saved in advance.

Clients are increasingly knowledgeable about this point. Something that is poorly understood in service businesses is that often clients are very knowledgeable about how quickly people need money, and what they will do for it. As your business gets going and you get used to a certain lifestyle, a certain income, then your need for money and the pressure that you might put on your clients will be very different from when you were starting out.

Maintaining Credibility

If you've worked in a company and then offer your services elsewhere, and if these services are outside the area in which you have worked before, then your clients might not see you as relevant. For example, if you've worked in marketing and are suddenly providing compensation advice, your clients may not see you as valid in that particular area, and you may not be able to sell your services to them. You've got to be seen to have an enhanced competence in what you do. If you move to a different sector it takes a while to establish credibility. You should emphasize your core skills and sell them first, showing at the same time that you can adapt to the requirements of others.

It is often hard to make a transition to a different, unrelated or just higher type of job if the people you will then be dealing with identify you with your previous role. For example, in a typical consultancy business, if you were a secretary and become a researcher, people would still treat you as a secretary and avoid giving you proper research work. It is best to offer your services to an organization which knows you only in your present role.

How to play politics is a big issue. If you make a mistake, you must admit it, and tell the truth. You must tackle and control the situation. You must get all the decision-makers together and agree the agenda.

Constantly Developing

As a one man band, you must always keep an eye open for new opportunities, but at the same time work to gain repeat business, including achieving new and different business with existing clients. You must show flexibility in taking on new assignments in new areas, and that you are moving with the times. You should always be careful not to take on work that is too difficult and which you will be unable to complete well. A job done badly is much worse than turning one down in the first place because realistically and honestly you know you cannot do it.

At the beginning you may find that running your one man band – especially the need to bring in new business constantly – is a real struggle, but you should see this as part of your learning curve. Most one man bands recognize the value of a good apprenticeship. They might not get paid very much at this time, but it stands them in good stead for the future. All one man bands have an important apprenticeship period. Not until you are a master do you actually make money, so it is important to stake out the area in which you want to be a one man band, and develop your abilities and standards. You can then use this experience to further market yourself.

Constant business development is one of the hardest tasks of a one man band, as you have to be good at executing work and marketing yourself at the same time. You must be seen to be around, but also get the work done. You must keep in touch with current and potential clients, while progressing your assignments in hand and not getting left behind. In marketing your services you have got to have the bottle to cold-call people. If your constant business development is successful, you'll soon have people cold-calling you. Each of us is only as good as our work and what our last client thinks, and therefore we must have a stake in what we do. Build on this in your business development activity.

At the same time you have to be disciplined, and have good organizational ability. You must build up your stamina and strength, but at the same time make the most of your contacts and your early mentors. You should have a strong competitive streak. This is all essential for staying in the game.

One of the problems with one man bands is that they can get out of date, and often don't think of acquiring new techniques, perhaps because they are isolated. In a larger group, this is easier. It is comparatively rare for one man bands to grow on their own, and many go 'off the boil' in three to five years. This is another reason to grow larger – perhaps one of the most important reasons – and is discussed further in the next chapter. After reviewing your first few months, you should consider further reviews, examining your on-going market research, making sure that the market is not leaving you behind. You will need to produce new marketing plans on a regular basis.

Growing

So far this book has concentrated on the concerns of those who want to keep their businesses small, but it may be that you feel you want to build your one man band beyond yourself. You may feel you need to share the load, to find someone you can work with who will help generate and complete business.

First of all you should consider the following questions:

- What will this growth mean for your business?
- How will you cope with handing over some of the power of running the business?
- What are the pros and cons of going into a business partnership with your spouse, boyfriend/girlfriend, son/daughter or other relative?
- How do you go about setting up a partnership agreement?
- What are the legal and taxation requirements?
- How do you protect your interest if the partnership fails?

You'll have to decide whether it is an advantage to be small or large. If it is as advantage to be small, then you can keep going as a sole trader, with relatively low expenses on your corporate image. If it is an advantage to be large, you can still run this as a one man business, but you need more status and infra-structure to make your business appear bigger than it is, especially if you have work overseas. Then you can set up a limited company.

You may find that you cannot get people to join you in building the organization the way you want it. This is why many one man bands remain one man bands. Alternatively the business may remain highly personalized and centred around you regardless of the number of people you may attract into it. It may be a big company but it may still only have you at the controls.

Coping with a mature one man band is a completely new issue. You want success, but success does things to your motivation, so you need to re-evaluate your goals from time to time, and either expand your business or cherry-pick from among your opportunities. You must progress or go stagnant. Losing control is one of the things people become paranoid about, worrying that they can no longer serve their clients. It can be hard to be emotionally detached from your business, even after you have diluted your equity by selling out and introducing others into it. Many one bands are totally unable to divorce themselves from their business. It can happen that a one man band business can be sold, perhaps to a larger company, and the former sole trader works for this larger company for a while but then leaves and sets up on his or her own again.

The Future for a One Man Band

One man bands can be very good for people who want to get an income for a certain period, and they are excellent for women and minorities; unquestionably they have done a great deal for many people. However, it is possible to argue that good one man bands move on. You either have to expand or something has to give. If you are good as a one man business you start getting more work and find it harder and harder to decide what to do; it becomes natural to look around to find other people to help, and then you are involved in other people working with you – and suddenly it's not a one man band anymore and, in many cases, no longer as much fun.

It is very hard to find a balance and to maintain the quality and the service, and this makes operating the one man band increasingly difficult. One solution is not to take on new work, but then there is something wrong with a one man band business that does not grow. It *has* to grow, yet it cannot grow too much.

One man bands are successful, in many instances, because they are small. They offer custom-tailored, cost-effective, personal service, and this is what a lot of customers want. When this changes they might not want what the business has to offer any more.

Employing Staff

Most one man band businesses are, by definition, owner-operated. But some will require staff to help with support systems. If you are unfamiliar with personnel matters, always take professional advice on recruiting, even at quite a low level. A Job Centre will help with free vacancy advertising and recruiting in most cases. Discuss employment legislation with a solicitor. Until you have a clear idea of your needs it may be better to offer staff temporary contracts rather than permanent ones, even though this makes recruitment harder.

Consult the Inland Revenue and Department of Social Security, and tell them you are becoming an employer. You will have to collect tax and contributions from your employees. You can sometimes avoid this administrative work by using self-employed subcontractors or by keeping wages below the current taxation limit.

As you hire staff or make partnership agreements you will find you make mistakes, so if it's not working you must cut your losses quickly.

Limits to Growth

You probably think, 'If I could earn x number of thousands of pounds a year, how will I ever turn that into half a million pounds?' The answer is that you never will, not on your own. There is a limit to the amount of work one person can do. If you go for expansion and you're keenly into building the business, this is where you truly get value, because you make your one man band business a corporation. But then you lose the freedom of the one man band. But, after all, you have to work out what the freedom of being a one man band actually is. It might be the freedom to do your own thing, but is this really freedom? Perhaps not, because you're completely blocked into what work you can get and what work you might get. If there are two or three of you, then you can all help to chip in.

Merging One Man Bands

There may be also be a case for putting your business in with somebody else's, so that you complement one another, each of you working in the sectors you want to be in and dove-tailing your working styles and effectiveness. Or you may choose to back your one man band business into a three man business and thus become a partner of that.

Why Change the One Man Band Set-up?

So, what motivates this type of crisis? It comes in two ways, either because you know you have a talent for the one man band you have set up but can't seem to get business, in which case you will want to bring in someone who is a good business developer, to get you more business; or perhaps you have more business than you can handle and therefore want to take on somebody who can help do the work and perhaps generate some new clients.

So, it's either that you have too little business or too much. If you've got just about the right amount of business, the question of having a partner doesn't really arise.

Not Enough Business

Taking each in turn, the situation where you haven't got enough business means that you're not being successful enough. Now, getting yourself a person who might get you more business is quite risky. On the other hand, perhaps the work isn't coming in because your service is very specialized and there is not a huge demand for it: in this case you should maybe broaden it more. So you may need to find someone who can broaden your service, or to find someone who is in an adjacent field of endeavour, in a business similar (or at least not dissimilar) to yours. It often may be that merging with someone else is the better bet, because trying to find somebody who will develop new business, a business-getter or marketing manager, is fraught with danger. And you really haven't yet established your one man band business successfully.

If you merge with other people you will of course lose some of your business identity. But if your business is not that successful and you haven't got as much work coming in as you want, you really have got a problem. So a merger might be the solution, but I think that this is only rarely true. Paying somebody to come in to try and develop more business, unless they've really got the nous, is tricky at best. You must also understand that he or she is probably going to demand quite a lot of you, and will most likely want a lead share of the partnership.

It could be that your business started off well but has not grown, and has in fact gone downhill, perhaps because you depend on assignments from big companies and they're cutting back, so you haven't been able to earn much. It could be that you know that a lot of companies would like to use you, but they're telling you that they haven't got the money at the moment.

Now, as a one man band business the market share you need is minuscule. Even if market conditions have been tough, there is always enough out there for you. It's not easy, and in a recession harder still, but in many cases it's probably your own lack of marketing effort rather than the market not being there that is at the root of your problem. You should target other markets, even overseas, and do something a bit more innovative.

It's easy to find excuses. Fundamentally, it boils down to the fact that people are thinking, 'Oh, he must be having problems because he's not very good at marketing and promoting himself. He's always going to be under-utilized unless somebody else can get the business for him. This is his strategic dilemma.' It's up to you not to let them start thinking this way. Remember that constant marketing is key. Look again at your business: would hiring another person really make everything all right? Or does the answer lie instead in increased effort on your part?

Too Much Business

What about growing a one man band because you've got too much business? This is when you really do need staff, and this is the most legitimate reason for expansion.

The soundest strategy is to go for people with technical confidence. You know what they can do, especially if you have used them on a freelance basis before. Go for somebody whose technical competence is higher than your own. He or she doesn't have to sparkle as much as you do with the clients; as long as his or her actual technical competence is higher the clients will see the additional value of using that person, because after a while they find your service better and better – you continue to offer personal service and at the same time all their technical needs are being seen to.

Also, as you get more experienced in doing your work you will know which are the hard parts and which the easy, and you begin to realize which parts could be done for you by someone else who is quite technically competent, saving the parts only you can do for yourself. An administrative person is a case in point. It may be that the administrator takes you a long way forward – is a good half-way house, as it were – but he or she will not demand the same kind of financial or managerial terms that a proper partner would.

The next level is to either hire someone on a full salary full-time or to make him or her a partner in the business. You might perhaps buy his or her services on a part-time basis to begin with, or check him or her out first by giving him or her occasional projects to do. If you decide to take this step you really must be sure to bring somebody in who is proficient in technical areas, as mentioned above – leaving you free to continue developing your client relationships.

Loneliness

You should not expand your business for the wrong reasons, and you should never hire staff to cure loneliness. It's very easy to be lonely in a one man band business; you are driven back on yourself a lot. It's not a problem if you are slightly introverted and therefore don't mind being on your own. Some people are genuinely self-contained, and even find that they get de-energized when they are with lots of people. Others, however, are more naturally extroverted; they get de-energized when they're on their own and only really feel on top when they're with people. An extrovert will find the need to talk to or be around people huge. He or she might, therefore, look to hire someone to overcome this need. This solution would only be worth it, however, if it makes him or her and the business more effective.

It's a mistake to want to grow your business just so that you have somebody around. You've got to be honest with yourself: admit that you're an extrovert and that you want somebody around because then you'll feel more at ease, less pressurized; you'll work better, get more business and be more successful. If all this is true for you, then hiring someone will be a positive move. Or you may feel, 'I need to be part of a team.' That's fine, too, as long as you know you have the business there to support a team. If you're going to have to invent things for people to do, however, if there really isn't work enough for two, or more, this might be frustrating, time-consuming and costly. If you expect to find yourself thinking, 'Now what can I get him/her to do next?', then the expansion isn't justified, it isn't business-driven. Reasons for growing a one man band should be positive.

Starting Again

If you feel that your one man band has failed, or that it's no longer what you want to do, there is nothing to stop you from starting again, and many of the people in our case study examples have done this. How can you start a similar business but create a different brand for it? How do you go about retraining yourself in another business? How can you avoid making some of the same mistakes again? Have you got it in you to be a constant entrepreneur?

Case study 5 deals with Anna, whose executive search business grew quickly from the beginning, mostly due to Anna's real sales ability and a high level of repeat business.

CASE STUDY 5: EXECUTIVE SEARCH CONSULTANCY

When Anna started her one man band, by her own admission she didn't take it very seriously at first. The subject (executive search) was serious, but she didn't approach it in a very textbook or classic manner. She thinks this is quite common among people who start businesses when they are young. She was only 28 at the time, and wasn't necessarily ambitious to make a huge amount of money. Now her one man band has become a large and highly-respected business, and is seen as one of the leading independent executive search firms in London. She grew the business rapidly, almost from the beginning.

Background

Anna had been working in another search firm and decided she wanted to leave – for no particular reason – and found she couldn't join another search firm very easily. So she decided to start her own. At that time the search business was dominated by middle-aged men; there were very few young people in it, and practically no women. Many of the search firms she approached with the idea of joining them thought that she was a joke.

Beginnings

In setting up her own business Anna wasn't consciously analysing the field or trying to find a gap in the market; she didn't even think she would necessarily succeed. Initially she saw her prospects in terms of three months, and thought that even if it were a total disaster it wouldn't really matter, she could always go and do something else.

People have to be driven by needs, and it's easier to set up your own business when your needs are few. When she was setting up her business her needs were relatively few in comparison with the men working in the same field, who for the most part had mortgages and families to support, and heavy overheads. She could afford to be a bit light-hearted when she set up her business, as she felt she had nothing to lose. It was not forced on her, and it was not the be-all and end-all of her life.

Rapid Initial Growth

Anna's one man band business grew quickly, but she never saw it as remaining a one man band business for long. One of her early policies, which she feels has been a factor in her success, was not to pay too much attention to what was happening in the market. However, she was offering something different, or at least felt she was; she was very confident because she was young, she thought she had a product that was different from that of the other firms, which were dominated by older people. Unlike the other firms she depended not on personal networks but on systematic research right from the beginning, trying to produce quality work and to be professional. By the end of her first year she had five people working with her, never having thought of the advantages or disadvantages of being either big or small.

Success Criteria

In looking at why one man bands succeed or fail, it can be quite difficult to pick out those characteristics that lead to success. Anna feels her business has succeeded through being choosy about the work taken on in the first place, whereas companies that have injected a huge amount of capital and have large debts to service have to take everything that comes along, more or less.

Much of the success of a business also comes from the personality of the person starting it. Anna felt she had nothing to lose and wanted to enjoy herself, and not work for people she didn't want to work for. From the beginning, the firm would allow few compromises. She found she had a streak in her that would say 'to hell with it' if she didn't want to work with someone. As time has gone on she feels she has learned to say 'no' more nicely, but she still says it! Of course, she went begging for work, and wouldn't just sit there waiting for people to knock on the door. But she has always taken a position of choosing who her clients were, and of considering why she wants their business, right from the very beginning. As a result, some clients have stayed for eight to ten years, ever since the beginning. Anna prides herself on working hard with them, and they have seen the value of her input.

Using Networking

Anna says that her firm made very few cold calls, even from the beginning, but found marketing relatively easy, as the nature of her work puts her in the market all the time. Sources, candidates and clients in executive search can be all interchangeable, so it is not usually necessary to make cold approaches. She did cold-call very high level people, however, in her non-executive director search work, ringing up the chairpeople of ICI and BP and going to see them. She feels that people at that level tend to be more accessible than many of the people working for them, and are generally courteous and helpful. She has found that they seem to like her professional approach, no doubt in part because they know it helps them, too.

Continuing to Grow the Business

Anna feels that she has been helped enormously in the growth of her business by the complementary skills of her group. She acknowledges her headhunting skills but is aware that a lot of her skills are instinctive and intuitive – 'thinking around corners' – and that she needs to work with people who use logic more, and think linearly; people who can put in mechanisms for the running and continued growth of the business. She has put in good systems from the standpoint of quality and expense, but above all has recruited people with different skills, and has helped them develop these skills. She needs people to run the business, because she is spending 90 per cent of her time in the market. She feels she has always been lucky in having found good people, so that she can do what she wants to do.

The Future

Many one man bands set up feeling they will always be independent, only later coming to the conclusion that good team work is essential in some fields and that you can't grow a business as a one man band. When you are expanding your business, however, you must search for people with whom you get on, and you must learn to delegate, which can be difficult if you're used to working on your own. A job is what you want to get out of it, and for Anna this has always meant doing a job she liked, and having a comfortable lifestyle.

Anna is confident about the future of her business. She feels that she knows what's going on, and is about 12 months ahead of the investment cycle and 6 months ahead the economy's turning point. She sees executive search as the first to respond to changes in the economy, followed by the behaviour of consumers, then industry, and then property. She would advise that every one man band be aware that things go up and come down, and that they try to plan for both bull and bear markets.

Start-up Costs
- Telephone installation – £200
- Answering machine – £150
- Fax machine – £500
- Computer equipment – £3,000
- Rental on premises – £5,000 downpayment
- Photocopier – £300
- Binding machine for reports – £150
- **Total start-up costs – £9,300**

Running Costs
These include telephones, photocopying, travel, office rental, entertaining, secretary (at about £18,000), researcher (at about £22,000); most of these costs can be passed on to clients

Typical Length of Time to Become Established
Three to six months

Typical Rate of Growth
30 to 50 per cent pa at first, then 10 to 25 per cent after the first few years

Typical Personal Income
£75,000–£150,000 upwards, even up to £350,000–£500,000 for a managing partner

Typical Turnover
£150,000–£500,000. It would be hard for a one man band business to bring in more. Firms with 15 professionals and a staff of 25 to 30 can have a turnover of £5m in this business

Partnership

Combining Your Skills
with Those of Others

In moving away from one man band status – but still staying small and tightly-controlled – it is important to expand the business carefully by including someone with complementary skills, perhaps as an employee but maybe more effectively as a partner. You have to be able to integrate with someone who has the talents you haven't and vice versa.

Once your one man band has become a partnership you will find that you fit into a certain role and your partner fits into another. One person in a partnership is invariably the more dedicated back office person, the other the more out-going, front person. For example, Stan Laurel and Oliver Hardy were an example of a typical partnership in that Hardy was a natural comedian who didn't have to work at it or intellectualize it at all, whereas Laurel would stay up all night handling the technical side of things such as the editing and some of the writing. He considered Hardy to be the genius, and Hardy knew that without Laurel's intelligence and hard work they would not have been a success: this is true partnership. It is important to understand and appreciate the knowledge, talents and skills of your partner.

Developing your one man band into a partnership is often a very good way to expand, as it can be a way of counterbalancing the skills and qualities of one man band people on their own. Many one man bands are good at getting the business going but may find it difficult to really build the business. There are many entrepreneurs who are good at starting things off, but are they good at taking them on to a further stage?

At what stage would you take on a partner? You could do so right at the beginning, or much later when you feel the need for other skills. But even after a long time you may value your independence and like working on your own so much that you want to stay a one man band.

Finding Partners

Getting partners is not about meeting people who are as good as you at bringing in new business; the ideal would be to get someone who is good at doing the business. Chemistry and competence are most important: you must get on with them and they must be good at what they do. Often you'll want somebody who maybe isn't a good business-getter but who is technically stronger than you in certain areas.

Getting Your Clients/Customers to Like Your Partner

You must also take into consideration that the clients want *you* to do everything. However, you, as a good front person, a good number one, can make the client relatively happy and keep him or her that way. That's the trick, that's what you have to do: you have to sell your new partner, who may not seem to clients to be as good or as appealing as you are, and then you have to make sure they continue to recognize your talents as well. Once you've got your new partner in with your clients, then they forget you or don't want you as much. The trick is to make sure clients value both of you equally.

In a certain respect, also, a second person can do the sort of background work the result of which you can then present to the client. There are some elements, like research, presenting statistics, doing mail outs, administrative and support work, which you can farm out without losing your one man band style.

Taking on a Partner

A big decision as a one man band is whether you take on partners or just 'helpers'. It's one thing taking on a secretary or somebody to help you with a bit of administrative or research back-up, but quite another to really invest in somebody else who will become a major force in the business, either in terms of helping you complete assignments or helping you get more business.

This is therefore one of the biggest – and often one of the most difficult – decisions to be made by a one man band. Unsurprisingly perhaps it is often a person's spouse who becomes the partner. This is in part because taking on a partner carries with it a big element of trust. Will this person be able to replicate the standard of work the client or customer is used to? Will he or she be able to build on the work done to date, and will the client like him or her? Will he or she fit into your working style, and what should you do about giving away a part of the business – should he or she have a share of the profits?

The basis on which someone is employed is also a very important decision, and one which you need to look at separately, as this differs significantly from setting up a partnership.

In case study 6 we meet Diana, who took on a series of partners to develop her presentation training company.

CASE STUDY 6: PRESENTATION AND MEDIA TRAINING

Diana began her career as an actress, but she gave this up when she decided that she wasn't really good enough to make it right to the top. She'd worked for Central Television and the BBC, especially programmes in the northwest of England, and she still takes on a lot of TV work, but she realized that her real vocation was in presentation training. When she met Peter – carrying out media training as his own one man band while also working as a newsreader for Granada – they set up in business together, and he is still a partner in Diana's presentation training company, Public Image.

Identifying a New Opportunity

Diana and Peter realized that there was a gap in the market, especially in the northwest, for high-quality presentation training. They felt that the main companies already operating in this market were mostly based in London, and lacked their credentials: Diana has acting and some journalistic experience, and Peter has even more journalistic experience. They were joined by another partner, Delia – also an actress – and also by Sarah, the fourth member of the team, who has specialist skills in presentation allied to business.

Outside Impetus

The company could not have been launched successfully without Diana, as she effectively got the business off the ground. The others have different and complementary skills, which have helped the business to develop.

Diana left school at 16 and initially worked as a dancer and entertainer on cruise ships such as the QE2. Then she got married (but divorced 10 years later) and had children. Her ex-husband was fairly well off, and they lived quite a comfortable life, until one day he lost everything through commodity trading. Because of their severe financial crisis (they were left with absolutely nothing), Diana had to go out to work. But all she had was a few O levels, and she felt completely unequipped to do anything.

At the time local and commercial radio had just begun, so Diana got an Equity card and did some commercials. She went to Manchester as a freelancer and worked for a radio company, enjoying the variety of the work. She was very new to all this, so it never occurred to her that she wouldn't be any good at it or that the work wouldn't come; consequently it always did. It was very difficult to build things up from zero, especially as Diana had two young children to support and absolutely no experience of being the breadwinner.

Setting Up

Diana found she was quite good at commercials, but knew she wouldn't be a good serious actress. The radio and TV work was a very good background for setting up the company, however, and once she'd started her own business she realized that she is quite hard working.

Diana found it relatively easy to make a gradual transition to being more involved with her company, but she has never made a complete break away from acting to business. Having her own business has given her more security, even though she hasn't got the extensive investment earnings she had before.

Diana feels she and her partners have had some lucky breaks in the business, especially with the advent of televising the House of Commons. There was a big article about them in the *Daily Telegraph*, along the lines of 'MPs rush off to charm school'. Although they don't like to see their company portrayed as a 'charm school', all publicity is good publicity. The principle behind the company is that your voice and your body are your only true means of communication; if you need to put your message across and have it understood these are the only instruments you have, and you must learn to use them effectively.

Running the One Man Band

The business takes up about 50 per cent of Diana's time, because she still likes to be in front of a camera, which she feels gives her continued credibility in her business and keeps her fresh. Part of her job is being able to inspire other people to present themselves well, and she can only do this if she is practising constantly. She likes the mix of work in her business and in television, but it is really all the same thing.

The company has been going six years now and is fairly profitable, although it took a couple of years to get off the ground, because Diana and the other partners were busy doing other things as well, and still are. Delia and Peter present *What the Papers Say* every week on TV. When the business was started it was just a side-line, now it is quite serious.

They target new clients carefully, mostly from among big companies. They also work for individuals in small companies and for public bodies and trade associations. Peter does a lot of one-to-one presentation training, particularly with Chairpeople's speeches, and works well with male clients, especially top businesspeople – but 90 per cent of the assignments are handled by Diana, Delia and Sarah.

Advantages and Prospects

One of the ideas behind setting up the business was for each of the partners concerned to have more responsibility for his or her own destiny. And everyone had to pitch in. Diana feels that in television work you can easily lose your job with a change of producer, and that this is a political decision and nothing to do with your level of competence. When you run your own business, however, if you lose a client it is largely your own fault.

With her business she feels much more in control, especially because she can have as much work as she wants. She feels that the ideal number of partners for Public Image is four; they can spread themselves around, offering training to a range of customers, and mostly working in twos. Part of their service it analysing everything within a client's video, and playing the video back for the client in private. They feel they offer a highly effective, personal service.

Diana doesn't want Public Image to get any bigger, as the partners work well together. They would find it difficult to integrate someone else, especially because that person might use different training methods. The partners are interested in body language, but have all had vocal training, and see this as very important too. Although they are a team, they see themselves as individuals, and are all equal in the company.

Diana is sure that presentation training is, overall, a growth area, but the training budgets of companies can be cut in a recession, and this has happened in some cases. Nevertheless she and her partners have found that they are reasonably recession-proof, because of the variety and diversity of their work. At times there have been big gaps to fill when they lose major clients, so they work at expanding somewhat so that they will be able to replace any clients they might lose. In this way they have some 'recession insurance' and also stay roughly the same size. They also sometimes bring in freelancers to carry out specific aspects of the business such as dress, appearance and assertiveness training, because they accept that they cannot do everything.

Diana's friends were not necessarily convinced that she could make a success of her business; many thought she wouldn't succeed because of a perceived lack of discipline. But she recognized the need to improve her weaknesses, and once she started the business she realized how satisfying it could be. She has now been working for 15 years, and feels that she has learned so much that she's now a totally different person. Running your own business makes you grow up and examine yourself. You have to know what you are good at, where your talents lie. Diana could have continued a broadcasting career, and she has made a conscious decision to maintain her links in that area, but she also wanted her own presentation training business. In addition she wanted to operate outside of London, and to be able to work from home, and she has been successful.

Generally, Diana feels she needs people around her, and she sees this as vital for the company, which offers a service that is a product of their combined skills. This helps them to fight for their markets, as everyone has to do. They emphasize the help their skills can provide for clients wanting to maintain their business edge, or even to change their company culture, if necessary.

She is now poised to take advantage of the introduction of subscription TV, and she and Peter are already involved in presenting *The Business Programme* on subscription TV for a company in Manchester.

Disadvantages

One drawback of having your own business is that you cannot afford to get sick. She used to suffer from migraines, but has found that she doesn't seem to get them so much any more, especially when she's working. The lack of a regular salary can also be a problem, especially if companies procrastinate about paying their invoices.

Generally Diana doesn't miss very much about her old life: she has a hectic social life and finds this as stimulating as work, but feels it would be nice to go on holiday more.

Why this One Man Band Succeeds

Many companies think they can just buy any training video and it will solve all their problems. Diana and her partners offer follow-up, encouraging each trainee to develop and grow, and this is why they get repeat business. They believe that it is good for companies to train out-of-house, as only a few companies have very good in-house training. Diana and her partners tailor courses to individual company needs, often working alongside the company's own in-house training departments. Public Image has grown into a small, successful, dynamic company, above all fostering their clients' confidence – as their motto goes: 'You cannot compete without confidence.'

Start-up Costs
- Telephone installation – £200
- Answering machine – £150
- Fax machine – £300
- Photocopier – £200
- Brochure – £500
- Stationery – £500
- Computer equipment – £2,000
- Rental on premises – £1,000 downpayment
- Video machines – £500
- **Total start-up costs – £5,350**

Running Costs
These include telephone, photocopier, travel, secretary
(only £4–£4.50 an hour); most of these costs can be passed
on to clients

Typical Length of Time to Become Established
Six to nine months

Typical Rate of Growth
20 to 30 per cent p.a.

Typical Personal Income
£35,000–£45,000 per partner

Typical Turnover
£500,000–£750,000 total once established

Going Global

Most one man bands will find they have enough on their plates developing business within their own town or city, but in some instances one person operations do a lot of work overseas. Are there opportunities for your type of work outside the UK? How can you develop business opportunities in Continental Europe, the USA, the Far East? There are legal and tax implications of overseas earnings which you need to be aware of, as well as the problems of working in countries without hard currencies. How can you enhance the value of your UK business by becoming more international, and become more international by enhancing your UK business?

International One Man Bands

Although it is difficult to envisage, there are many examples of successful international one man bands. Journalism and freelance writing can be adapted to almost any market where your native language is spoken, or if you are fluent in others; photography is also international. Import/export businesses are international by definition, and are very successful operating between places where goods are made cheaply – such as the Far East and Asia – and the UK, where they can command high prices compared with the cost of manufacture locally.

Another international possibility for one man bands is helping non-British people set up businesses in the UK and other countries. One man bands are ideal for offering specialist consulting advice. Those who have experience of companies in other countries, or who may themselves be immigrants, can offer a very sought-after service. They can help with providing contacts, preparing market research, sourcing suppliers, and with many other services. Such one man bands can also help individual expatriates settling in the UK from overseas who need advice and introductions.

Richard's recruitment and consulting business took off when he decided to break into the Eastern European market.

CASE STUDY 7: RECRUITMENT CONSULTANCY IN EASTERN EUROPE

Richard was forced to go into a completely different line of business after coming out of an industry he had worked in for a long time. Although this appeared to be a problem at first it has been an advantage in the end, as Richard is now in a fast-growth area, running a recruitment consultancy in Eastern Europe, an area of the world now opening up to the West in leaps and bounds. He didn't seek to be a one man band originally, but now enjoys it very much, and it is also very rewarding financially.

From a Smaller Corporate Sector

Richard worked in a computer consultancy which turned into an agency, putting IT people out to clients. During his work there Richard gained experience of IT recruitment both in the UK and overseas. Their people were like temps, but tended to stay in the companies where they were sent for six to twelve months rather than just a week or so.

An International Dimension

Richard recruited IT specialists for jobs in the UK, across Europe and in the Middle East. In Europe he hired IT people for public sector contracts in the Benelux, and also for the European Space Agency in Germany. His company worked especially for the big European institutions, agencies and computer manufacturers. They would put out tenders to a number of recruiting firms, and won many of these.

The Start of the Trail

At this point Richard could not have imagined that he would want to set up on his own, and never saw himself as an entrepreneurial one man business. However, circumstances conspired to change his mind, when his company was bought from its parent company, a major British plc, in a management buy-out. An eminent City figure helped assemble this, and the group was run privately under his guidance for a number of years. Richard was included in the MBO as a minority shareholder, ran the major operating unit within the company, and was appointed to the board of directors for the group. In 1985 the company was bought by another major public group on a five-year earn-out arrangement.

Leaving the Corporate World

All the executive shareholders were working on service contracts and were under the five-year earn-out arrangement for their shareholdings. The objective over this period was to grow the group to the maximum size possible, thereby maximizing the potential value of the shares. The arrangement did not work well, however, and towards the end of the period many conflicts arose as the shareholders and the management began to have different objectives. This culminated in virtually all of the executive shareholders, including Richard, parting company with the group after having sold their shares, and in most cases receiving substantial compensation for the ending of their service contracts. Richard feels that the management made a big mistake doing this, as it resulted in the loss of precisely those experienced individuals who would have been able to steer the group through the recession which was to follow.

For the sale of the shares, the largest shareholder in the group collected literally millions of pounds, and all the directors did very well on their original investments, which had appreciated by about 400 per cent. Richard was 35 at the time. One of the conditions of his leaving agreement was that he would not attempt to operate in competition in Europe for two years, and although the settlement and the sale of the shares were substantial, Richard could not just sit back and relax. He had to find an alternative career.

Contemplating Starting a One Man Band

Richard then landed some freelance research work for a small headhunting firm which soon after won an East European assignment in financial services, to find bankers to work in Poland,

Czechoslovakia and Yugoslavia. On carrying out this assignment Richard realized that there was tremendous potential in Eastern Europe for this service. He soon became frustrated by his client's lack of vision, and decided to focus on this area himself, making using of his major asset, his Eastern European origins and Polish heritage. As the situation unfolded in Eastern Europe the opportunity of a lifetime presented itself to him, and he became determined to capitalize on it.

The Break

A headhunter whom Richard had met during his search for a position in London had been especially interested in his story, and gave him the break which turned out to be a major turning point. He advised that it was probably futile to team up with a London-based company, and instead introduced Richard to his firm's Austrian counterpart. The Austrian company had a very entrepreneurial owner who had the vision to target Eastern Europe as a major opportunity, and who was already considering opening offices in the region.

To others it may have seemed too early to begin developing a business in Eastern Europe, but acting almost as pioneers Richard and his Austrian client began a number of assignments. Richard started to work on two projects in Czechoslovakia, and then took on the first of many in Hungary. At this point he began to travel extensively in the region, as well as in Austria and throughout Western Europe, marketing the service.

Richard realized that with his recruitment background and Polish heritage he could do well in this field. Most of the Slavic languages are closely related, and therefore his Polish helps a lot. Hungarian, however, is totally different, and very hard to learn. German comes in useful in this region, and Richard is working on this now that his major client is Austrian. He was initially concerned that his Polish would be rather rusty, but found it was better than he had imagined, and generally people have been very supportive. It was also strange to visit Poland; it was like going back in time to the 1950s. He suffered for a while from a lack of business vocabulary, but manages well now.

The outcome is that Richard has been able to develop with his partners quite a significant executive search business in Eastern Europe, obviously in a growth phase, whereas by contrast search in the West has not grown substantially.

Why this One Man Band Works

Retaining his services suits Richard's clients, as they do not incur the fixed costs of someone permanently on the payroll, and he himself prefers to work on a percentage of the fees generated for the assignments he is involved in. He finds this keeps him motivated, and encourages him to bring in the clients himself, as he can obtain a higher percentage for these.

The projects he takes on are very difficult, as little information is readily available in the Eastern European markets, and this makes it quite out of the ambit of the average headhunter. Richard feels it's an advantage that he has specialized in this area and is not saddled with responsibilities elsewhere.

Future Prospects

Richard's current clients in Eastern Europe are talking about making him a partner now, and he has presented a business plan for opening a joint venture in Poland. He has particular views on how the business should function for the whole of this region, both now and in the future. This should take his business out of its one man band phase and grow it into quite a substantial unit. However, he is still not entirely sure about this move, as he feels he might like his business to remain small and controllable.

Advantages

Richard feels that there is a great contrast between working on your own and being in a big company where so many things are being done for you, things you just don't appreciate at the time. In a large company you are very cushioned against reality, and generally people have no idea how much work is involved in running your own business. Your perspective is very different when you have your own business. By contrast, it is easy to lose motivation when you are spoon-fed in a big company.

The advantages of having his own business have included the fact that he can capitalize on a new trend very rapidly. He was certainly in the right place at the right time. As far as he is concerned, the advantages of being a one man band are that he is independent, well remunerated, the work is exciting and he has a sense of achievement in a pioneering field. He is highly individual in his work – even unique – and is in a market that still has a great deal of scope for further development.

Disadvantages

Richard feels that his biggest disadvantage was having to set up his one man band while still having a young family and significant financial obligations. This means he can't risk-take as much as he would like. Richard also finds that the administration of running his own business and being alone are very onerous, especially VAT, tax and reclaiming expenses. This is all very time-consuming, and he dislikes most of it, so he is now using a part-time accountant and passes on a lot of the work, although of course he still has to brief him.

Advice

Richard emphasizes that running a one man band is a huge commitment, and advises anyone considering it to ask him- or herself if the investment of time required will be worth the risk. If you can't or really don't want to put the time and effort in the one man band will inevitably fail. Many people who talk about having a one man band business simply do not realize how hard you have to work to make it succeed. Richard also points out that planning your approach and creating a proper business plan is essential, and that it's vital to research your potential market carefully.

You must also make sure that your partner/family are behind you with your venture, as without their crucial support it is hard to make any real progress. You should forget completely about days off, holidays and time to yourself for the foreseeable future, and this can be very tough on your family. You should keep to your core business area and specialize in one thing so that you can focus in and become a specialist, with something unusual to offer. You should re-appraise your services continuously and never become complacent, and above all find something you enjoy doing, otherwise you will not be able to sustain it.

Start-up Costs
- Telephone installation – £200
- Mobile phone – £200
- Answering machine – £150
- Fax machine – £500
- Computer equipment – £3,000
- **Total start-up costs – £4,050**

Running Costs
These include the telephone, travel, entertaining (which can be passed on to clients) and a part-time accountant (approximately £8–£10 per hour)

Typical Length of Time to Become Established
Six months

Typical Rate of Growth
30 to 50 per cent pa

Typical Personal Income
£50,000–£75,000

Typical Turnover
£50,000–£100,000

Selling Out

Do you feel you want to keep this business going as it is, or do you want to expand further, or even sell out? How do you attract good offers, and get a good price? Is it possible to sell your one man band at all, given that it's chief asset is you? Is selling out more likely to mean that you will just be going to join a company, and the business will disappear? Or will the integrity of the business be retained as part of another, perhaps bigger organization? Will you have to join this organization too for a certain period? Is this what you really want to do?

Linda has found that it was a good idea for her to sell out her financial services business, especially because due to changing legislation it is now very difficult to run this type of operation as a one man band.

CASE STUDY 8: INSURANCE AND INVESTMENT SERVICES

Linda began in the business of independent financial advice, life insurance and pensions when she was 22, earning commissions while working for a large brokerage company. Later she formed her own company, which she recently sold to a financial services group. She established her one man band because it enabled her to continue in the work she knew, with more flexibility in terms of where she was based: most of the time she was able to work from home. She has four children, and is convinced that she wouldn't have been able to juggle her family and career commitments as easily had she been working for a large company.

The Start of the Trail

Linda met a life insurance salesman who tried to sell her a savings plan, demonstrating his full sales presentation techniques in the process. It did not seem very difficult to do. The saver-plans were sound financial products, offering tax relief and other benefits, and to Linda it seemed that selling insurance would be a most attractive way of earning a living. She also liked the idea of being self-employed, and had already thought about having her own business. She was technically too young (under 25), but was told that all she had to do was to learn the script of the sales presentation and present it to the branch manager. She felt she had nothing to lose, so she learned the script and performed her presentation, and was immediately taken on. She decided to settle in London, and rented a flat in Hampstead.

Since then, Linda feels she can honestly say that she has never looked back. She had a particularly good first three months, even being voted 'trainee of the month'. She admits that she was caught by the hype. This was the late 1970s, when large insurance groups were emerging and growing strongly, and were employing many young people working on a commission basis.

Developing: Role of a Mentor

After three months Linda's branch manager left to form his own company, and asked her to join him. He was an important mentor, and she was glad to follow him. Linda was one of five people at the start-up of his new brokerage firm, and became a unit manager herself within a year. In running the office she found that the manual systems she had learned stood her in good stead. She believes that good clerical systems and good O & M (organization and methods) should be taught to everyone at school. Systems are very important, especially in selling, which requires good organizational skills and discipline. The combination of discipline and selling skills has been key to her success.

In the start-up brokerage company, where she worked for four and a half years, Linda took on a variety of roles: trainer, recruiter, manager. At the same time she was constantly involved in selling plans, pensions and capital investments, and was moving more and more from insurance into investments.

By the time she became branch manager there were 30 consultants in the company, and Linda began to feel it was time to move on and develop her own financial planning skills. It was very hard work and quite draining, as the company constantly had to recruit and train new people to offset the turnover of staff. There is often a rapid staff turnover in the financial services industry, as very few can make the grade. During the 1980s economic boom, too many young people in financial services thought they could earn large rewards while remaining self-employed, but very few actually made it.

Discipline, Background and Skills

While she was working at the brokerage company, Linda would start each morning cold-calling potential clients, aiming to approach 25 people every day. This was hard work, but it was justified by the end results. Some people she cold-called were rude, but it was important not to mind this too much; she maintained the outlook that any phone call could lead to an appointment. She soon discovered that it was necessary to telephone at least four people to produce one appointment, and each one called could be the one to produce a commission. Linda realized that if she could complete six months' work in one month, then she could earn potentially six times more than was expected. So she aimed to make four appointments every day and see at least 15 people a week, and found she was able to sell her services to at least one in three people she met.

Another discipline which Linda learned, and maintained in her own business, was her constant attention and dedication to her clients' needs. They became very loyal as a result and, she suggests, felt very guilty if they had to use anyone else. She kept her clients for ten to twelve years, in many cases, and many of them referred her to still more business.

In selling financial products such as insurance, Linda discovered that although clearly many people require the service, they can feel uncomfortable – or even nervous – about being sold to, and that this has to be borne in mind when approaching potential clients.

The Catalyst

After working for this brokerage company Linda then joined a brokerage offering a more comprehensive financial planning service. This business expanded quickly, and in two years developed from a small partnership to having 16 directors.

Linda was to work for this brokerage for four years, during which time she and her husband moved to Surrey and she had her first baby. Although they employed a nanny at home, she breast-fed her baby for eight months, during which time Linda tried to carry on working. Eventually, however, she found the commuting was just too much, and decided to have two months off. This turned out to be the catalyst she'd needed. Linda made the decision, in 1985, to form her own business and work from home. Her first moves were to buy a photocopier and hire a secretary.

Setting Up

In retrospect Linda thinks starting up on her own was the best thing she ever did. Although she thought her client base would disappear if she left London, she found it did not make any difference. She carried on doing the same work she had done before, although of course she had never done it entirely on her own before, even though she had always worked on commission. She became an independent financial adviser, selling a range of financial products, and starting out as a sole trader. The business grew rapidly, and she formed a partnership with her husband after six months. He opened an office in East Grinstead while she continued to work from home.

To be a successful one man band, Linda considers that it is necessary to be good at marketing and selling, and to combine these skills with substantial business acumen, because one person has to be able to handle all the tasks, and hold the business together. The attractions for her included the chance to meet people from a wide range of industries and from across all sectors. She has the outgoing personality to do a job like this, and enjoys meeting people.

Selling Out

Having firmly established her business, Linda felt that the small business market was particularly good, and that there was considerable demand for small businesses, so she sold her business to a larger financial services group and became an authorized representative for them.

She liked having her own business, and saw many of her clients as friends and was very keen to keep them, so there she experienced some conflict about selling the business. Yet she is satisfied with her decision to sell. She travels into London frequently, as even though she can talk to loyal clients over the telephone she likes to visit the new ones, and enjoys going to see them in their own environment even though it might be more efficient to encourage them to come to her. She likes to feel accessible to her clients, as many people make financial decisions on the spur of the moment and it is necessary therefore to be there to prevent her clients from going off-course with their financial planning.

Linda felt that a major disadvantage of being a one man band was that the business was dependent on her being in constant good health. If the owner of a one man band falls ill for a long period of time, the bank can foreclose on the business, staff can lose inspiration and the whole company can founder. It was when she was pregnant with her fourth baby that she decided to sell out, after 12 years of hard work. She did not build up much capital, but did develop a very good client base, and has become a director of the company which acquired her business. They gave her capital in return for bringing in an infrastructure. One immediate result of selling out was that she found she could go on holiday, and could have time off without worrying that the business would collapse. Having more capital she has also been able to hire more staff, and to delegate the jobs she didn't like doing. In the past, with her own company, the staff had to be paid even when she was on holiday and not earning, so she tended to dispense with holidays altogether.

During the time of her one man band Linda didn't save very much capital, and still harbours a desire to have several thousands of pounds in the bank, especially to pay the school fees for her children. One of her private assets is a property in West London which is rented to tenants, and this at least brings in some income. Linda would not say that in her case being a one man band made her rich, but that was not why she did it.

Harking Back

Linda regrets losing some aspects of her one man band: now that she's part of a large group means she can't look after her clients as well as she used to. A one man band business that is sold to a larger group can become constantly tied up in Board meetings. In Linda's case this has meant that she is not able to return her clients' telephone calls as promptly as she would like to, and finds herself involved in big company politics and inter-company balances, and is beginning to hark back to the simplicity of the one man band days. She likes the idea of capitalizing every five years on what she has done, but one needs to take clients with one to be successful. People want financial planning and they want products which will last a reasonable amount of time, normally at least ten years, and they want the person who provided these products to stay with them. Linda points out that you cannot often sell and take your clients with you.

Advantages and Disadvantages

In her one man band business Linda built up her knowledge of her sector considerably, and has developed an interesting mix of qualities in the process, a combination of business sense and flair for selling – qualities which do not always naturally occur together. As a one man band, you need an eye for detail: paying wages, organizing the cleaning woman and running the whole show.

One problem Linda faced in the past was that she looked too young to advise older people about their finances, so she had to wait until she had more experience and had built up a client base in the broking business before she felt she could set up on her own successfully.

A new problem which has emerged over the last few years has been the saturation of the financial services market; there are too many financial consultants, and many of them have a poor reputation, which has affected the whole industry. People say 'Oh no, not another life insurance salesman'. It is hard to be proud of being in this line of business. People see talking about insurance as the fastest way to clear a pub. When she began Linda was very self-motivated, and at that time it was certainly a rising market and many people were interested in entering it. But in recent years the business has been hard hit by the Financial Services Act. Last year one fifth of all independent financial advisers closed down or merged with others. So the market is shrinking, but Linda believes that if you are determined to stay a better market will develop in the long run.

Note

Since the introduction of the Financial Services Act it is no longer possible to set up a one man band business as an independent financial adviser in the way that Linda did. It is now necessary to offer proof of financial adequacy and to demonstrate your independence by offering a very wide range of products.

One way to operate is to join an umbrella organization (such as the DBS Group or Burns Anderson). It is also essential to be a member of FIMBRA, which can cost as much as £5,000 a year, and it can take approximately ten weeks to arrange registration. It is impossible to start up from scratch and make money as an independent financial adviser, as FIMBRA membership is only possible after three years of training, and it takes at least two to three years to become established prior to becoming independent. Faced with all these requirements, many people get discouraged and give up within the first three months. An easier route to take is to work for an insurance company and become a company representative or tied agent. Then it is necessary to be authorized through LAUTRO and abide by its rules.

If you are determined to be independent, one solution is to work for a large financial services group on a freelance basis, officially being self-employed and even working from home. Increasingly, however, this way of working is being challenged by the Inland Revenue, which maintains that a self-employed person should be working for a variety of clients, not just one. Working in the insurance industry is another good way of preparing to become an independent financial adviser, but there will be a period of supervision, and the necessary three years' training for FIMBRA membership.

Start-up Costs
- Telephone installation – £1,000 (several lines)
- Answering machines – £300
- Fax machines – £700
- Photocopier – £700
- Computer equipment – £5,000
- Stationery – £1,500
- Office furniture – £1,500
- **Total start-up costs – £10,700**

Running Costs
These include telephone, travel (which cannot be passed on to clients but must be met from commission income)

Typical Length of Time to Become Established
Immediately, if work can be carried over from a former position

Typical Rate of Growth
40 to 50 per cent at first, then 15 to 25 per cent after a few years. If you concentrate more on serving existing clients than on attracting new business this growth rate should remain steady

Typical Personal Income
£25,000–£45,000

Typical Turnover
£40,000–£65,000+

Business-to-consumer One Man Bands

INTRODUCTION

As was true for the business-to-business case studies we have examined so far, all these businesses are (or have the potential to be) full-time, have relatively low start-up costs, and can be run by one person (although you will need an accountant and perhaps some other professional advisers, and possibly some support staff as well). There follow 16 business-to-consumer case studies: each is unique, and together they offer a varied cross-section of some of the great number of opportunities and range of possibilities available within the business-to-consumer market.

Some of the subjects of our case studies began because they'd been made redundant or were unable to find work; others simply felt dissatisfied with being in a large company or working for someone else, and saw a one man band as an opportunity for a more satisfying and worthwhile way of earning a living. Some were young people just starting out, others had almost reached retirement age. All of them spent some time analysing their skills and the qualities they thought they'd need to be able to run a one man band: high on the list were a need for independence, determination, wanting to do something different, wanting to prove themselves, wanting something interesting and stimulating, and wanting to express themselves more. Often they were people of slightly unusual backgrounds, from off the beaten track.

Market research was a necessary preliminary in all cases, although some found that the demand for the services they could offer was already there, without their needing to do much investigating. Most people set up a one man band in a field related to their previous activities, but not always. A significant proportion made a total break and went in for something completely different, although it was usually something they'd had some experience of as a hobby or outside interest.

The amount of research and work put in on a business plan also varied. These elements were not considered crucial by those who turned their corporate careers into one man bands, nor by those who needed no financing. Some were able to set up their businesses with personal funds, and to grow the business by ploughing back profits. The businesses are all, by definition, low-cost anyway. Equipment was minimal in each case, although stock of products was needed in some instances. But the value-added service offered by the individual person was always the most important ingredient for success.

Most of the businesses started up as sole traders, and the majority have stayed this way. Forming a limited liability company was the option chosen by those with an ambition to grow their businesses and eventually to be more than a one man band. This is more common for business-to-business one man bands, as you will have seen.

All of these people experienced the problems of pitching for business, although often early business leads were easier than expected. It was frequently the case that business came in before they were ready for it, and that they created their one man band business in response to market demand. First assignments and first clients/customers always played a vital role in getting the business off the ground.

Actually running the business was seen as exciting but tiring, and much harder work than expected. Some experienced difficulties in serving a number of clients/customers at once while marketing for business at the same time, but all found that good work meant good referral business. Cash flow was always a problem to some degree, and few of the one man bands have reached a mega-rich, very comfortable stage. Almost by definition a one man band remains hungry for business and insecure in outlook, however healthy its bank balances; it is the kiss of death to rest on one's laurels.

A number of the people in our case studies grew their one man band beyond its original size, but all are still dominated by the personality of the founder. One man bands are inevitably totally identified with the person who started them.

CASE STUDY 9: ADULT EDUCATION/TEACHING

Background and Influences

Marcia teaches English Literature and History to adults under the auspices of her own one man band business. She started doing this work when her children left home and she found herself with more time on her hands, and a need for more company and interaction with others and more of a sense of purpose in life.

Marcia studied these subjects at university, and although she had always stayed interested in them she had never done much with them; she also felt that she would be a good teacher. She discovered that offering her skills and knowledge in adult education could be a readily saleable product. She was also influenced by a friend, an accomplished music teacher, who had set herself up in business and had lots of students. She found, through asking around, that most adults who had missed out on secondary or higher education would most readily take to English Literature and History.

Preparation

Marcia checked with her local authority to make sure that it was permissible for her to offer her teaching skills; because she was not necessarily training people for specific examinations it was agreed that she could go ahead and set herself up as a freelance teacher. Her next problem was locating a venue. She thought that at first she would use her very large dining room, as the table had enough space for 12 people and she thought that this would serve her well (she didn't really want to have classes larger than this). She thought about making use of the local school, but as she thought she might like to run courses in the daytime, when the school would be busy, she had to rule this out. She also felt that the school wouldn't seem very comfortable and attractive to the kind of students she wanted to attract. She looked under 'Halls' in the Yellow Pages, but they all seemed rather large and, she estimated, probably rather expensive.

The Product

Marcia invested in subscriptions to a number of teaching magazines, especially *Education* and *Training and Education*, which gave her

ideas in structuring a course to offer. At first she planned a course
of six one-and-a-half-hour lessons covering a variety of topics within
English Literature and History. She picked appealing and varied
topics in which she had a particular interest, and found videos to
help illustrate each one. She spent some time carefully preparing
extracts of these videos. She also thought of practical exercises to
go with each class, so that each student could each make his or her
own contribution.

Marcia decided to run the course in the evenings, and picked
Wednesdays from 7.30–9 p.m. She decided that this day and time
would be best because it didn't clash with any particularly popular
television programme, and would give people time to have their
supper and still get home from class before it was too late. She also
thought it would be a nice idea to offer a glass of wine and some
'nibbles' at the end of the first class.

Advertising and Promotion

Marcia advertised her courses in the local newspaper and in shop
windows. She decided to charge £2.50 per person per class, payable
at each class or at a discount if a student paid for the whole course
at once, so that the total would be £12 rather than £15.

Launching the Service

Marcia was thrilled when for her first evening 15 people turned up,
of which five paid the £12 to do all the classes. Therefore, in her
first evening her takings were £60 for the five who paid in advance
and £25 from the remainder, totalling £85. Only two of her students
dropped out the following week, but they were more than replaced
by three others who had heard about the course from those who
had already attended.

Marcia found the first course quite difficult and demanding, but
at the end of it she felt much more confident and able to run the
whole thing again easily. She has now been running her course for
two years, and has brought in more people through advertising more
widely and networking through local societies and groups such as
the Women's Institute.

She has made slight variations in the content of the courses and
the topics covered, to keep herself interested and to attract old
students back, and has started to have some former students coming
back again. She was approached by the local college to teach there,

but decided to carry on doing her own thing. She enjoys devising her own courses and running them her own way.

Advantages and Disadvantages

Marcia sees the advantages of her business as being the minimal outlay – just £50 in advertising and less than £50 in hiring videos, photocopying handouts and the occasional few bottles of wine and food, and was pleased that there was no delay in payment, as everyone either paid in advance or on the evening of each class. She found that the teaching fitted in well with her other activities, although her husband did occasionally complain about the noise and invasion of the house on a Wednesday night.

The downside, Marcia found, was that the course needed a lot of preparation, and it was difficult to estimate demand in advance.

Profits

She found that her profit per course was not large, especially at the beginning when she had advertising costs and the need to borrow the videos, but she was able to reduce her costs per course to around £50, therefore making around £200 profit per course. She found she was able to run her course for 22 weeks of the year, which allowed for three courses a year.

The main benefit, she feels, has been all the new friends she has made, and the confidence and satisfaction she has gained. The extra pocket money has given her a new feeling of independence, and this together with the teaching has almost made her feel transported back to her university days!

CASE STUDY 10: ADVANCED DRIVING METHODS AND TECHNIQUES

Background and Influences

Tony runs his own advanced driving tuition business. He had always loved driving, and for this reason had joined the army (to drive tanks) and the police force (to drive police cars and vans). But Tony didn't like the regimented lifestyle of these pursuits, and wanted the freedom to do his own thing. He thought about being a taxi driver, but wanted something a bit more unusual.

When he heard about the charges levied by the local driving school, especially for teaching someone more advanced skills, beyond the normal road test standard, he thought this sounded quite remunerative. Also, although regular driving tuition was readily available for learner drivers, advanced driving tuition for experienced road users seemed to be in short supply. Tony felt that with ever-busier roads and more difficult driving conditions for drivers to cope with, his services could be in great demand. He also thought he would teach drivers of specialist vehicles, such as motor cycles, commercial vehicles, and even how to tow caravans and boats. He'd done all these things in the army and the police.

Preparation

Tony took out membership in the Institute of Advanced Motorists, and gained approval for his proposed service from the Department of Transport. He sought information from the motoring associations (the AA and RAC), and spoke to their staff about the sort of advanced driving techniques required; they and their literature were very helpful in refining his product.

The Product

Tony developed a series of short courses to appeal to a wide range of advanced learners. These included 'Advanced Traffic Management' for people who suddenly found themselves having to do a lot of city driving; 'Trailer/caravan/boat towing' for those who had acquired these vehicles and wanted to know how to tow them safely; 'Motor-cycle Handling' for relatively experienced motor cyclists who wanted to refine and develop their techniques; and 'Commercial Vehicle Driving' for those who found they needed this skill in their job. Tony had also done some driving on the Continent, in France and Germany, and thought he could offer some short courses on this, although this would be in the way of mainly verbal advice rather than practical demonstration.

Tony also offered a course on 'Safer and More Economical Driving', teaching techniques for reducing the risk of accidents and saving on petrol and wear and tear, so a student could develop good driving habits and keep costs down. This course included instruction in controlling a car, overtaking, night driving, dealing with skids, and driving high-performance diesel and automatic cars safely. He also offered a course on 'Quick and Easy Basic Maintenance', so that his customers could save on their garage bills for minor repairs.

Tony decided to run each course as four separate hours of tuition, to be scheduled to suit the convenience of the customer, charging £15 an hour so that he would make a total of £60 per course. The customer's own car, van or motor cycle would be used in each case, saving wear and tear on Tony's own vehicles and minimizing the problem of providing cars. However, Tony had a range of vehicles which he could use if necessary, if a customer wanted to learn a specialist skill before he or she acquired the relevant vehicle.

Advertising and Promotion

Tony knew that although acquiring these kinds of motoring skills was an important growth area, advanced driving tuition was a new idea and might take a while to get established. So he prepared a detailed advertising campaign to create awareness for his services. Again, the AA and RAC were supportive and allowed him to enclose a small flyer about his services in their magazine for members, especially as he promised to promote their services among his customers in return. He also organized a leaflet drop in all the homes in his neighbourhood with at least one car. In addition he advertised in the local press, his advert stating in a practical and appealing way that he could help all drivers improve their driving and make it safer, more enjoyable and more economical. His courses, his advertising argued, were geared towards saving the customer money on motor insurance, petrol and maintenance costs. In this way Tony was selling his service as a range of benefits, not just as simple driving tuition.

Launching the Service

On the day that his first advertisement appeared, customers began to telephone Tony to find out more. He took six bookings on his first day, the courses on 'Advanced Traffic Management' and 'Safer and More Economical Driving' turning out to be most profitable. News of his services spread by word of mouth, and Tony even found himself teaching elementary driving to people who had failed their road tests repeatedly. After about six months Tony found that he was handling about six or seven bookings a day, which matched his capacity.

Advantages and Disadvantages

Tony realized that the long-term success of his one man band would depend on building up a good reputation for providing useful, relevant skills that people needed. He also found the hours long and the work quite demanding, but his business did give him a great sense of freedom, and of achievement in really being able to help his customers, who often became friends in the process.

Profits

Tony spent £100 on printing flyers to be inserted in AA and RAC literature and to be used in the leaflet drop, and a further £50 on advertisements in the local press. Running the courses was very profitable: working out at £90–£100 a day, including weekends (in fact, weekends were more popular than weekdays, as many of his customers were too busy to have a class in the week). There was no expense on handouts or printed course materials, and Tony found that he gained in proficiency and found the work easier as time went on. The need for expenditure on advertising was reduced as the courses were up and running, and within the first month his takings were pure profit and the use of his own vehicles was minimal.

CASE STUDY 11: ALARM INSTALLATION FOR HOMES AND CARS

Background and Influences

Eamon had a tough upbringing in a rough neighbourhood, and his brother had fallen into bad company and had ended up in prison, convicted of burglary. Eamon reacted very strongly against this, and was so determined not to follow the same path that he decided to go into burglary prevention. He knew a lot of insider information from his brother and his friends, and realized he could put this to good use and earn money in the process. Eamon worked in an electrical shop and knew that (a) he could sell, and (b) he could easily understand how burglar alarms worked. He had been bored sitting in the shop all day, and had long been thinking about having a job where he could be out and about more.

Preparation

Eamon read as much as he could about burglary prevention products. He was amazed at the degree to which the prevention of burglary and vandalism had become such big business, with many different products and services available to combat the threat. He discovered that the fastest-growing area was the supply and fitting of intruder alarms in houses, followed by car alarm systems. Alarms used to be only for rich people's homes, but Eamon found that their use was rapidly descending the social scale, and that alarms were being considered essential by anyone with a largish property and valuables to protect. And not even just by them: many people hated the idea of intruders breaking into their homes, even if they didn't have much worth stealing.

Eamon also found that alarm technology had progressed to the extent that installation was comparatively quick and easy. All he would have to do was develop his selling skills and demonstrate that he could make a trouble-free, reliable job of installing the alarms. He knew that he would have to be good at explaining to his customers how the alarms worked, but he didn't think that this would be a problem. He had good selling skills, a basic electrical knowledge, some money available for advertising and stock, and his own car. He joined the National Supervisory Council for Intruder Alarms, which was useful for the advice it offered him on the range of products available. He found that he didn't need precise electrical qualifications, because the systems worked on low voltage rather than by being directly wired up to mains electricity.

The Product

Eamon decided to offer a limited range of home and car alarms, including the bottom-of-the-range models for customers who were undecided about whether or not to have an alarm, and whose decision would therefore be affected by price. He also offered a state-of-the-art model, if only to show customers how amazingly sophisticated burglary prevention equipment could be. All were quick and easy to install, causing minimal disruption. Eamon found some good alarm component suppliers in the *Exchange & Mart*. He found that most systems were basically the same, operating from an electronic control box and wired to detectors at possible points of entry in the home, with the alarm raised by an outside bell or siren. Even the car alarm systems were not so different. Thus the products were quite easy to understand. The alarm component suppliers also provided detailed instructions, often operating a 'hotline' to help with problems. The work mainly would involve laying cables discreetly, drilling holes and mounting connectors. The quality standard for alarms is BS 4737. Eamon also offered within his fee a repair service, annual maintenance inspection, and a special deal on parts.

Advertising and Promotion

Eamon realized that widespread advertising would be necessary, and first of all targeted middle-income range homes, which didn't have a home alarm but lived near people who did. He had some flyers printed and, noting which homes didn't have an alarm already, dropped in a leaflet. He felt proud that he wasn't casing the joint to see which places could be ripped off, as he knew his brother had done on many occasions. Many people were out in their gardens as he was leaflet dropping, and several times he engaged them in conversation, with the result that even before he had any stock people had expressed keen interest.

He also advertised in the local newspaper and put a small card up in various shop windows. In addition he made a small stand for himself outside a major supermarket, stopping people as they entered or left and endeavouring to convince them of the value of an effective alarm system.

Launching the Service

Right from the beginning enquiries began to come in, and Eamon found that everyone who telephoned him was already convinced of the need for an alarm. He followed up his leaflet drop and found that in one out of three homes he had visited, people wanted an alarm. He was helped considerably by a heavy crime wave in the area, triggered off by widespread redundancies in several local factories. Every time a break-in was reported in the local paper Eamon cut the article out and stuck it in a clippings book which he could show to customers. It was amazingly effective. After six months Eamon increased the range of alarms offered, in response to his customers' needs. He found an alarm component supplier who could offer him a free design service: Eamon would send a sketch of his customer's property to the supplier and the supplier would design the alarm and quote a price for providing the parts. Eamon then added his labour costs, and found he could mark up the price considerably and still offer value for money.

Advantages and Disadvantages

Eamon found that selling alarms was very much a growth area, and he had no trouble finding customers. The business was easy to set up and to run, except that he found the paperwork quite complicated and that it took a while to learn about the products. Fortunately, he remained friends with his ex-colleagues in the electrical shop, and they helped him with the business administration. Overall, Eamon was amazed that the business was much simpler to organize and run than he had thought it would be.

Profits

The most expensive alarms come to between £600 and £800 (including installation) for a medium-sized three-bedroomed detached house. At this rate Eamon found after six months that he could make about £700 a week, with a major expensive alarm at least once a fortnight and several small home and car alarms every week. He has also continued to market strongly, spending about £100 a week on promotions.

CASE STUDY 12: SELLING ART
Background and Influences

Caroline had always been very interested in art, and knew that she was good at enthusing others. She had studied art history at university and was quite a good painter in her own right. She was told that selling art could only be a part-time job, but she was determined to make a full-time living out of it. She had worked in a gallery, but had felt that it was restrictive, and was frustrated by the fact that she had no say in the works being chosen for sale. She was also poorly paid, when she knew that the margins on paintings were very high.

Why couldn't she sell paintings from her home instead? She lived with her parents, who had a large country house which included a sizable studio that she used for her own painting. She was an only child of fairly wealthy, quite indulgent parents, who were anxious that she should be happy and able to express herself.

Preparation

Caroline began preparations by cleaning up and redecorating her studio and, first of all, arranging a tasteful exhibition of her own work. Then she set about choosing artwork to buy. Through working at the gallery, and through her friends from university, she tracked down several artists who produced the sort of work she liked and who seemed likely to become more sought-after in the future. She also found out about art importers, to provide a further source of artwork at a low price.

The Product

Caroline decided that there would be a good market for works of art whose style and subjects fell somewhere between clichéd reproduction and the really avant-garde. She wanted to offer artwork that was appealing and attractive to fairly conservative tastes, targeted at newly-rich businesspeople who knew little about art but wanted to own some tasteful originals which would accumulate value over time and which would in the mean time look nice in their homes.

Caroline bought ten pieces to start with, from her contacts at the gallery and at university. She also offered the advantage to customers that they could view the artwork in the comfort of Caroline's studio without having to trail around the shops, at a time that suited them, including evenings and weekends. She would also advise on where and how the piece should be hung or displayed for maximum advantage, and help customers to build up their own collections, finding special works on request.

Advertising and Promotion

Caroline advertised her gallery in the local press, giving her telephone number only so that people would ring her to make an appointment to view. She targeted young, up-and-coming businesspeople, advertising her service to them by putting a card on the notice board of the local health-and-fitness club, the golf club, and in the pages of the programmes sold at the local theatre. She also got coverage in the local societies and cultural groups. She sent special flyers out to promote the idea of artwork as the perfect gift for Mother's Day, Valentine's Day, Christmas and birthdays. One of her best sources of promotion turned out to be free: the referral by word of mouth of satisfied customers, once her business had got going.

Launching the Service

Caroline found there was no shortage of people wanting to see her collection, and she was thrilled that in her first week she was able to sell four pieces, one painting at £500, two at £100, and a small engraving at £50. Her artist friends were equally delighted, and several of them agreed to meet the customers who'd bought their work at Caroline's studio, and this often led to further sales. After a while, she found that she could make even greater profits by selling imported artwork, which she would then frame. In the *Exchange & Mart* she found suppliers of artwork from India, Thailand and China, and chose those which she thought would appeal most to Western tastes. Caroline found that about 80 per cent of visits from people who had telephoned resulted in a sale, and that she could price paintings and other work between £30 and £250, with a few at £500. She was even able to sell some of her own paintings – much to her amazement – because they had been painted for her own amusement and she'd not considered them commercially viable.

Advantages and Disadvantages

Caroline discovered that she had targeted her market segment well, and that art was very popular among wealthy young businesspeople. Her choice went down well, and she found she was really adding value by deciding which pieces matched each customer. Her overheads were low since she was able to show the works in her own home. The business could easily have been limited by lack of space, but this wasn't a problem to Caroline because she had the large studio, which also meant that her business didn't intrude on her parents' lives too much. She thought that if this became a problem, she could rent some space in a shop, but liked the freedom of running her own business from home.

Profits

The cost of promotion and buying the works of art in the first instance was fairly high, but Caroline was able to recoup her initial expenditure after a month. She had spent £200 on advertising, and had bought ten pieces, costing her £1,000. In addition she already had 20 paintings of her own. In the first month she made a profit of £1,500, and from then on she built up a steady business, selling five or six pieces a week.

She was able to make between 50 and 100 per cent profit on the paintings, and her own paintings were almost entirely profit, except for her expenses in canvas and paints. In terms of selling imported pictures, she found that she could buy a 18 x 24 inch oil painting on canvas from a wholesale importer for about £8, added to which was the cost of framing, about £15. Thus her typical product cost could be as little as £23, and she would then calculate a price based on the quality of the work, and on how appealing and attractive its theme was. Many of her £8 paintings could be sold for £100 or £150, because of their carefully-chosen themes. She always offered visitors tea and biscuits (or wine and canapés, depending on the time of their visits), but this was a minimal expense and usually absorbed into the family household expenses.

CASE STUDY 13: CAR BROKING

Background and Influences

Jack was running a garage selling petrol and new cars, and over the years became aware that motor vehicle sales were becoming increasingly competitive, so much so that customers have begun to expect that they will always get a discount on a new car. Jack found that he was constantly being undercut by a new breed of car salesmen, known as car brokers. Car brokers offer new vehicles for sale at well below list price. How do they do it? Basically, by shopping around a number of well-known, appointed dealers for their best trade price on a specific car for ready sale. Thus, the car broker is able to offer his customers among the public a wider choice of vehicles at prices much lower than most customers could negotiate for themselves, while keeping a sales commission for himself.

Jack was in a pub one lunchtime, and found himself propping up the bar next to two chaps who were clearly car brokers. He was amazed at how they could so easily undercut him on prices, and how simple the business seemed to be. They had built up good relationships with dealers up and down the country who were only too glad to offer them cars at a lower price in order to attract the manufacturers' big incentives, which are always based on unit sales.

Jack was getting fed up with the big overheads of the garage. It didn't seem to be making much money, and he was having a lot of staff problems. It thought it would be nice to have a job which would give him independence.

Preparation

Jack gave up running the garage, and set up a small office at home for his new business. He already had good motor trade contacts, and he spent some time telephoning them and telling them about his new business. Many of his dealer friends were glad to sell cars through him if it meant they could be moved faster. Jack subscribed to *What Car?* and analysed his future competitors by looking at their advertisements. He also joined the Motor Manufacturers' and Traders' Association, thinking this could be useful for further contacts. Then he acquired a large collection of Yellow Pages directories and motor dealer listings.

The Product

Car broking works by placing advertisements offering new cars at a discount greater than that offered by the franchised dealers. When customers respond to an advertisement placed by a car broker, the service is explained to them: they are dealing with a broker who can obtain the car they want at a lower price. The broker makes a note of the car they want, and their telephone number. Then the broker telephones a large number of dealers holding the franchise for the make of car the customer wants. After a number of enquiries have been received, the broker then approaches dealers, explaining that he or she is a broker and asking for a good price on the model his or her customer wants. The better you are at negotiating, the better a price you will get, and the larger your margins and higher your profits will be. Most dealers are anxious to sell quickly, and will offer a broker a good price rather than wait for a walk-in customer. This is especially the case now that the industry is suffering from considerable over-supply and dealers are being offered more and more enhanced incentives from the manufacturers to move stock.

Advertising and Promotion

Jack realized that comprehensive advertising was vital for the success of his car broking business, and took space in a number of motoring periodicals, finding their addresses and circulation details in *Benn's Media Directory*. He also advertised the specific models of cars he knew he could get especially good discounts on.

Launching the Service

As a result of one of these advertisements, Jack received a telephone call as soon as he had set up his business from a potential customer who had already contacted three dealers in his neighbourhood in his search for a new SEAT Toledo. The recommended price was £8,999, and the dealers were offering modest discounts of only £20–£50. Furthermore, none of them stocked a Toledo in the colour he wanted. Jack knew which dealers stocked Toledos, and which of them was likely to offer him a good price. Jack telephoned six dealers locally and nationally, including one who stocked the car in his customer's favourite colour for only £8,090. Jack charged the customer £8,599, and the vehicle was delivered three days later. The customer made a good saving (£400 off the manufacturer's recommended price), and Jack made a profit of £509, after just six telephone calls and an initial outlay on his advertisements. Word soon spread around about the good prices and fast service Jack offered, and he began to wonder why he hadn't been doing this before.

Advantages and Disadvantages

Jack found that his knowledge of the car trade was very helpful, together with his good telephone manner. Jack was known as quite a smoothie, and developed good relationships with customers, especially women, who wanted to pay a better price for their new car but weren't very confident when it came to tough negotiating with hardened dealers. Jack's overheads were low and he was able to build the business up to a high profit level, much better than when he had owned the garage.

Profits

Jack was soon able to make several deals a week. Some took longer than others to come through, and sometimes the customer could be slow in paying or would want to pay in instalments. But this is largely the dealer's problem, because he collects the money and pays Jack his commission. In a good week Jack can make around £1200 in commission, but his advertisements can be expensive (he usually spends about £200 a week on these). He advertises not only his service as a broker and the actual discounts he can get, but specific cars which he knows he can get particularly cheaply from friendly dealers. Jack's profit increased as time went on by moving up-market to more expensive cars, and by expanding his dealer network.

CASE STUDY 14: CAR CLEANING AND VALETING

Background and Influences

Greg had always been a practical boy. He wasn't particularly bright but he was hard-working, entrepreneurial, reliable and friendly. He hadn't been able to get a job on leaving school, so his father, who ran a small garage, helped him to set himself up in business cleaning cars and offering a car valeting service. Greg soon built up a network of satisfied customers who liked their car to be clean inside and out, and who appreciated his friendly and personal service. Many of these were people who occasionally had to offer lifts to their own customers and who thus had particular reasons for wanting to keep their cars as clean and smart as possible. Car valet work can be one of the most successful and profitable one man band cleaning services, as a volume service and contract work can be achieved far more easily and for a far smaller investment than is true for many comparable cleaning activities.

Preparation

Greg, helped by his father, realized the enormous potential demand for this service, and began asking around to see where customers could come from. He needed premises which could take several cars, but luckily had his father's own garage forecourt to use. His father also supplied him with the necessary equipment, asking that he should be reimbursed when Greg started earning some money. The forecourt could take six cars, with hot water pressure available for cleaning car exteriors and an electric point for operating a carpet steam cleaner for interiors. These were the only major items Greg needed. He could have hired the carpet steam cleaner from a specialist supplier, but he decided, with his father's help, to acquire one, because he would need to use it constantly. He looked up

'Cleaning Materials Manufacturers and Suppliers' in the Yellow Pages and found a direct-from-the-factory outlet where he could buy one at almost cost price.

The Product

Greg's car valeting service was aimed at the top of the market, at those owning expensive and prestige cars who would want regular and frequent use of his service. He also aimed it at the contract market, where he could provide valet services for a fleet of cars through just one arrangement. He offered a range of services, such as the whole of the car (in and out) or the exterior only, with a special top-of-the-range service which including polishing all the chrome and fancy bits on prestige sports cars. He also offered coach, lorry, van, motor cycle and caravan cleaning, at special prices by negotiation.

Advertising and Promotion

Greg put an advertisement in several local newspapers, and stuck small postcards advertising his services in shops, especially those selling motor accessories. He had his father's friends and contacts, but he also spent some time canvassing trade customers directly, including new and used car dealers, car hire firms, taxi firms, car auctions and fleet operators. He found their addresses, sent them a small leaflet which he had had printed, and then phoned them up. Many expressed a keen interest in his service, even those who already used a valet service. His progress in getting customers was helped considerably by his special offer to do one valet job for free, challenging his potential customers to match the quality and thoroughness of his work for the same price. Many people admired him for his initiative.

Launching the Service

Even from his first day, thanks to his father's friends and contacts through his garage work, Greg was able to attract several customers. He took a great interest in each car, and got to know the likes and dislikes of each customer. Some liked air freshener to complete the job, some liked a fresh shampoo smell to the seat covers – if they were sheepskin or removable ones – and some cars were harder work than others, with ash trays to empty. He was lucky in that his father's staff in the garage would help him answer customer enquiries and take bookings, but he made himself available as much as possible to do this too. He found that most people wanted the complete inside-and-out service, and that there was also some demand for caravan cleaning, as he started up at the end of the holiday season when people wanted to put their caravans away for the winter in a clean and tidy state.

Advantages and Disadvantages

Greg found that the great advantage was that volume contracts were easy to get, and that whole garages and companies were only too pleased to use his services, especially those that had suffered from poor-quality valet services in the past. Greg's cost-effective service also appealed to their tighter budgets. No special skills were required on Greg's part, so there was no time lost training, but as he built up experience of valeting he found he could complete work on each car faster, while still doing a very good job. It would have been a big disadvantage if he'd had to supply his own area on which to clean the cars and his own equipment right from the start, but in due course he was able to pay back his father for the equipment, and start paying a small rental fee for the use of the forecourt space. He found there was some competition, but the need in the market was strong, and he could keep going with the customer base he managed to develop, which remained loyal due to his personal and reliable service.

Profits

Greg built up contracts with four local franchised car dealers to clean all their new and used vehicles, as well as having other, occasional customers. He found he could clean thoroughly eight cars a day, or 40 a week, maximum. The used cars would be quicker, costing £22 each, while the new cars and those requiring special service would take longer, and could cost as much as £30. Greg's takings reached £1,040 a week based on half the cars being done at the cheap rate and half at the expensive. He spent about £100 a week on advertising for the first few months, but then was able to start paying back equipment costs–£1,000 – and a weekly rental of £100 for the use of the forecourt.

CASE STUDY 15: CONTACT SERVICE FOR HOBBYISTS

Background and Influences

Rob was really crazy about train-spotting, and he knew he wasn't alone. In fact, he knew over a hundred other locomotive buffs. He had worked in a local shoe factory but he had really hated it, spending all day just looking forward to the evenings and weekends when he could read his train books and visit stations all over the country. Nevertheless he had to keep the factory job to earn a living, as he hadn't done very well at school. He was fairly quiet and introverted, but was hard-working and dedicated, and good at the things he was genuinely interested in. He was a great expert on trains, and his rather anxious parents often worried about the fact that he didn't seem interested in anything that would make money.

However, when he hit upon his contact service idea Rob found he was able to earn a living from his hobby. He'd heard about pen-pal services before, and had actually met one of his best train-spotting friends through a pen-pal in Canada whom he had started writing to while still at school, and whom he hoped to meet one day. His friend had told him about a new service popular in the USA which helped bring together hobbyists and enthusiasts in all forms of sports and hobbies. Rob saw that there was great scope to develop such a service among train-spotters in Britain (and maybe Europe), which would make use of his great knowledge of train-spotting and his talent for careful organization and administration without his having to leave his desk. The fact that he had fairly little money and resources didn't seem to matter too much.

Preparation

Rob already knew about most of the media read by train-spotters, but looked up *Benn's Media Directory* and *Willing's Press Guide* (at his local library) for more ideas about places to advertise. He set up a small filing-card system to keep note of all the contacts he could develop. He also found out about other people running similar services, in ship-spotting, stamp-collecting, bird-watching, fishing or photography. He then prepared a small leaflet explaining his service, and the benefits for all those interested in trains. He also had an application form printed, for those who were interested to fill in.

The Product

Rob found his contact service easy to operate. All he had to do was put people also interested in train-spotting in touch with one another for discussion, friendship, and sharing insights. Rob was able to offer added value, by virtue of his in-depth knowledge of trains, in matching people with very specific – even esoteric – needs. Those filling in his application form were asked to give personal details of their hobby, especially in terms of the trains in which they were most interested and the area in which they lived, and were asked to pay a one-off fee, in exchange for which they were promised a contact. Rob was fully aware that train-spotters tend to fall into various categories: those who like steam trains and those who prefer 125s; those who like travelling on trains and those who like just looking at them; those who go all over the country in search of trains and those who just sit at home and read about them. His job was to match these different types of train-spotters up, using his judgement to decide who would have most in common with whom.

Advertising and Promotion

Rob advertised in the specialist train-spotting press, and also put up one of his specially-printed cards at every railway station he visited, as well as in every modelists' shop and anywhere else he thought train-spotter might go, such in the as souvenir shops accompanying special railway exhibitions. There were also towns and junctions which were particularly special to train-spotters, and Rob made sure that his card was prominently displayed in all of them. Rob thought there was a potential for several thousands of members in due course.

Launching the Service

Rob was amazed at how many completed forms began to arrive in the post each day. It wasn't as easy as he'd thought to match them up, however, as people had such varied interests, but the more information he received the easier it was. He soon decided to dispense with his card index system and invest in a small computer. He was able to buy a second-hand word processor for only £200, and developed his own programme. Each applicant was sent the name of at least one compatible enthusiast in the first instance, while he sent the applicant's details to two or three others. If the recipient had no success in following up the contact details Rob sent, he sent another at a cheaper rate. Rob also got in touch personally with several of the people who wrote in, and was able to organize a get-together for those in his region. This led him in turn to editing a short newsletter for those interested in keeping in touch, which he gradually extended to include potentially all those who had written in.

Advantages and Disadvantages

Rob was able to test the viability of his contact service for a small initial outlay, and when he found it was successful he was able to pack in his job and do it on a full-time basis. The capital requirement was low, and the potential was indeed great. He was worried that as it was a new idea it might take time to get established, but there was a lot of initial enthusiasm. It needed motivation and tenacity on his part, but he was so keen on his hobby that this wasn't a problem.

Profits

Rob charged £20 for a first contact, and a further £10 (which he promoted as a 'privileged member's rate') for each subsequent one. In the first month almost 300 people wrote in, earning him nearly £6,000, less £100 for printing up leaflets, application forms and advertisement cards, and a further £150 for advertising. His computer and discs cost him £250. The number of new applicants tailed off slightly, but by the end of a year Rob had 2,000 people on his books, and was then able to diversify and increase his business with his monthly newsletter, for which he charged £5 per year subscription. Over half of his hobbyists subscribed, so he made a further income of £6,000, reduced to £4,000 after paying for printing and postage.

CASE STUDY 16: DATING AND MATCH-MAKING AGENCY

Background and Influences

Margaret is a very caring, warm person. She is half-Italian, and has a great love of life, being romantic and affectionate by nature. She married quite young, to a tall, blond English boy, and truly enjoys the married state. She has always thought that she only began to live after she was married. As a result, she feels that just about everyone else should be married, and that couples who are falling out should be helped to get back together again, whenever possible.

Margaret had spent a while working as a marriage guidance counsellor when she noticed the emergence of a number of dating agencies, set up to put couples together. She thought she could have more fun, gain more satisfaction, and make more money this way. She had also learned in her marriage-guidance work that many of the couples' problems stemmed from the fact that they were very ill-matched in the first place.

Preparation

Margaret soon realized that good dating bureaux were in demand. She thought she would operate from home, in the first instance at least, because she had a small spare room to use as an office and a pleasant reception room in which to meet singles and to introduce prospective couples. Her home address was quite prestigious and respectable. She started to plan her advertising campaign, and acquired an inexpensive computer on which to set up a database. She was quite tidy and well-organized, and was confident of her administrative ability. She consulted media and press guides to decide which newspapers and magazines to advertise in, and prepared forms to be filled in, with space for the applicant's interests and the sort of person he or she was looking for.

The Product

Margaret offered a considerate, confidential and discreet approach for people of all ages and backgrounds who did not want to go to big agencies but instead wanted a personal service from a warm, friendly and understanding individual, someone who would give them confidence. She wanted to attract people who ordinarily would not dream of going to a dating agency, who had never been to one before, and who would not want to place an advertisement directly themselves. She made it plain from the beginning that she wanted clientele who were quite serious about forming long attachments, preferably marriage. She realized that she might lose some customers this way, but preferred to do this, knowing that a good, up-market reputation was very important. It also seemed likely that more serious clients would be willing to pay higher fees, and would stay with the service until they found the perfect partner.

Advertising and Promotion

Margaret advertised her dating agency – 'The discreet and individual way of finding your perfect partner' – in the sort of magazines that appeal to the kind of serious, fairly discerning people she sought to attract. She thought she would target the slightly older end of the market, including people who had been too busy pursuing successful careers to find a mate and who had slowly realized how lonely they were, as well as people who had been widowed, or who had divorced or split up after their children had grown up and left home. Margaret also produced a short, tasteful brochure, fully explaining the service.

Launching the Service

Margaret's telephone continued to be busy from the moment she placed her first advertisement, and she was amazed at how many people there were who found themselves single and didn't like it much. She asked people about their likes and dislikes, the nature of their work, how they spent their leisure time, and the sort of person they could imagine as their dream partner. Margaret tried to classify these responses as scientifically as possible, to make it easier to match people up. Her computer helped her produce lists of people who might be compatible.

Margaret introduced a £50 signing-on fee, subject to her decision that an applicant was serious and committed to finding a partner. After three months a further £40 would be needed for more introductions.

She told all her first clients that it might take a few months for her database to attract enough possible partners, but as the numbers signing on grew rapidly she found that she was able to send out details of introductions after six weeks. She insisted on meeting most of her 'singles', and her shrewd assessments of their characters and needs helped enormously in their achieving successful friendships and, in many cases, marriages. She found that she had to extend her service to help younger people find partners, too. A number of mothers also came to her for advice when they were concerned that their sons or daughters did not seem to be having much luck in attracting potential partners. Margaret also started videoing her Case interviews with potential partners, to be shown to other clients.

Advantages and Disadvantages

Margaret found the business to be very satisfying and quite lucrative, but that putting the right people together could take a lot of thought and good judgement. She had to be very careful to avoid potential clients who didn't take her service seriously, who weren't interested in long-term relationships. She had to turn down people who were clearly looking for casual relationships, or who just wanted an attractive escort without any serious commitment. There were other agencies with different aims which could supply these. She was particularly diligent about avoiding taking on anybody who was married already and only wanted a bit of fun on the side. Part of her product was her serious attitude to the long-term fulfilment of her client's needs.

Profits

Margaret found that 200 people had signed up in the first six weeks, all paying their £50. This totalled £10,000, from which she had to deduct £300 for her brochure, £200 for application forms, and another £500 for advertisements. She had also spent £500 on her computer and discs. Subsequently she spent £500 on a video recorder and blank videos.

She found that she was able to bring in at least 20 more people a month without having to spend more on advertising, as news of her service spread by word of mouth, and that the business would bring in about £20,000 a year.

CASE STUDY 17: FANCY DRESS HIRE

Background and Influences

Joanna loved giving and going to parties. Throughout the year, parties with a fancy-dress theme were becoming more and more popular. Besides St Valentine's and Halloween, parties were often being thrown to raise money for political or social causes – such as elections or wars/disasters in various countries. Those on the party circuit had a great need for a wide range of fancy-dress outfits, and it was always a problem finding a shop that would stock the particular outfits they needed. The problem often was that the shop wouldn't have an outfit in the right size, or wouldn't have the right design for a particular theme, or would be closed just at the time the outfit was needed (for a party thrown at short notice). Joanna pinpointed a fun and potentially lucrative way of making money, something much better than her sales assistant job in a designer clothes shop.

Preparation

Joanna had a spare room at home to use for storing outfits, and her house was in a fairly quiet part of town, with plenty of parking space outside. She already had a large selection of her own outfits, and enjoyed dressmaking, so she went to work on making more. She then advertised and asked around for outfits no longer needed, including old wedding dresses (which could be dyed and changed to use as ball-gowns). She went to a number of theatrical suppliers and bought costumes, attended theatrical auctions, held when a specific production reaches the end of its run, and visited an army surplus store and found some attractive old uniforms, both formal and tropical. She also went to jumble sales, especially in quite up-market parts of town, and rummaged through for colourful and exotic bargains. She had a big automatic washing machine and good laundry facilities at her home for washing the costumes after use, and a couple of streets away there was a specialist dry-cleaning shop which would offer her a good deal in return for her giving them a lot of business. She also purchased dress-makers' forms and mannequins on which to display the costumes.

The Product

Joanna would choose and hire outfits which she would then clean, press and sub-hire out. She recognized that a fancy-dress business was a good one to run from home, and that she could help people with a personal service designed specifically for their requirements. She thought she would hire out to people going to parties or for amateur theatricals, and keep the business fairly small. She started with 50 costumes, following some traditional fancy-dress trends of clowns, policemen and panto horses, but adding her own ideas of more modern and contemporary tastes, and reflecting current politics worldwide.

Advertising and Promotion

Joanna consulted media and press guides, and placed advertisements in the magazines read by top socialites and fashionable party-lovers, such as *Vogue* and *Tatler*, and also in theatrical magazines, including *Drama* and *New Theatre Quarterly*. She even held a few of her own fancy-dress parties, to gauge demand and to get the ball rolling. She found that business increased through word of mouth as a result of her growing reputation for good presentation, and because she offered an interesting, diverse choice, as well as flexible opening hours.

Launching the Service

Joanna assembled her collection of costumes and held a small cocktail party to launch her business. From then on, customers began to flood in, especially as the party season was well under way. She had a separate fitting room, kept fresh and clean, and was prepared to stay open all the hours her customers required, especially when they had to go to a party at short notice. Joanna started a booking scheme for costumes, and would hire them out by the day, charging a deposit and accepting the remainder when the costume was returned the next day. If people were late returning garments they were asked to pay extra penalty costs, especially if it meant that Joanna lost the chance to hire out the costume to someone else. Joanna found that if she could get people to come and see the costumes they were generally captivated, especially if they tried some on. Then they would suddenly remember a function they had been invited to, for which one of the costumes was ideal, and so Joanna had a 'sale'.

Advantages and Disadvantages

Joanna found that the same costumes could make her money several times over, especially the tuxedos and ball-gowns, and also the theme clothes, such as schoolgirl outfits, the historical costumes, and the military uniforms. Her one man band did need some investment to get going, but she had plenty of costumes to start with and was quite adept at making more. Demand could be limited when fewer parties were being held, but at these times Joanna could focus on amateur theatricals instead. She found that having a wide range of friends helped, as they were the sort of people with a need for her service, and were in any case well-disposed towards her and keen to at least see what she was up to.

Profits

Amassing the collection of costumes cost Joanna £500, and she spent another £100 on dummies, £200 on advertising, and £200 on printing leaflets and handbills. Luckily she did not have to pay out for use of a studio, and was able to take care of most of the laundering costs herself. In terms of fees charged, a very up-market and expensive costume would cost £25 (comparing well with the £40 charged in other shops), while a simpler outfit would cost only £10. If Joanna spent a lot of time advising people on the most suitable garment, and especially if she had to carry out any minor alterations, then she put another £5 on the bill; late returns incurred a 50 per cent surcharge. With 50 customers in her first week Joanna made £800, broke even after three weeks, and thereafter made a steady income of around £650 a week, even after continuing to advertise her service. She enjoys the freedom of her new career, and sees her service as genuinely helpful and quite unique.

CASE STUDY 18: INTERIOR DESIGN

Background and Influences

Jean has always had a flair for design and for being creative, and has certainly made a wonderful home for herself and her family, but she never thought of doing anything with these talents – that is, until her children had grown up and left home, and she'd begun to feel rather bored. She was particularly inspired by an old school friend, whom she hadn't seen for many years, who came to visit and who was very complimentary about Jean's home. This friend talked of a woman she knew who had set up a commercial interior design company, and said that Jean's work was already better than that of her friend. Jean gave her friend's comments a lot of thought, and invested in some interior design magazines. She could see that designer homes were becoming increasingly in vogue, yet not everyone could afford the outrageous prices charged by the most up-market designers.

Preparation

Jean built up a library of interior design ideas, and attended a number of trade shows, as well as visiting show-houses and -flats in her neighbourhood. The range of fabrics and finishes was now so extensive that there was clearly no limit to the range of possibilities, except those set by a customer's purse. Jean had not realized that her ideas could make her money, as she hadn't attached a value to them before, but she could see that others were doing this successfully, even when their ideas were not that striking. Jean was surprised at the knowledge she had built up over the years, especially her ability to visualize designs in a particular setting, and knew she could pass on her enthusiasm to others. She also had a large touring car and plenty of storage space at home.

She applied to join the British Institute of Interior Design (1c Devonshire Avenue, Beeston, Nottingham NG9 1BS), and spent some time at the Design Council (28 Haymarket, London SW1Y 4SU) looking at examples of good design and collecting information. She attended the Ideal Home Exhibition and smaller local shows, and got up to date with the products available by visiting relevant shops and warehouses. Jean then wrote to manufacturers and suppliers, and built up a collection of brochures and product details. She bought a copy of *Decorative Art and Modern Interiors*, an annual reference guide, and subscribed to *Homes and Gardens*, *House and Garden* and *Ideal Homes*. She also found out about a range of decorators and builders who would be able to carry out her ideas. She found out about design courses on offer at local colleges, and enrolled for the one which seemed most appropriate.

The Product

Jean offered advice on tasteful and innovative designs tailored for individual customers' requirements, and supervised the implementation of these designs. She would sell a dream of a perfect house, advising customers on how this could be achieved given the range of products commercially available, for an affordable price. She would cost out all the services ahead of time, so that customers could budget accordingly. Her service offered state-of-the-art design ideas at more down-to-earth prices, without an excessive mark-up.

Advertising and Promotion

Jean took out advertisements in the main design magazines and locally (also in the Yellow Pages), targeting the neighbourhoods where people were conscious of good design and making the most of their homes. She held a coffee morning in her home for friends and contacts who might help her to spread the word around, and gave a talk on the subject at a number of local societies.

Launching the Service

Jean started the business by advertising and targeting a leaflet drop, and received a good early response, especially as she launched her business in the spring, when people were thinking about spring-cleaning and revamping their homes. She set about getting commissions, and once people expressed interest she visited the room(s) to be designed and discussed the tastes of the client in terms of colours, fabrics and furnishings. The first half-hour of consultancy was free, but if the client wished to commission her, Jean's charges would begin, and she would outline a unique creation for them. She would start with the basics – ceiling, walls, floor – and then move to specific objects and features, including lighting and curtains. She would draw designs professionally (the course she was taking helped her gain proficiency in this), adding swatches of fabric and examples of colours, and photographs of particular items. The colour photocopying service offered by her local print shop was very helpful here. The resulting 'design report' would be presented to the customer, and any last-minute adjustments would be made before the builders and decorators, whom Jean would supervise closely, were brought in. She became very involved in each interior design creation, taking photographs of the different stages of the work, and took a great pride in the successful implementation of her ideas.

Advantages and Disadvantages

Jean found that her ideas and advice were highly-valued, and that her fees were not queried. It also cost her relatively little to establish the service. Her design ideas and imagination were stretched to the limits, but she enjoyed this. Although initially it took a while to become well-known, once word got round she had plenty of enquiries for her service. It was clearly not a mass-market service, limited instead to an elite group, but within this group there was a lot of scope for charging big fees.

Profits

Jean decided to establish quite high fees, as her customers could clearly afford them, and set them at £30 per hour. She would also charge the customer 10–15 per cent of the builders', decorators' and electricians' fees in return for supervising them and making sure that any problems arising during the course of the work were quickly solved.

Jean found that she could earn £500 for designing a large sitting room, and up to £2,000 for an entire house, to which was added the 10–15 per cent of the cost of carrying out her design ideas. She could easily make £1,000 a week after offsetting the start-up costs for the course, books, advertisements and leaflets, which totalled around £750–£1,000.

CASE STUDY 19: PARTY AND ENTERTAINMENT ORGANIZING

Background and Influences

Pauline is a very fun-loving and capable mother of three who spent several years as an expat-wife, during which time she acquired a lot of experience organizing parties and entertainments. She planned parties for several hundred guests in the most far-flung parts of the world, often negotiating with suppliers through an interpreter.

Pauline is a very active person, well-organized and with a great eye for detail, and when her husband retired and her own social whirl slowed down she realized how much she would like to continue to be involved in the world of party-giving. A friend of hers asked for her help with organizing a major function to mark the departure of her eldest son for a job overseas, and Pauline found that not only did she enjoy herself, but that she was very good at it. Her friend made it widely known that Pauline had helped with the organizing, and before she knew it Pauline had a string of customers wanting her service. The logical step was to create a small business, and Pauline soon did this, with the help of her accountant son.

Preparation

Pauline built up a library of magazines – which included reports on various functions that had been successful – to get ideas and to develop a profile of potential customers. She found out all about local suppliers of food (including cakes and specialist items), drinks, ice, decorations, and even entertainers and musicians, as well as sources of liveried waiters and people to serve the food. She found most of these suppliers in the Yellow Pages or through their advertisements in magazines. She also bought a range of books on giving parties, including dinner parties and more informal gatherings.

The Product

Pauline knew how important good planning was to successful parties, and she offered her expertise in organizing a range of types of party where nothing would go wrong and everyone would enjoy themselves. She would arrange exclusive and up-market cocktail parties, big family celebrations, smart dinner parties, and even children's birthday parties. She could take away the burden of responsibility and worry from a busy host or hostess, exuding a confidence that all would be well by virtue of her experience and capable manner.

Advertising and Promotion

Pauline targeted her future customers carefully by advertising in quality magazines, and by passing the word around. Because of the success of the first party she organized, and her large number of contacts, promotion was not difficult. She also described her service to potential suppliers, so that they could mention her if their customers – who dealt with them direct – complained about the problems of organizing their own parties.

Launching the Service

Pauline's first event once she had officially started her business was a wedding reception in a large country house.

She researched all the suppliers and checked their references, and spent a long time with the hostess to gain an idea of her taste and style, and what she wanted. Her daughter was marrying an American, so the theme of the reception was a coming together of these two nationalities, with typical British and American fare and decorations, together with music and decor to support this theme. Most of Pauline's work was done on the telephone, to suppliers. She quoted a price that included the costs of using all the suppliers, and added a 20–40 per cent margin to cover her own fees. She knew the impression this particular hostess wanted to give, and the atmosphere she wanted to create.

Subsequently, Pauline organized parties in hired rooms in restaurants and night-clubs, working with the management, and even hired river-cruising boats and a local museum as settings. Pauline would handle everything: from the printing and posting of invitations, through the booking of the entertainers and organizing the food and drink, to the decor, flowers and the small gifts and mementoes for those attending; she would even hire security people, if necessary. On one occasion, Pauline organized chauffeur-driven limousines from the local airport for an important overseas visitor for whom a special party was being given.

Advantages and Disadvantages

Pauline found the chief advantage to be that her service didn't seem like work – and she soon discovered it could be very profitable and was quite a growth area. It required a lot of organizational ability, but she has never been short of this. The main disadvantage was being dependent on suppliers – who can and do let you down – but Pauline learned to be careful to check their references and keep others in reserve in case of emergency. Coping with last-minute disasters became one of her specialities!

Profits

Pauline decided that she was not seeking to make a vast income but would mostly offer her service for her own fun and satisfaction. She worked out a scale of charges ranging from £250 for a children's party up to £1,000 for a massive family get-together which more than 300 people might attend. Charging around £5–10 per person was a good guide. She found that throughout the year there would be wedding and birthday parties, with Christmas as a high point, and that she could regularly make £500–£600 a week organizing a range of parties. She spent little on advertising, as news of her service spread by word of mouth.

Pauline also charged a mark-up on the services of the people she hired for each party. She found it convenient to base her charges on the total cost of the whole party. One large, spectacular party with special effects cost Pauline £1,800 to organize, taking into account all the costs of the suppliers, and on top of this she put her own mark-up, with the overall total coming to £2,500. Thus a party costing £600 would bring Pauline a profit of £500 or so. She has found it very hard work and could not possibly run more than two or three at the same time, but it has been so profitable that this has not been necessary.

CASE STUDY 20: PHOTOGRAPHY

Background and Influences

Steve trained in photography at college, but found he got bored working in a lab doing developing and printing, and wanted to go out on location more. The location work he managed to get from his company was mostly photographing houses – for the local estate agent – as well as taking pictures of factories and products for brochures. He found there wasn't enough interaction with people for his liking, and he was very poorly paid. He was also fed up with the noisy, industrial town where he lived, and felt restless. Out of the blue he received a postcard from an old college friend who'd visited a seaside town and had decided to stay there, and was working making souvenirs and crafts to sell to tourists. He wrote to Steve, saying 'Why don't you come too, and try making money by taking photographs of tourists? You could always use those photographic model boards with cut-out heads!'

Steve fancied the idea, and visited his friend, initially just for the weekend. He liked the place so much he decided to stay, and thought he would try to set up a small one man band photographic service, aiming to get work all through the season.

Preparation

Steve discovered that traditional street photography used to be very popular in the past and has since been revived, especially in traditional old-fashioned tourist resorts. It seemed very simple. All he would have to do was to visit areas which were very popular with the old-fashioned type of tourist, and take with him a selection of cut-out photographic model boards for people to pose alongside of. Obvious choices for models were famous celebrities and politicians, whom a person could stand next to and pretend to be with, or the rather clichéd but popular fat lady in a bathing costume, policeman, clown, traffic warden or astronaut with a hole cut out for the head.

There were lots of other possibilities, and Steve, being quite clever at carpentry, could easily make the plywood supports so that the photographic model boards would stand upright.

The Product

Steve thought he would try out his model board photo service as a sideline initially, offsetting this by offering a more formal facility for taking photographs of families and children on holiday. He could stay with his friend, and if the whole thing didn't work he could always go back to his old job. Steve already had a good quality camera and tripod, and sound photographic skills. He could get on well with people and put them at their ease, and he was also good at persuading people to do zany things. After all, having your picture taken with a different body is quite a wild thing, and not something that everybody would want to do. But he guessed that people on holiday would be quite relaxed and might fancy doing something for a laugh.

Advertising and Promotion

Steve put some signs up among the advertisements for general holiday attractions, and also put an advertisement in the local newspaper, but his best source of custom was just standing by the pier with his models. People always stopped to look even if they didn't have their picture taken, and had a good laugh at the expense of others who were brave enough to try.

Launching the Service

First of all, Steve checked with the local authority about whether he would need a licence. They said it wasn't necessary, but that it was just as well he had asked them as they liked to know what was going on. He made a set of six photographic model boards and constructed a box to carry them in. Each model was divided into sections that could be assembled quickly, and he took pictures of his friend and various neighbours posing with the model boards, so that his customers could see what the photographs would look like. He found a good place on the sea front which wasn't too windy, where a large number of people congregated, near the entrance to the pier.

Steve assembled his Mrs Thatcher model first, and immediately potential customers began milling around. Straight away, several people wanted to have their picture taken, and paid the total cost of £5 in advance. Steve made a note of their names and addresses, carefully numbering each photograph. At the end of his first day, he found he had taken over 150 photographs, and he was thrilled at the number of people who wanted their pictures taken. The sunny weather helped, and people particularly liked his fat lady in a bikini model, as well as his Fred Flintstone, Marilyn Monroe and Incredible Hulk. Steve rushed home and did the developing and printing, putting in with each finished picture a price list for enlargements and further copies. Then he posted them the next day, having charged the customer for the postage in advance. He found many customers coming back for more copies and for enlargements, and discovered he was kept very busy taking photographs all day and developing them and any reprints and enlargements at night.

Advantages and Disadvantages

This service depends on fine weather and a good tourist season at the chosen resort, but once underway the overheads are comparatively low. Steve found his outgoing and humourous personality helped. It would not have worked in more sophisticated resorts, nor if he had been less of a salesman. Photographic experience and being able to do his own developing and printing increased his profits substantially.

Profits

Steve's costs included making the photographic model boards, which cost him £30 each, or £180. His photographic chemicals for the developing cost another £50. He already had his camera and developing equipment, but he had to buy films and photographic paper, which cost another £100 per week. But he found that with 150 people per day, he could make £750 – but this was a good day, and when the weather wasn't so good his takings could go down to about £100. But overall, he found it was a good business and was able to augment the work out of season by taking portrait pictures, pictures of babies and pets, as well as doing weddings and other celebrations. It was certainly better than working in a lab in the big city.

CASE STUDY 21: PROOF-READING AND EDITING

Background and Influences

Keith is quite a scholarly person who loves reading and has very wide interests. Above all he has an eye for detail and a very precise approach to everything he does. He studied English language at university but never did very much with it. He was working as an administrator with the local council and was fairly bored, feeling that his talents were not really stretched, but he liked living in the country and working quite near to home, as he is not particularly outgoing or adventurous.

Keith is a good writer, and worked for a while on his local newspaper, but found that the only way to get on as a journalist would be to go to London, and this Keith just didn't want to do. Once, on one of his infrequent trips to the county town he was attending a book launch party, and chatting to the author. He was very intrigued when the author said how much she would value someone who could proof-read and edit well, as these tasks were so time-consuming they left her with hardly any time to write all the books she was hired to write, let alone make sure she'd caught all the errors, inconsistencies and ambiguities. Keith immediately fancied the idea of this sort of work, and offered to proof-read and edit her next book. She was delighted, and turned out to be very pleased with his work, and helped him to find other authors to advise. A number of publishers also provided him with more work.

Preparation

Keith discovered that editing and proof-reading was a small market niche which he could exploit successfully to bring in an excellent return. He particularly liked it because he could work from home. He bought a copy of *The Writers' and Artists' Yearbook* so that he could target authors by writing to their publishers. He studied how corrections should be written, and talked to other authors he knew about the way their books were edited and proof-read. Keith found that this could be an ideal business, having minimal overheads and offering an enjoyable and entertaining way of earning money out of his interest in reading.

The Product

Keith decided to target professional and amateur authors and writers, rather than to work directly for publishers. He knew that most of these authors weren't very good at tightening up the style of their manuscripts or checking them for inaccuracies. Keith realized that there was a lot of scope for this one man band, especially as so many books were being produced each year and the number was continually on the increase. He knew that there would be strong competition from people with professional experience, but he could offer a personal service to a range of authors, providing speed and accuracy and perhaps undercutting other very expensive editors. Keith was aware that he would need only a handful of prolific authors to have enough regular work for a part-time business, and that if he could attract more and more authors he would be able to edit as a full-time job.

Advertising and Promotion

Keith knew it was important to advertise thoroughly, and found several newspapers and magazines which he knew were popular among authors. He also went about getting an entry for himself in *The Writers' and Artists' Yearbook*, as well as in various media directories. He also contacted a number of publishers and asked to be put in touch with their authors, and joined a local writers' group and mentioned his services to them, asking them to pass on the message to their other author friends.

Launching the Service

Keith's first customers were existing friends and contacts, especially those referred to him by the author who had first suggested the idea of editing and proof-reading to him. Very soon after he decided to launch his service (calling himself an 'Editorial Services Consultant'), he received a variety of manuscripts on different topics, including a novel about living on a remote farm in Africa and a textbook about biotechnology. Keith read the manuscripts, looking for grammatical, spelling, typographical and layout errors as well as for inconsistencies and contradictions. He simply marked anything that seemed to be amiss in the margin for the author's attention, following the standard editorial and proof-reading markings (which are explained in *The Writers' and Artists' Yearbook* and in any good dictionary).

When he'd read the manuscripts through thoroughly Keith would return them to the author, who would then check all his comments before sending the manuscript back to the publisher. Most authors found the cost of hiring Keith well worth while. Some of Keith's authors were able to gain instant acceptance of their manuscripts because of their accuracy and quality, and the fact that he had already edited and proof-read them meant that they could be published more quickly. Keith's work could make all the difference between a speculative piece of work being accepted or rejected. He was also able, once he knew his authors well, to suggest improvements to their style and content, and was ultimately able to become almost an adviser and consultant to his closest authors.

Advantages and Disadvantages

Keith had a great interest in reading and a lively mind; this would not be a job for someone who gets bored easily or who has only a narrow range of interests. Some books are inevitably fairly dull and dry, and there is a great need for self-motivation and -discipline to be able to sit down hour after hour reading. Good concentration and an eye for detail are also essential, as without these it would be impossible to do the job successfully.

Profits

Keith would charge about £100–150 per manuscript on average, according to its length and technical sophistication. He would charge less for a novel than for a textbook, even if they were of the same length. Some manuscripts he could read in four to five hours, whereas some would take twice as long. Keith's start-up costs were fairly minimal: he paid £200 for his entries in the main media directories and another £200 on small advertisements. He found he was able to work on four or five manuscripts per week, and could make £650–750 in a good week.

CASE STUDY 22: PROPERTY RENOVATIONS

Background and Influences

Mike had been working as an estate agent, and noticed that as the building of new houses was slowing down, the demand for renovated property became stronger. Several people were coming to him with properties to sell which they had renovated themselves, and he was impressed with the level of profit they were achieving despite the overall slump in the housing market. He had always thought that opportunities to renovate old houses were few and far between, and also that you had to be a property tycoon to be able to afford to buy them. But not any more. Prices were coming down considerably, and there were many opportunities to acquire dilapidated old properties and transform them into exciting new homes, often ones with real character. Through his work as an estate agent Mike knew a lot about the sort of houses that were most in demand, and the locations that were most popular; he also had many contacts in the building fraternity. As the estate agency business continued to slump Mike was made redundant, and started his one man band with his redundancy money.

Preparation

Mike discovered that the demand for renovated property was indeed increasing, and that the market for improved older properties was probably better than it was for new buildings. Mike was no big property financier, nor was he an experienced builder, but he didn't see why he couldn't buy and renovate an old property and sell it at a good profit. It would take some capital expenditure, but he had his redundancy money, and once he had got started there could be a constant flow of new income coming in from resold properties.

The Product

Mike would create new value in the housing market by doing up old properties which might otherwise lie empty and useless. He felt he had the necessary management skills as a result of his experience in the estate agent's, and he certainly had the ability to present proposals and arguments to both buyers and sellers fairly convincingly. He had the capital to buy his first house, and, if this turned out to be necessary, he thought he probably could organize a syndicate of people who would be interested in investing with him. Once he had made some income on his first deal, he felt sure he could bring in other investors. He knew there would be a demand for the renovated houses, and could identify the sort of people who would want to buy them. He thought he could make a good profit by virtue of his market knowledge and management skills.

Advertising and Promotion

Mike already had good professional contacts, and through working as an estate agent he knew of specialist media such as the *Estates Gazette*. He also bought himself copies of a number of books on property renovation, having first checked the resources available at his local library.

Launching the Service

Mike was able to launch and run his business from home, and after his first successful renovation was able to start up a syndicate. The other people in the syndicate were working and therefore too busy to organize the renovations, so Mike added value and made money through his organizational and management skills. He found it was important to have a team of professional advisers and use them to do the actual work. Mike's job was to recognize the potential in a derelict property and to be able to acquire it using money from the syndicate. He found that he was able to raise mortgages and overdrafts from banks to help with the financing, too, and that a number of building societies were also interested. Some estate agent friends were helpful in telling him about properties suitable for renovation. He hired a good solicitor to advise him on the laws affecting development, and a surveyor for advising on whether or not buildings could be renovated economically. Mike also had a number of friends who were architects and builders, who could undertake the renovation work, under Mike's direction. Finally, Mike used an accountant to arrange financing, prepare the accounts, deal with tax and apportion profits between the syndicate members.

Typically Mike would begin by advertising in the 'Business Opportunities' columns of newspapers, to find people who might wish to join the syndicate. He would then look for properties, and would instruct his surveyor to analyse their renovation potential. Then the builder and architect would prepare a costing for him, and he would arrange and supervise the necessary work. After it was done he would be able to put the property on the market, and finally he would divide the proceeds between himself and the syndicate members, allowing for an organization and management fee for himself.

Mike was able to build up a successful business concentrating only on residential property: organizing syndicates, using only trusted and experienced professional advisers, and working only as supervisor. He never actually undertook building work himself, but was always around to make sure it was proceeding satisfactorily.

Advantages and Disadvantages

As far as Mike could tell, the advantages included a very high return and the fact that property seldom loses value, so he was unlikely to lose the benefit of his investment. The only problems might have been caused by planning and building regulations, which make it difficult to change the established use for a building. However, Mike found that by concentrating on the domestic market he was able to avoid any of these complications.

Profits

In a typical renovation, five investors would provide £10,000 each to buy a derelict house costing £30,000, with the remainder being spent on renovating and converting it. If the renovated house could then be sold for over £100,000, this would represent an attractive return. Mike found that he was able to go for more expensive properties all the time, and became more ambitious in his renovation project. There are examples of property renovators who have started off with a modest £20,000 or £30,000 – by mortgaging their own home – who have built up a portfolio of properties worth a several million pounds.

CASE STUDY 23: REPAIR AND REFURBISHMENT

Background and Influences

Allen was very practical and capable. He had been made redundant from his coal-mining job, and didn't want to have to move to get another mining job. He was also anxious to avoid mining, as it was a dangerous job and he'd already suffered a few injuries.

Allen had always been good at repairing equipment and appliances around the house, and many of his friends brought in various electrical items for him to mend. Many of them were considered beyond repair, but Allen always had a knack of getting them to work again. When he lost his job, one of his friends (whose fridge Allen had recently mended) half-jokingly said he should go into the repair and refurbishment business, especially if he could buy such goods very cheaply, do them up and sell them again. Allen decided to give it a try, and his reconditioned appliances are now enjoying new leases on life all over his locality.

Preparation

Allen was able to base his business basically on junk that he could turn into money. Most of the items he repaired were worth nothing broken, but after reconditioning were actually quite valuable, sometimes more valuable than new, because many were old models that weren't being made any more. He had a small workshop at home which he could use, and a good selection of tools. He was interested in electrical and mechanical items, and was quite imaginative about fixing things. As a start he went about collecting magazines and journals, such as *Do-It-Yourself*, *DIY Today*, *Electrical and Electronic Trader*, *Mechanical World*, *Electrical Yearbook* and *Manufacturers' and Merchants' Directory*, to provide himself with some background information.

The Product

Allen was able to refurbish broken and apparently useless items and re-sell them at a large mark-up, almost equalling the price of new products. In some cases Allen's reconditioned goods were seen as better than new, because the original models were better made than those currently available. The products Allen repaired included lawn-mowers, vacuum cleaners, TV sets, bicycles, motor bikes, washing machines, refrigerators, cookers, fans, shower units, mixers and many more.

Advertising and Promotion

Allen advertised his service for mending broken items – asking as well for items needing reconditioning and restoration – first in the local newspapers and then on postcards which he placed in shop windows. He also opened a market stall, which became one of his most useful promotional assets.

Launching the Service

Straight away many people brought in items needing repair, and Allen was also able to buy items from auction and garage sales as well as acquiring some through his advertisements. Occasionally he found things could not be repaired, but even then they could always be cannibalized for spare parts for other products. With more complicated products Allen would phone up the manufacturers and ask for suggestions on how to repair them. Very often he would receive enough information in this way to be able to mend them.

Sometimes Allen had to use new parts to mend something, but where possible he would bought them second-hand. Often a cleaning job was all that was necessary: electrical items would magically begin to work again once they had been cleaned thoroughly and their connections restored. His background in electrical items meant he could always test products for safety. Allen had inquired at the local council for permission to undertake this work, and they referred him to the Electricity Board, which allowed him to carry on because he had electrical experience, although any repair work on large or complex items had to be cleared with them, and they would charge him for this. Even so their fee was worth it on large items, and did not reduce his profit very much.

Once they had been reconditioned Allen was able to sell his products by advertising in the classifieds and at his small stall in the local market. This stall was also a good source of items to be repaired, because passers-by would see it and be reminded of goods they had at home that were broken or damaged. Allen found that there was a good potential in second-hand goods, especially in mechanical items such as lawn-mowers and washing machines. They were often breaking down and being discarded when there was really only something fairly insignificant that was wrong with them.

Advantages and Disadvantages

The chief advantages for Allen were that not many people were offering his service, and that his special knowledge and skills were a great help. If he had just relied on friends bringing him items to mend, then his profits would have been limited, but instead he was able to make real money by buying faulty or damaged household goods cheap because they were regarded as virtually worthless.

Profits

By buying broken and unwanted items at auctions, second-hand shops and through advertising, as well as going to retailers and buying goods that had been traded in, Allen found he was able to repair products and then sell them for twice the money he had paid for them. It was fairly rare for him to find he couldn't mend something, and he enjoyed the challenge of this sometimes difficult job. In a typical week he could make up to £500, based on an average of £30–£100 profit per item. The market stall cost him £50 a day, and he spent another £50 on advertising. The need to advertise decreased as news of his service spread by word of mouth. He already had the necessary tools, so the main input was his time and skill. He liked meeting people and found the work comparatively untaxing, and enjoyed pottering around in his workshop, especially compared with the noise and heat of the mine.

CASE STUDY 24: MAKING AND SELLING SANDWICHES

Background and Influences

Gianni arrived in Britain three years ago and worked at his uncle's deli and restaurant. He enjoyed serving the food and chatting to the customers, but he felt he would like to run his own restaurant. This seemed very expensive and beyond his reach, but one day he had a new idea when one of his regular customers telephoned and asked if he could deliver his favourite pastrami special, because he was stuck at his desk working on an urgent assignment. Gianni soon realized that he could run his own sandwich service to many other customers who were too busy to get away at lunchtime. Gianni wasn't that great a cook, but he knew how to make appealing sandwiches in a variety of interesting combinations, and he had lots of marketing ideas. Before long, he was delivering 'Gianni's Goodies' to several nearby offices, shops and other establishments, augmenting his sandwiches with a range of cakes and confectionery, all with an Italian style, packed in a distinctive lunch box with an Italian flag which he designed himself. Customers liked his cheery manner and reliable service, and the fresh and well-presented food, and were quite happy to pay the small extra involved.

Preparation

Gianni found that food retailing was one of the fastest-growing businesses around, and that he could make money selling sandwiches made with ingredients supplied at a discount by wholesalers, adding his own special touches and providing additional snacks and confectionary. He knew he would be good at selling his service, and was friendly and enthusiastic.

First Gianni went to the local council and got a licence to run his sandwich service. He worked out that he could start each morning by buying his raw ingredients and snacks, then prepare the lunches, then go on his rounds. He designed some attractive cardboard lunch boxes, with which he could make up lunch packs tailored to each individual, putting together an appealing blend of sandwiches, fruit and cake or some biscuits, according to individual tastes.

The Product

Gianni would offer really appealing sandwiches delivered to his customers' desks or work-stations, on time and with a smile. He would offer whole-lunch combinations, such as his favourite bacon-and-avocado sandwich served with a chocolate wafer biscuit and crunchy apple. He also offered a real Italian-style pastrami speciality, a tuna-and-cucumber on brown wholemeal bread, a vegetarian item, a variety of cheeses and pickles, and other popular or unique combinations. He developed a new menu every week, comprising six to eight different sandwich fillings which always included meat, fish, and typical Italian and vegetarian selections. The price of the sandwiches varied according to the cost of the ingredients, and his service was fresh, friendly and punctual. He targeted a fairly small area, so that he could serve it well without having to travel far.

Advertising and Promotion

Gianni advertised in the local papers and magazines which he knew were read by people in offices and factories. He also printed leaflets for distribution, giving his telephone and fax numbers. Gianni's leaflet was designed so that customers could fill in their requirements and fax it to him, so that he could arrange their special order and deliver it at the specified time.

Launching the Service

Gianni launched his service after a short advertising campaign and after gaining assurances from a critical mass of customers at his uncle's deli that they would try him out to see how good his lunch boxes were, and how extra convenient it was to have their lunch delivered to their desks. He often found that once a couple of people in an office wanted his lunch packs he would soon get many other customers, and quickly found himself serving a dozen or more people in several different offices. People got so they looked forward to the contents of his red, green and white cardboard lunch boxes, which announced cheerfully that 'Gianni's Goodies' had arrived.

In winter Gianni would introduce hot soup in sealed containers, finding that traditional home-made minestrone was by far the most popular. He found that his small van was very helpful for delivery and that he could fill it with enough lunch boxes to serve a large number of customers. A number of his customers only needed his lunch boxes two or three times a week, but others would want them every day. In several offices, Gianni could be guaranteed to sell everything in his large basket to hungry workers. As time went on, he offered pies and crisps, and also developed more Italian specialities, since his customers seemed to like his Italian theme.

Advantages and Disadvantages

Gianni's service would not have worked but for the quality and freshness of the sandwiches, and reliable delivery. Gianni had to get up early to buy the ingredients and make the sandwiches, and it could be a rush to deliver them all at peak lunch-hour times. Nor could people be relied upon to want his lunch boxes every day, but he was able to build up a loyal client following, especially by varying the menus and range of snacks.

Profits

Gianni found he could mark up the cost of raw materials by 100 per cent, and sell a pack of sandwiches for between £1 and £2.50, depending on the ingredients. Gianni found he could produce 200 sandwiches a day, which he could sell for a total if £350, and make takings of another £200 on snack items. For this income of £550 per day, he need spend only £200, due to buying items in season and using his deep freeze. His hot minestrone soup could be made for 20p a cup, but he could sell each cup for 75p to £1.00 (depending on whether the 4- or 6-oz cup is chosen). His other costs included disposable plates, cups and cutlery, his advertisements and leaflets, and the fax machine. But he found he was able to pay off his start-up costs in the first month, and then to spend less than £100 a week on packaging.

Index

Of further interest . . .

CAREER TURNAROUND

How to apply corporate strategy techniques to your own career

JOHN VINEY & STEPHANIE JONES

Have you been made redundant and feel unsure about the future? Is your industry going through a tough time? Have outside influences forced you to rethink your career? Or perhaps you are secure in your job but need a new challenge? Here is *the* book for anyone who wants to revitalize their career, start taking positive action, and try something entirely new.

In this highly original approach to self-improvement, leading headhunter John Viney, and international business writer and lecturer Stephanie Jones, take these key elements of successful corporate strategies and explain how effectively they may be used to transform individual lives and careers:

- Mission Statements
- Objectives and Goals
- Personal, Company and Market Audits
- Market Research and Networking
- Product Development and Branding
- Attracting Investment
- Implementing Change

This astute strategic advice is illustrated with case studies of people from different countries and different industries who have successfully turned their careers around, proving that this approach and techniques can and do work.

Career Turnaround is a practical and inspiring guide to achieving positive and effective change in your career.

THE 12-DAY MARKETING PLAN

Construct a marketing plan that really works — in less than two weeks

JAMES C. MAKENS

Here is a complete, step-by-step blueprint for building a superior marketing plan for your product or service. In these pages, you will find ready-to-use forms, tables and worksheets that cover every planning function, including competitive analysis, pricing strategy, sales promotion, advertising, budgeting, forecasting and much more. Just fill in the facts and *The 12-Day Marketing Plan* writes a comprehensive, tailor-made marketing plan for you.

This unique time-saving guide will help you develop a marketing plan that:

- Positions your product or services for maximum sales
- Determines your best pricing strategy
- Manages your distribution channels to their best effect
- Evaluates the cost-effectiveness of your marketing operation
- Selects the most effective advertising and sales promotion strategies
- Identifies problem areas in your marketing effort.

In *The 12-Day Marketing Plan*, you will find time-saving worksheets to help you conduct an internal audit . . . analyse competitors . . . develop marketing research strategies . . . and much more.

And, because all the worksheets are organized in the order that you will use them, you won't have to worry about overlooking a relevant point or skipping a critical step.

WHO DARES SELLS

The ultimate guide to selling anything to anyone

PATRICK ELLIS

Who Dares Sells is the book for ultimate success in the business of sales. It will show you how to sell anything to anyone, anywhere in the world. Read it, live it, and this could be the best investment you ever make!

Who Dares Sells is all about creative, dynamic selling principles, tactics and techniques. It reveals the most effective methods known today of achieving successful sales, including:

- the effective use of psychology
- how to deal with 60 different types of buyer
- how to plan for success, achieve and maintain it
- sales pitfalls — and how to avoid them
- how to use colour, graphology and neuro-linguistic programming
- revolutionary closing techniques
- how to read non-verbal signs in a buyer
- how to sell yourself!

Patrick Ellis is an international sales expert who, after a lifetime in business, has decided to reveal the secrets of his success. Twelve years in the writing, *Who Dares Sells* is everything anyone will ever need to know about selling — in one definitive volume.

CAREER TURNAROUND	0 7225 2478 1	£6.99 ☐
THE 12-DAY MARKETING PLAN h/b	0 7225 1969 9	£22.50 ☐
WHO DARES SELLS	0 7225 2718 7	£9.99 ☐
THE SHORTER MBA h/b	0 7225 2507 9	£25.00 ☐
GET THAT JOB!	0 7225 2692 X	£4.99 ☐
CLIMBING THE CORPORATE LADDER	0 7225 2533 8	£5.99 ☐
DO IT!	0 7225 2695 4	£7.99 ☐

All these books are available from your local bookseller or can be ordered direct from the publishers.

To order direct just tick the titles you want and fill in the form below:

Name: _____

Address: _____

_____

_____ Postcode: _____

Send to: Thorsons Mail Order, Dept 31V, HarperCollins*Publishers*, Westerhill Road, Bishopbriggs, Glasgow G64 2QT.
Please enclose a cheque or postal order or your authority to debit your Visa/Access acount —

Credit card no: _____

Expiry date: _____

Signature: _____

— to the value of the cover price plus:
UK & BFPO: Add £1.00 for the first book and 25p for each additional book ordered.
Overseas orders including Eire: Please add £2.95 service charge. Books will be sent by surface mail but quotes for airmail despatches will be given on request.

24 HOUR TELEPHONE ORDERING SERVICE FOR ACCESS/ VISA CARDHOLDERS — TEL: 041 772 2281.